Beginning Microsoft Excel 2010

Abbott Katz

Beginning Microsoft Excel 2010

ISBN-13 (pbk): 978-1-4302-2955-1

ISBN-13 (electronic): 978-1-4302-2956-8

Printed and bound in the United States of America 9 8 7 6 5 4 3 2 1

President and Publisher: Paul Manning
Lead Editor: Ben Renow-Clarke
Technical Reviewer: Simon Murphy
Editorial Board: Clay Andres, Steve Anglin, Mark Beckner, Ewan Buckingham, Gary Cornell, Jonathan Gennick, Jonathan Hassell, Michelle Lowman, Matthew Moodie, Duncan Parkes, Jeffrey Pepper, Frank Pohlmann, Douglas Pundick, Ben Renow-Clarke, Dominic Shakeshaft, Matt Wade, Tom Welsh
Coordinating Editor: Kelly Moritz
Copy Editor: Janet Gokay
Compositor: MacPS, LLC
Indexer: BIM Indexing & Proofreading Services
Artist: April Milne
Cover Designer: Anna Ishchenko

Distributed to the book trade worldwide by Springer Science+Business Media, LLC., 233 Spring Street, 6th Floor, New York, NY 10013. Phone 1-800-SPRINGER, fax (201) 348-4505, e-mail orders-ny@springer-sbm.com, or visit www.springeronline.com.

For information on translations, please e-mail rights@apress.com, or visit www.apress.com.

Apress and friends of ED books may be purchased in bulk for academic, corporate, or promotional use. eBook versions and licenses are also available for most titles. For more information, reference our Special Bulk Sales–eBook Licensing web page at www.apress.com/info/bulksales.

Downloadable workbooks for this book are available to readers at www.apress.com. You will need to answer questions pertaining to this book in order to successfully download the workbooks.

Contents at a Glance

Contents

About the Author

 **Abbott Katz** A native New Yorker, Abbott Katz currently lives in London and has introduced Excel to numerous corporate and university classes on both sides of the Atlantic. He has written for a wide range of publications, including New York Newsday, the (UK) Times Higher Educational, and insidehighered.com, and holds a doctorate in sociology from SUNY Stony Brook in New York. Prior to moving to London in 2005 he served as the Deputy Chair of the Sociology Department at Touro College, while at the same time teaching the introductory computer course at Queens College. His interests include jazz and baseball, but like all Americans, he remains utterly clueless about cricket.

About the Technical Reviewer

 **Simon Murphy** is a freelance software developer specialising in integrating Excel with other enterprise resources. He has been doing spreadsheets forever, having started in the 80s, and mainly works in the financial analysis and reporting arena. He also runs a successful business selling Excel add-ins via the internet.

Simon spoke at the inaugural Excel User Conference in Dallas Fort Worth in 2005, and regularly speaks and contributes to the European Spreadsheet Risk Interest Group (eusprig.org), the worldwide authority on the risks inherent in commercial spreadsheet use.

XLAnalyst, the spreadsheet risk assessment tool that Simon developed is one of the most popular spreadsheet audit tools in the market.

Simon is also a member of the Microsoft Office Developer Advisory Council, and helped steer the developer features of Excel 2010. He has an MSc in Software development and his main consulting interest is around performant User Defined Functions.

Acknowledgments

It's a truism, but it's true nonetheless: Writing a book nowadays calls upon a team effort. Blog away in solitary bliss, but writing – and assembling - a hard-copy book is something different. The name you see attached to the book's title identifies but one of its contributors, and it's only proper that I acknowledge those unfailingly congenial, if anonymous, teammates whose work would otherwise go unsung.

First, all due thanks to Apress Lead Editor Ben Renow-Clarke, who was there at the book's inception, and has lent a continually helpful hand to the project. Coordinating Editor Kelly Moritz has offered her non-stop assistance, across six time zones no less, and Copy Editor Janet Gokay has delivered spot-on grammatical and stylistic counsel. Technical Reviewer Simon Murphy asked the right questions, and often supplied some of the answers, too.

Closer to home – much closer – my devoted wife Marsha granted me the time and space to pursue this literary chore, even if it meant neglecting my other chores – even more than usual. (I did manage to mow the lawn today, though.)

And speaking of spaces, a writer's desk these days is wherever his laptop alights, and so a number of venues should be cited and thanked as well, including the Bewick Centre in Gateshead (thanks to Sholmi Issacson), assorted tables on the East Coast and Grand Central train lines, a clutch of Starbuckses (check that plural, Janet) and the British Library.

On the other hand, of course, blame for any and all of the book's shortcomings reverts to the guy with his name attached to the title.

Introduction

Welcome to *Beginning Microsoft Excel 2010*. No; you're not a dummy, but you may be new to this vast, empty, rectangular world of columns and rows that Excel spreadsheets comprise, and you may be just a little bit intimidated, too. You may have a couple of questions as result: What do I do, where, and how?

Those are big questions, and the answers to them don't come in the 25-words-or-less variety; but *Beginning Microsoft Excel 2010* tries to make the answers easier to understand by erring on the side of *explanation* over the click-here, click-there, bullet-pointed mode of book instruction. Knowing what's going on in your workbook, and why, makes the prospect of constructing this, and your *next,* workbook that much less daunting.

Beginning Microsoft Excel 2010 isn't to be read as a spreadsheet "bible," the kind of work that catalogues each and every command the application has to offer. That kind of book surely has its place, of course, but if you're starting out with Excel — and I'm speaking as an Excel instructor — you need to know the important basics, and then some — those capabilities which can get you up and running and doing real work, and pretty soon. As a result, and given the proverbial limitations of space, a good many decisions had to be made along the way about what to omit, as well as what to include. Excel is, after all, a vast application, and something tells me you're not prepared to pay for a few thousand pages worth of detail about the whole shebang.

If you're not entirely new to Excel, but are leapfrogging instead to the 2010 version from Excel 2003 or some prior release, you too may be in need of a bit of orientation — especially to the Excel ribbon-based motif of commands, part of what's called the Microsoft Office Fluent Interface, discussed in detail in Chapter 1. It's a different look to and means for accessing the Excel commands you already know, and that variation on a tried-and-true theme is off-putting to some. Hang in there, and it'll begin to make sense.

Also new to Excel (and Office) 2010 is what's called the Backstage View, an area that gathers in one place some important commands you may need to carry out sooner or later — for example, saving, document retrieval and sharing, and printing options.

CHAPTER 1

Introduction to Excel

Making the Acquaintance

It's here—Microsoft Excel 2010, the latest take on the spreadsheet program that millions of people use worldwide to process, calculate, and display information in countless ways, and for countless reasons.

As with so many computer terms, "spreadsheet" has its roots in the hard-copy world, harking back to the outsized, columned, paper ledgers in which bookkeepers recorded invoices and other financial doings. But with the advent of the PC, those green-tinted pages eventually gave way to an electronic "sheet," one empowered to do far more than its 17" x 11" forebearers, and to do so with far more data, and at far greater speeds.

Unlocking Your Inner Worksheet

It's true of course that many Excel users spend a good deal of their time adding columns and rows of numbers, and while that's a critical task, and one Excel performs with surpassing ease and accuracy, that's really just the beginning. Once you merge your understanding of what Excel can do with what I call the "spreadsheet imagination," you'll begin to discover there isn't much you *can't* do with the application. (There are limits, though; I've seen someone compose a CV on Excel...Not recommended). There's little doubt that enormous numbers of Excel users badly underutilize the potential sealed within the program, even at their current skill level, and so it's worth knowing that every boost to your understanding can only work to your advantage.

Here's an example of what I mean. Suppose you want to track your family expenses for the calendar year. Sure—at first blush that sounds like little more than an old-school, standard, add-these-rows-and-columns type of task. But think about it—if you could, you'd also likely want to break your expenses out both by category and date. So instead of a simple history of payments that starts out looking like Figure 1–1:

Date	Expense	Sum
01/11/2008	telephone	7.31
15/11/2008	Central Heating	17.00
15/11/2008	Property Tax	232.00
15/11/2008	Life Insurance	29.00
15/11/2008	Medical Insurance	96.00
15/11/2008	Plumbing Insurance	6.24
15/11/2008	Water	65.00
23/11/2008	Cleaner	25.50
23/11/2008	Food	30.00
23/11/2008	Food	7.00
23/11/2008	Food	16.00
23/11/2008	Food	14.00
23/11/2008	Food	4.00
23/11/2008	Newspapers	2.00
23/11/2008	Newspapers	2.00
23/11/2008	Sewing	10.00
28/11/2008	Savings	40.00
30/11/2008	Car Maintenance	58.00
30/11/2008	Cleaner	30.00
30/11/2008	Clothes	21.00
30/11/2008	Contents Insurance	300.00
30/11/2008	Eat out	17.00
30/11/2008	Food	45.00
30/11/2008	Food	11.00
30/11/2008	Food	2.00
30/11/2008	Home Insurance	900.00
30/11/2008	Newspapers	4.00
30/11/2008	gas	38.00
30/11/2008	Sewing	10.00
01/12/2008	telephone	7.00
07/12/2008	Breakdown Insurance	115.00

tion | **Actual Expenses** / Chart1 / Monthly Breakd

Figure 1–1. Sample family budget expenses

you could, once you've powered up that spreadsheet imagination, tweak the data to look like Figure 1–2:

Sum of Sum	Date												
Expense	Jan	Feb	Mar	Apr	May	Jun	Jul	Aug	Sep	Oct	Nov	Dec	Grand Total
America trip					264.00								264.00
Annual subscriptions		20.00						45.00					65.00
Breakdown Insurance											115.00		115.00
Car Insurance	281.00												281.00
Car Maintenance								6.00	3.00		58.00		67.00
Central Heating	17.00	17.00	17.00	17.00	17.00	17.00	17.00	17.00	17.00	17.00	17.00	17.00	204.00
Child Tax Credit Repay	12.50	12.50	12.50	12.50	12.50	12.50	12.50	12.50	12.50	12.50	12.50	12.50	150.00
Cleaner	128.00	125.00	95.00	90.00	127.00	76.00	70.00	70.00	94.00	135.00	55.50	30.00	1095.50
Clothes	133.00	24.00	26.00		76.00	48.00	39.00	158.00	115.00	3.00	21.00		643.00
Contents Insurance										347.00	300.00		647.00
Dental Treatment					55.00								55.00
Donation												150.00	150.00
Dry Cleaner						8.00	6.00			18.00			32.00
dry cleaning		7.00		12.00	12.00	8.00							39.00
Eat out	25.00	66.00	10.00		17.00	16.00		62.00	20.00		17.00	14.00	247.00

Figure 1–2. Those same figures, broken out by expense category as well as month

Here the expenses are indeed totaled by category, and cross-tabulated by month as well. And as new expenses are incurred and recorded on the spreadsheet, all the new numbers recalculate immediately and update the category and monthly totals. And you'll agree that knowing how much money you spent on food in July illuminates your budgetary picture more sharply than a simple, bottom-line total of all your costs.

Here's another example. Suppose you're a teacher who wants to construct a spreadsheet that calculates students' averages across five exams. For starters, your spreadsheet might assume this form, shown in Figure 1–3:

Student	Exams 1	2	3	4	5	Average
Alice	67	96	67	100	85	83
Derek	82	89	45	93	67	75.2
Dorothy	73	70	93	65	93	78.8
Edith	81	48	52	75	76	66.4
George	90	67	84	59	77	75.4
Gordon	90	86	89	77	94	87.2
John	83	96	60	63	70	74.4
Mary	77	78	80	90	100	85
Paul	61	91	68	61	99	76
Ringo	89	80	79	82	77	81.4
Class Averages	79.3	80.1	71.7	76.5	83.8	

Figure 1–3. Student grades for five exams

Now, that's a perfectly lucid and serviceable read on the data, complete with an alphabetical sort of student names. But with a bit of formatting derring-do and a jot of number-crunching savvy, you could come up with something like Figure 1–4:

Student	Exams 1	2	3	4	5	Average	
Alice	67	96	67	100	85	83.0	︿︿
Derek	82	89	45	93	67	75.2	⌄⌃
Dorothy	73	70	93	65	93	78.8	⌄
Edith	81	48	52	75	76	66.4	⌄
George	90	67	84	59	77	75.4	⌄
Gordon	90	86	89	77	94	87.2	⌄
John	83	96	60	63	70	74.4	⌃
Mary	77	78	80	90	100	85.0	／
Paul	61	91	68	61	99	76.0	∿
Ringo	56	80	79	82	77	74.8	／
Class Averages	76.0	80.1	71.7	76.5	83.8		

Figure 1–4. The same grades, this time formattted to highlight the highest grade in each exam. Each set of student grades is also charted.

What additional information does the revised gradebook provide? Well for one thing, it singles out the highest student score on each test, backgrounding that score with a reddish tint (note the shared top honors in tests 1 and 2; the color choice is your call). For another, our new and improved gradebook tacks on a mini-chart called a Sparkline alongside each student's average, capturing her trajectory of test performance—a rather cool feature that's not exactly new, but which *is* new to Excel 2010. (Note Mary's steady upward performance slope, for example.)

Now imagine these features applied to the gradebook for a class of, say, 200 students, and note the ease with which you could identify top scorers, and how cogently those 200 Sparklines could delineate each student's progress. And Excel isn't afraid of big numbers, either; think about a university registrar using Excel to compile the course grades of, say, 20,000 students, each one treated to his own Sparkline. Why not? It's a striking way to deliver the big picture in fine-grained form.

The Pep Talk

Now, are the spreadsheet skills I've applied to these examples the kinds of things you can learn right away? Well, maybe not *right* away; but with a modicum of determination and reflection and some concerted practice time, the skills begin to build. After all, everyone starts at square one.

Excel is a vast application, and there's always more to learn about it. There's a batch of features you *have* to know in order to be able to use Excel productively; there's also a large trove of features that are very nice to know, but not quite as indispensible. No one expects you to learn all there is to know about the software, and your spreadsheet needs might be rather unprepossessing, after all. I know you can keep a secret, and so I may as well confess in the interests of transparency that I've never calculated a right-tailed student's t-distribution with Excel. But the tool for doing so is there, however, and somebody out there *is* using it. On the other hand, I *have* used other built-in formulas (called *functions*) named INDIRECT, RANDBETWEEN, and SMALL, and a raft of others that might actually help you do the work you need to do—even if you don't realize it yet.

This book will strive diligently to introduce and explain the have-to-knows and many of the nice-to-knows, too—but all the while keep in mind that, in the matter of spreadsheets, more really *is* better. Know more about Excel, and your ability to add value to your data analysis will burgeon.

This is an important point. Learning more about Excel imparts a different kind of empowerment from the sort you'll experience by mastering, say, Microsoft Word. In the latter case, expertise generally serves a greater task—the business of writing and communicating. Knowing how to fashion a table of contents may be a very good thing indeed, and it's something you might need to know; still, that bit of technical wisdom won't help turn you into John Updike. But learn how to batch up a pivot table (and that's what we used to re-present the budget data you see above) and your central spreadsheet mission—portraying and interpreting your data in intelligible and informative ways—*will* be enhanced.

Interacting with the Interface

So let's begin to describe what you'll see once you actually fire up Excel 2010. Turn on the ignition and you'll be brought to a broad expanse of white space, bordered by a sash of buttons, shown in Figure 1–5:

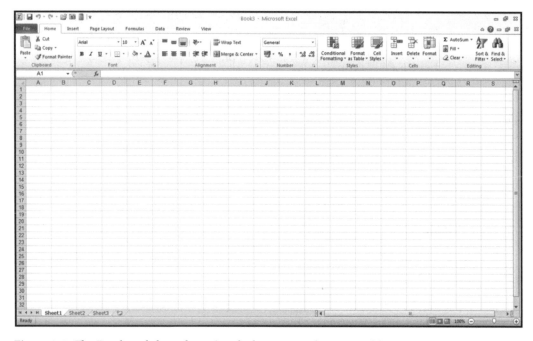

Figure 1–5. The Excel worksheet, featuring the buttons on the Home ribbon

Now, if you're a somewhat experienced Excel user—or *particularly* if you're an experienced user—you may find the above tableau a bit disconcerting, depending on the version of Excel you've been using to date. That's because, starting with Excel 2007, the program's interface underwent a rather dramatic overhaul, one which called for a measure of unlearning on the part of veteran users in order for them to get reoriented to the new regime (and, in a real sense then, beginners may be operating at something of an advantage, since there's nothing for them to unlearn).

Practiced users of the 2003 and prior releases had to, or will eventually have to, wean themselves off this familiar command setup, seen in Figure 1–6:

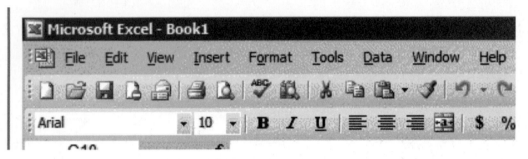

Figure 1–6. The older Excel menu bar/toolbar interface

This now-venerable interface started users off with a row of commands on top (the menu bar) and two tiers of buttons tucked immediately beneath them, called the Standard and Formatting toolbars respectively. As many of you know, clicking any of the named commands on the menu bar unfurled a drop-down menu that sported a column of additional commands, e.g., Figure 1–7:

Figure 1–7. A traditional Excel drop-down menu

And the toolbar buttons? Nuances aside, they basically supplied an alternative means for accessing the same commands inlaid in those drop-down menus. For example, in order to begin the process of opening a file you could have clicked File ➤ Open on the Menu bar, with the Open command appearing on the resulting drop-down menu. Or, you could have clicked the Open button instead on the first strip of toolbar buttons, as shown in Figure 1–8:

Figure 1–8. The traditional Excel Open file button

which would have done the same thing. Again, the commands on the menu bar were more or less emulated by the toolbar buttons, giving users two ways of bringing about whatever it was they wanted to do. (In fact, there were and are often *more* than two ways, because a welter of keyboard equivalents for these commands were and are likewise available; but we're confining our introduction to the commands you'd actually be viewing onscreen).

Because this command structure remained in place for years in the Office programs, users learned it and grew at home with it. But according to Microsoft's own literature, there were problems. As new command options proliferated across successive Excel releases, and as these were assigned their places on the drop-downs and/or toolbar buttons, the job of actually finding commands became rather a burdensome task—in part because a lengthy array of *additional* toolbars also lay in waiting in the background, to be ushered onscreen at the user's discretion.

And there was another problem, one I've encountered more than once in the course of my instructional stints. Some newcomers to the older Office programs assumed, understandably, that the menu bar commands—again, those topmost names such as File, Edit, View, etc., you see on the upper tier—were merely captions describing the *toolbar* buttons nestled immediately below them. But they aren't. And so Microsoft decided that a rethink was in order.

Tab Talk

The result was embodied in a new interface that first made itself known to users with release 2007, and with it came a new vocabulary: Tabs, Ribbons, Groups, and the Quick Access toolbar. *Tabs* are the headings, eight by default, that hold down the upper part of the interface, and that bear a genetic resemblance to the nine menu bar command headings topping the older interface. Indeed four Tab names—File, Insert, Data, and View—reproduce four menu bar names, as shown in Figure 1–9:

Figure 1–9. The new-look tabs

And what do the tabs do? With the exception of the green-hued File, each tab, when clicked, sports a collection of buttons that are more-or-less coordinated around a general spreadsheet objective (what the buttons actually do will be detailed in the later chapters). The Home tab, for example, the one whose contents are automatically displayed when you enter Excel, comprises a collection of buttons that in very large (but not exclusive) measure reprise buttons you'll see on the old Standard and Formatting toolbars in previous Excel releases. Buttons that help you change the appearance and position of text and numbers, and that copy and paste data—all staples of those two earlier toolbars— appear here.

Moreover, the contents of each tab are further organized into titled *groups*, clusters of buttons which are even more closely themed, for example, the Font group within the Home tab is shown in Figure 1–10:

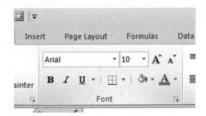

Figure 1–10. The Font button group

Users need to keep this basic understanding in mind: tabs contain groups.

Note that some group buttons are embellished with a small, downward-pointing arrow, but others are not. Click those arrows and you'll be brought to another set of related command options—ones associated with the original button. For example, click the down arrow attached to the Sort command and you'll see Figure 1–11:

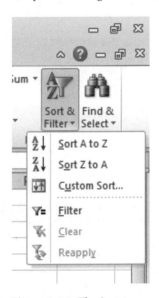

Figure 1–11. The Sort command drop-down menu

This list presents you with a set of options for sorting columns of data. These arrow-driven commands are perhaps the closest thing you'll see to drop-down menus in release 2010.

Click a button with *no* arrow alongside it, on the other hand, and its action is often carried out on the spreadsheet immediately. Alternatively, click an arrowless button and you'll be presented with a dialog box requiring additional user action—but without the kind of sub-menu shown in Figure 1–11. Click the **B** button you see above in the Font group, for example—there's no arrow there—and any data you've selected on the spreadsheet acquires a boldfaced appearance right away, with no additional options from which to choose. Note as well that if you simply roll the mouse over any command on the ribbon, a small but helpful description of what that command does, called a ***tooltip***, materializes.

Another point about tabs. By double-clicking any tab you can submerge, or minimize, the buttons populating the tabs in order to streamline the appearance of the top of your worksheet, as seen in Figure 1–12:

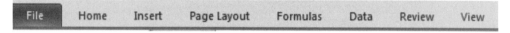

Figure 1–12. *The 2010 tabs, after having minimized the button groups*

(You actually need to double-click a tab twice to achieve this effect. The first double-click takes you to the button contents of the tab on which you've clicked; the second double-click minimizes all the buttons.) Double-clicking any tab heading returns all the buttons to view (you can also minimize by right-clicking anywhere among the tab names and selecting Minimize the Ribbon on the resulting dropdown menu. You can also minimize the ribbon by clicking the caret-like up arrow in the upper far-right of the screen, right above the ribbon. Clicking that arrow a second then restores the ribbon to view.

Something New, Something Old

In addition, some—but not all—of the groups populating the tabs feature a small, right-pointing arrow in their lower right corner, revealingly called the dialog box launcher, see Figure 1–13:

Figure 1–13. *Where to find the dialog box launcher*

If you simply rest your mouse atop one of these arrows without clicking yet, a small description of what's going to happen after you *do* click bobs to the spreadsheet surface. In the case of our group above, the description states, "Shows the Font Tab of the Format Cells dialog box" (along with a keyboard equivalent of the command you're about to execute). Go ahead and click, and you'll call up this object shown in Figure 1–14:

Figure 1–14. The Format Cells dialog box

Look familiar? If you've used any of Excel's pre-2007 releases, it should. What's you're seeing is the good old Format Cells dialog box, the same object that would have made its way onto your screen via the menu bar command/drop-down-menu sequence in the older versions. This dialog box, and others like it that have seeped into the 2010 interface, make a retro visit to the predecessors of Excel 2010, as if to afford discombobulated users a friendly, tried-and-true alternative to all those newfangled tabs and groups they're faced with now.

And this continuity—the availability of dialog boxes from earlier Excel generations—divulges a kind of open secret about Excel 2010 to users of the pre-2007 era: Once you drill down beneath the Tab-Group interface and reach the commands that actually make something happen on the spreadsheet, you'll find that many—though certainly not all–of these commands, particularly those in dialog boxes, are virtual replicas of earlier ones. The fact is that much of the DNA of earlier Excel generations has been encoded into 2010, pointing us to the conclusion that Excel 2010 isn't quite the radical break with the past you may first take it to be. The wheel hasn't been completely reinvented, even if the hubcap has been restyled.

Keeping Tabs…on a New One

On the other hand, even if you're coming to Excel 2010 from the 2007 rendition, you'll quickly observe one significant departure from that latter interface—the debut of the File tab, distinguished from all the other tabs by its conspicuous green cast. The File tab supplants the 2007 Office button—perhaps destined to go down as a one-hit wonder, having come and gone with that release alone (See Figure 1–15.)

Figure 1–15. The Office 2007 button

The suspicion was that too many users mistook this button for nothing more than an inert logo when they first saw it, and not as the repository of important commands it actually was (my wife, a moderately experienced user, tells me it took her ages to figure out what the button did). In any case, click the 2010 File tab and this time you *won't* roll out one more array of buttons atop your screen; instead, you'll see something like Figure 1–16:

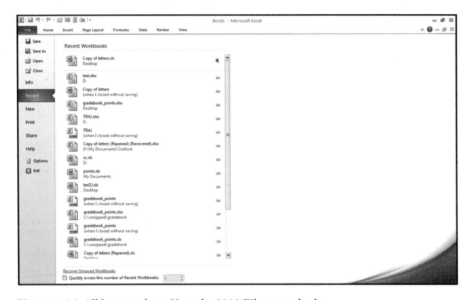

Figure 1–16. All buttoned up: How the 2010 File menu looks

Clicking File, the rough—very rough—equivalent of the pre-2007 menu bar command with the same name can bring you to a number of notable destinations gathered in what's called the Backstage:

- For starters, it presents you with a list of recently accessed spreadsheets, so you can swiftly retrieve them again.

- It offers up basic Office commands that affect files, such as Open, Save, Save As, and Close.

- It warehouses various printing options.

- It contains numerous default settings, e.g., the typeface and font size in effect when you start any new spreadsheet. Of course, the defaults are there to be changed, as you see fit. For example – if you want to change Excel's default font, click File ➤ Options ➤ General, and then enter the appropriate font and font size choices in the drop-down menus.

- It furnishes Excel's Help component.

And File allows you to customize your ribbon in a variety of ways, either by enabling you to fashion new groups you can then post inside the existing tabs (quick review: *groups* are the subdivisions of tabs) or freeing you to customize new tabs altogether, by selecting, grouping, and subsuming commands under a new tab name of your devising.

That last point also reminds us that Excel is stocked with a rather prodigious array of commands that, by default, *don't* appear on any tab. But they're all listed here in the deeper recesses of File, to be added to tabs by users who need them, as shown in Figure 1–17:

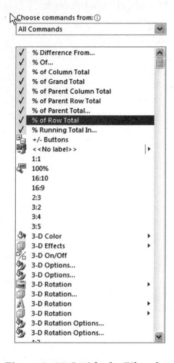

Figure 1–17. *Inside the File tab, where all of Excel commands are listed*

Figure 1–17 captures but an excerpt of all the available commands; and while you may not need to import too many of these into your tabs, remember the knowing-more-is-better credo. There are some cool capabilities stored in that list—capabilities you may one day decide you'd like to use.

Cool QAT

All of which segues into the Quick Access Toolbar (QAT), a rather mild-mannered strip of buttons you'll find lining the upper-left perimeter of your Excel screen, as seen in Figure 1–18:

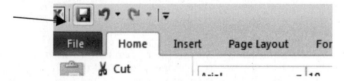

Figure 1–18. *The Quick Access toolbar*

Apart from demonstrating Excel's tenacious attachment to the word "toolbar," the QAT plays a valuable role in enabling you to access important commands easily. Stocked with but three buttons at the outset—the ones which execute the Save, Undo, and Redo commands—the QAT can be tailored to store any other command buttons—ones you presumably want to use often. The idea is that you can post any existing, tab/group-based command to the QAT so that the command remains available even when you go ahead and move on to a different tab.

For example, suppose you're a pivot table devotee, and while you know that the command for designing a new table is housed in the Tables group of the Insert tab, you want to able to activate a pivot table at any time—even if you now find yourself in, say, the Data tab. By right-clicking your mouse on the Pivot Table command (important note: unless otherwise indicated, all mouse clicks in this book call upon the left button) and clicking the Add to Quick Access Toolbar option shown in Figure 1–19:

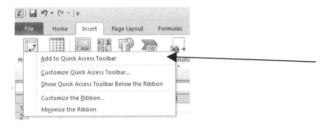

Figure 1–19. Where to add commands to the QAT

you can dispatch a copy of the Pivot Table command to the QAT, where it makes itself available whenever you want it (Figure 1–20):

Figure 1–20. QAT access to the Pivot Table command

No need to revisit the Data tab; just click Pivot Tables on the QAT instead—and there's your pivot table.

You can also install any command onto the QAT from that master list of all Excel commands catalogued in the File tab.

Understood in Context

Now there's one more component of the 2010 interface you'll want to know about, one which appears only on occasion. When you add certain elements to your spreadsheet—e.g., one of those pivot tables, or a chart, or a Sparkline, or a graphic object (say, a shape or a picture), and return to that object and click on it, a command name alluding to that object suddenly pokes its head atop your screen. What does that mean? Well, let's return to our grading sheet, complete with those student-performance Sparklines. Click on any cell containing a Sparkline, and you'll trigger this display (Figure 1–21):

Figure 1–21. The Sparkline Tools tab

Click that amber title (the color varies by whatever object you're working with) and a *new* set of tab contents barges onscreen, overriding the tab with which you'd been working to date. What you see now instead is a battery of options devoted to Sparklines alone (Figure 1–22):

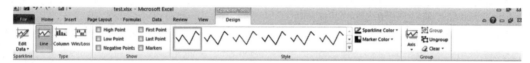

Figure 1–22. Sparkline tool buttons

Complete your Sparkline revisions, click on any other, non-Sparkline-bearing cell, and this tab disappears, returning you to the previous tab. Whenever you click any Sparkline cell, that tab revisits the screen (again, how Sparklines actually work is to be taken up in a later chapter). Thus these object-specific, now-you-see-them-now-you-don't tabs give you swift access to the commands for working with some special spreadsheet tools—exactly when you need them.

Alt-ered Consciousness

Now let's add an important navigational note to the proceedings. We've spent a good deal of time in the company of our trusty mice, ambling across the 2010 interface with those redoubtable pointing devices leading the way. But there's also a keyboard-based means for accessing all of the above elements:

Tap the Alt key, and these lettered or numbered indicators suddenly attach to the tab headings and the QAT (Figure 1–23):

Figure 1–23. Alt keyboard options

Then tap any one of the letters/numbers you see called Key Tips (this time without Alt), and that tab's contents display. Thus if you tap A as we see it here, the Data tab's buttons will appear, each command of which is then *also* lettered. Then tap any one of *these* letters (and note some commands comprise two letters—these should be tapped rapidly in sequence), and the command executes, as shown in Figure 1–24:

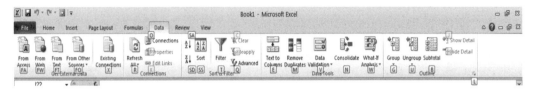

Figure 1–24. Inside the Data tab: Alt key options

Thus if I type **SD** now, a selected range will be sorted in descending alphabetical order (and don't worry what that means if you aren't sure. Sorting is to be explained later. But note that **SD** = Sort Descending). And once the command does its thing, all the letters disappear. And if you initiate the whole process by tapping Alt and then have second thoughts about it, simply tap Alt a second time, and the letters vanish—no harm done. Thus the Alt approach offers one more way of getting the same jobs done—but this time with no mouse required, if you're so inclined. Commit a few of these Alt-ernatives to memory and you should be able to speed some of your basic, recurring tasks as a result (and just for the record—the Alt technique in subtler form also works in the pre-2007 releases of Excel, too).

A couple of other points before we wind up. The way in which the ribbon's contents appear on your screen will depend in part on your screen's resolution (I speak from experience). Your button captions may thus be positioned differently from ours, and so the screen shots in this book may not precisely correspond to what you're seeing. So rest assured: you're not hallucinating, you just have a different screen setting. And here's something else that you won't see in previous Excel versions: when you select text (defined broadly, here, as including numbers as well)—that is, when you actually highlight the text, as opposed to simply clicking on a cell—you'll see a dim, apparition-like toolbar looming a bit above the cell. Lift your mouse just a bit, and the toolbar—called a mini-toolbar—resolves sharply on screen, as shown in Figure 1–25:

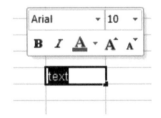

Figure 1–25. The mini-toolbar

The mini-toolbar supplies you with speedy access to standard text formatting option buttons — bold, italics, etc. Click one and the change is made. If, on the other hand, you find this utility literally gets in the way, you can turn it off by clicking File ➤ Options ➤General ➤ Show Mini Toolbar on Selection, and unchecking the box.

We can begin to figure out how to pour our data into that massive space—and make the data work for us.

So let's begin.

CHAPTER 2

■ ■ ■

Getting Started and Getting Around the Worksheet

More Addresses Than the Phone Book—Cells, and How to Get There

Let's start at square one—literally, by returning to Excel 2010's blank worksheet, which is what you'll see when you enter the program, as shown in Figure 2–1:

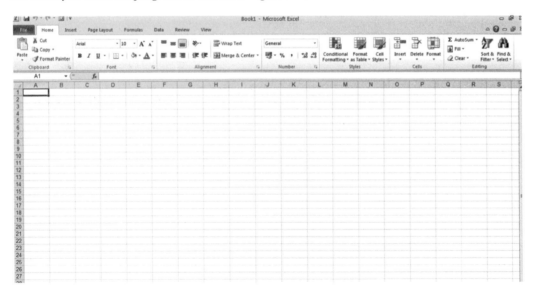

Figure 2–1. The 2010 worksheet, or at least part of one

And, as you scan this rather panoramic scene, we'll trot out a few more of those have-to-know concepts, ones you'll need to keep in mind in order to steer your course across all this territory spread out before you. You're looking at a ***worksheet***—or more strictly speaking, part of a worksheet, an integral part of a ***workbook***. A workbook, simply put, is really Excel's name for a file, the kind of object you'll find listed in My Documents, e.g., familybudget.xlsx. What Microsoft Word calls a ***document***, then, is what Excel calls a workbook.

By default, the workbook is outfitted with three identical-looking worksheets, all of which are represented by tabs (not the kind we explored in detail last chapter) in the lower-left corner of the workbook, as shown in Figure 2–2:

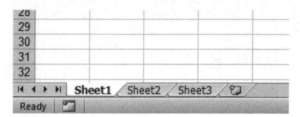

Figure 2–2. *Keeping tabs on the worksheets*

You can supplement these three start-off worksheets with additional ones if you wish, or delete them (though you can't delete all of them, of course; otherwise you'd have nothing left), and you can even hide a worksheet. Why might you need to use several worksheets? For example, a university professor might want to assign a sheet to each of the classes she's teaching, listing each roster of students and their grades on each sheet. And for ease of data entry and review, all the sheets could be designed and formatted identically.

As you can see, the worksheet comprises an enormous grid, criss-crossed by lettered columns and numbered rows. Each intersection of a column and row is called a ***cell***, each of which in turn bears an ***address***, identified very simply by its unique combination of column letter and row number. Thus in Figure 2–3 the ***cell pointer***—that thick-bordered rectangle that gallivants across the worksheet—finds itself in cell C7:

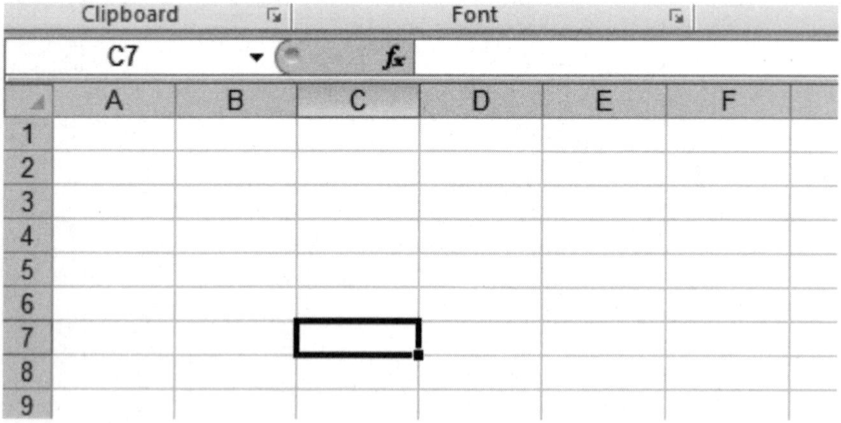

Figure 2–3. *Selecting cell C7*

You'll note of course how the respective C column and 7 row headings have changed colors, denoting the current position of the cell pointer. A little less obvious, though, is the C7 (it's never 7C, by the way) posted in the upper left of the screen shot. As you can see, that sliver of space up there, called the *name box* (and why it's called the name box is to be explained a bit later) records the whereabouts of the cell pointer; and the two kinds of indicators—the column/row-heading color change and the name box cell reference—make it easy to know exactly where you've situated the cell pointer.

And as for the cell pointer itself, its position marks that point in the worksheet where data will go when you begin to type. Thus if I type the number 56 in our screenshot, it will be posted to cell C7.

And as we earlier observed, the worksheet is large—very, very large, consisting of 16,384 columns and exactly 1,048,576 rows. Do the math and you wind up with over 17 billion cells, a preposterously huge number that will likely far, far exceed any purpose you and I might bring to a workbook; and given your computer's memory allotment, you probably couldn't fill all those cells even if you wanted to. Put another way—if I wanted to view the entire worksheet at one time on my screen, I'd need a display about 800 feet wide and 1.6 miles long, give or take a football field—and try to sit with *that* in economy class. And remember just for the record that *each* worksheet in the workbook boasts another 17 billion cells—so if you need to catalogue the stars in the Milky Way, for example, you've come to the right place. Just make sure you get a RAM transplant first.

But you may be bothered by a more practical issue: since we run out of letters at the 26th column—letter Z, that is—what do we call column 27, for starters? Answer: That column is assigned letters AA, followed by AB in column 28, etc. Sidle over to the 53rd column and you get BA, and so on. By the time you puff into column 701—ZZ—your next stop is AAA, with the lettering finally coming to rest at XFD—the 16,384th column. Thus an address such as

LPW34734

is perfectly legal, even if you never park your mouse in that cell—and you probably never will.

Getting Around

In any event, you'll need to know about the ways in which you can transport the cell pointer to the various cells across the worksheet. Perhaps the simplest means for doing so—and you may well be able to figure out some of these techniques by yourself—is to click your mouse on any cell you wish. But if you need to click a distant cell—say, LA345—you need to get there first, and you'll find yourself a long way from that locale when you first get into Excel and find yourself in cell A1. One way to traverse all that space is to click any of the four horizontal or vertical scroll buttons lining the far and lower-right sides of the workbook, as in Figure 2–4:

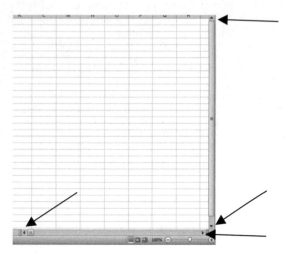

Figure 2–4. The four scroll buttons

Click one of these and the worksheet slides one row up or down or one column to the left or right in the indicated direction. And if you click a scroll button and then continue to hold the left mouse button down, the worksheet skitters rapidly in the chosen direction, until you release the mouse. You can also click either of the two scroll bars that sit between the two pairs of scroll buttons shown in Figure 2–5:

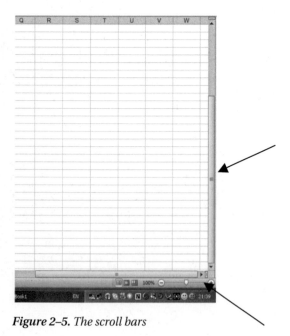

Figure 2–5. The scroll bars

Click either of these and keep the mouse button down. Then pull, or drag, the scroll bar across or down, depending on which bar you've selected; the worksheet speeds in the direction you've chosen—but only as far as you've already travelled. That is, if you're currently in column X, for example, you can only scroll horizontally between that column and column A. Note in addition that when you drag a scroll bar, Excel displays an accompanying caption, one which notifies you which row or column is going to end up in the leftmost column or the uppermost row onscreen once you release the mouse button. Try it and you'll see what I mean.

But remember this: *neither* scroll option—neither the buttons nor the bars—will actually take you *into* a new cell. To illustrate the point: suppose I click cell C5 and then ride my scroll bar to say, column AH. This is what you'll see, in Figure 2—6:

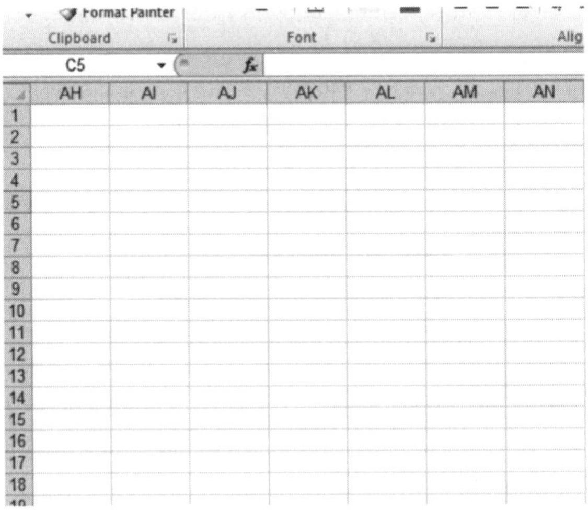

Figure 2–6. Now you see it, now you don't: Cell C 5 remains selected, even though you've scrolled quite a way beyond it.

You've made it to column AH, but look at the name box, the field that always records the current cell pointer location. You're still "in" C5, even though you can't even see that cell onscreen right now. And, as a matter of fact, if you begin to type now, that data will be installed in...cell C5 (and note that row heading number 5 is colored, reminding you that this row continues to be occupied by the cell pointer).

The larger point, then, is that scrolling will only enable you to *view* new areas of the worksheet. If you want to actually *move* into cell AH1, for example, you'll still have to click it.

As you may have gathered, then, there is a kind of hit-or-miss quality to mouse moves. Clicking or dragging or scrolling in the direction you want to go, in the hope of landing *precisely* in the cell you're seeking, can be something of a challenge—particularly if you want to travel a long way across the worksheet. If I need to deposit the cell pointer in cell AB367, for example, and I'm starting cell from D8, I may have to do quite a bit of clicking and dragging until I end up at that address—if I rely on my mouse.

Key Points

But Excel supplies us with a range of *keyboard* navigational maneuvers that also allow us to home in on the cell we want; and again, some of these are rather self-evident. First, pressing the Enter key bumps the cell pointer down one row—though keep in mind it is possible to change the direction an Enter press takes. By clicking the File ➤ Advanced ➤ After Pressing Enter command, you can actually redirect the Enter press to head left, right, or even up, instead of down. And if you uncheck the After Pressing Enter box, pressing Enter won't move the cell pointer at all, leaving it in the cell in which you just typed. Press any of the four arrow keys and you move in the appropriate directions (and thus the Down arrow and Enter keys are equivalent here). Press Tab and you head one column to the right. Enter the Shift-Tab combination and you set out in the opposite direction—one column left; and so these Tab variations thus emulate the Right and Left arrow keys, and Shift-Enter lifts you one row up.

To encompass broader stretches of the worksheet in one fell swoop, press the Page Up or Page Down keys. These zoom you up, or down, one *screen's* worth of rows; just remember that, because you can modulate the heights of rows (something we haven't learned yet) the number of rows you'll actually span in that screen's worth with will vary. A far more obscure set of keystroke pairings—Alt-Page Down and Alt-Page Up—take you one screen's worth of *columns* right or left, respectively, though because you can also widen or narrow columns the number of columns across which you'll travel will vary, too.

Note in addition that if you *hold down* any of the above navigational keys instead of merely pressing them, the cell pointer will career rapidly in the direction you've chosen. Thus hold down Page Down, for example, and you'll streak down the worksheet at breakneck velocity.

Now here are two more slightly different but surprisingly useful keyboard navigators. Press Ctrl-Home and Excel will always deliver you back to cell A1, irrespective of your current location. What's valuable about Ctrl-Home? Well, if you find yourself the spreadsheet equivalent of a million miles (or cells) away from home, Ctrl-Home immediately rushes you back to the worksheet's point of inception—that is, cell A1.

And for a kind of flip side to Ctrl-Home, there's Ctrl-End, a slightly trickier move. Tapping Ctrl-End ferries you to the last cell in the worksheet containing *data*, that is, the lower-rightmost cell in which any kind of data at all is currently stored. Thus, if you've typed 476 in cell XY567912 and nothing else beyond that spot, Ctrl-End will take you exactly there. There's only one problem with Ctrl-End: if you delete the 476 from cell XY567912 and then press Ctrl-End, you'll *still* be sent back to that cell - even though it's currently empty. In order to let Excel know where to find the last data-bearing cell on the worksheet now—wherever it may happen to be—you need to save the worksheet first. Then press Ctrl-End, and you'll find yourself face-to-screen with the "new" last cell in the worksheet.

And the name box we introduced at the chapter's outset also plays a navigational role. Click the box and then type any cell reference, e.g., D435 (by the way—cell references aren't case sensitive; you could type d435, as well), as in Figure 2–7:

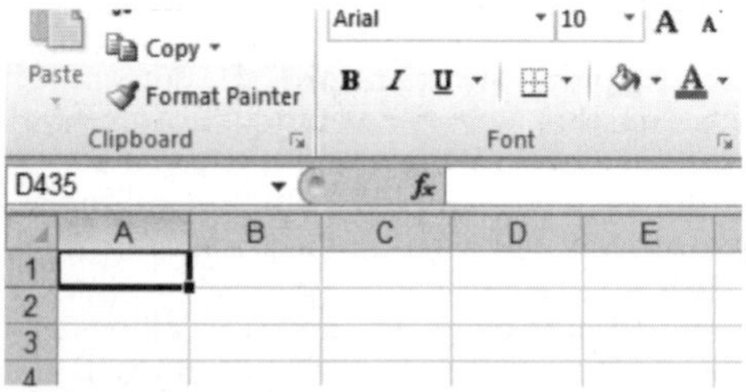

Figure 2–7. Using the Name Box to navigate to a cell address

Then press the Enter key, and Voila! Excel surges directly into D435. This method, then, provides a high-speed route to precisely the cell you want, no matter how far away; and unlike scrolling, it places you right smack-dab *into* the cell.

And for a similar but not identical means for pinpointing a particular cell, press the F5 key and this Go To dialog box appears, as shown in Figure 2–8:

Figure 2–8. The Go To dialog box

Type a cell in the Reference field, press Enter, and again the cell pointer rockets to just that address. And if you think Go To is a virtual clone of Name Box with nothing new to offer, that isn't quite true. If you use Go To repeatedly in the course of your current spreadsheet session, it compiles a list of all the destinations you've previously visited with that command, as shown in Figure 2–9:

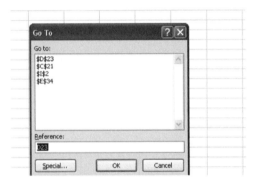

Figure 2–9. *Getting to a cell via Go To*

Click any of the addresses recorded and click OK, and you'll be returned to that address (those dollar signs will be explained in a later chapter). (Go To also does a number of other more exotic things, too, such as flagging all the worksheet's cells with formulas in them, if you need to know that sort of thing.)

Here's a table summary of these options we've described (the list is not exhaustive, by the way, but will surely do for now):

Table 2–1. Cell Navigation Techniques

Technique	Type of Movement
Mouse	Enables user to click any cell
Scroll buttons/bars	Moves to a new area of the worksheet; but does not directly select any cell
Enter key	Moves one cell down
Shift-Enter	Moves one cell up
Tab	Moves one cell to the right
Shift-Tab	Moves one cell to the left
Arrow keys	Moves one cell in desired direction
Page-Down/Up	Moves one screen's worth of rows up or down
Alt-Page Down/Up	Moves one screen's worth of columns right or left
Ctrl-Home	Always moves to cell A1
Ctrl-End	Travels to last cell containing data (the lowest-right such cell on the worksheet)
Name Box	Moves to cell whose address you've typed in box
Go To	Moves to cell whose address you've typed in Reference field

Ranges: A Select Tool

And now for something if not completely, then at least slightly, different. To date, we've explored a variety of ways for meandering across the worksheet, all of which bring us to one particular cell at journey's end. But Excel also provides us with the means for occupying more than one cell at the same time. What does that mean?

Well, it means that it's time to dust off another one of those have-to-know concepts. This matter doesn't originate with Excel, of course, but history aside, spreadsheet users very often need to visit, work with, or be able to identify a *group* of cells at the same time. Why?

The reasons are several. For example, a user may want to change the font that currently appears in a large cluster of cells. Having the ability to bring about that change simultaneously in all those cells is obviously a great deal more efficient than having to revise each cell individually. After all, what if you wanted to change the font for, say, 50 million cells?

In addition, Excel users very often need to perform some sort of mathematical operation on a gaggle of cells at the same time. Indeed, isn't adding rows or columns of numbers—the classic Excel task—exactly what we're talking about here?

So in order to do this kind of work we need to be able to define ***ranges*** on the worksheet. Strictly speaking, a range is any collection of cells that has been selected or identified at the same time. But more conventionally put, a range is a set of *adjacent* cells that exhibit a rectangular shape—and the concept is far simpler than it sounds.

Figure 2–10, for example, is a range:

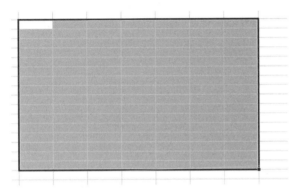

Figure 2–10. *A typical range*

As is Figure 2–11:

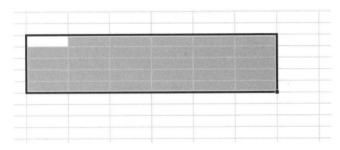

Figure 2–11. *Another range example, this one narrower and shorter*

And so is Figure 2–12:

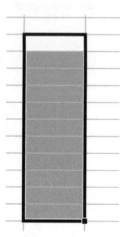

Figure 2–12. One column, eleven rows

You're doubtless getting the idea. Our cell pointer—and that's what it is—stretches when it selects a range, serving as its perimeter; and with one clear exception, a bluish fill color identifies exactly those cells that populate the range (and why the very first cell in a range remains white is a matter to be revealed later).

And so here's the point behind all this: if I want to change the font in a range of cells, I can select those cells I want as illustrated above, and then go ahead and issue a font-change command. And as a result, *only* the cells in the range will be affected.

And how do you go about selecting cells in a range? It's rather easy—and again, both mouse and keyboard approaches stand at the ready. If you're mouse-inclined, click the first cell of the desired range—which is, typically, the upper-left cell in the block of cells you want to select. Keep the mouse button down, and pull—or drag—across and/or down the cells you want to incorporate into the range. When you're done, release the mouse button, and the blue-blanketed range remains selected.

You can also select an entire column by simply clicking a column header—that is, the alphabetized area in which the columns are named. Doing so highlights that column, as in Figure 2–13:

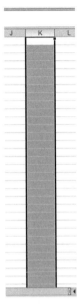

Figure 2–13. *An entire column selected*

Yes—all one-million-plus cells in the K column are now selected (hope you weren't expecting a fold-out showing them all). And you can select a row by clicking one of the numbered row headers on the side of the screen. And by clicking the column/row header area and dragging across or down that area, you can select multiple columns or rows.

And if you opt for keyboard cell-selection approaches, first select that upper-left cell, using any navigational means you wish. Then hold down the Shift key, keep it down, and press any of the keyboard arrow keys in the direction of the cells you wish to select. For example, you can first press the Right and then the Down arrows, thus enabling you to describe a range of as many columns and rows as you wish. Just remember to keep the Shift key down throughout the process. When you're done, release the Shift key and observe your range, decked out in blue. (Just keep in mind for the record that you could start your range selection by clicking what is the upper-*right* cell of the desired range, and dragging *left* and down and/or up. It's just that most people—at least those who speak and write English—tend to think left to right.)

But I've been holding out on you. There's yet *another* way to designate a range, and that alternative takes us back once again to the name box, along with an important data entry principle. If, for example I type this:

D13:H23

in the name box and then press Enter, cells D13 *through* H23 will be selected, turning that tell-tale blue (with the exception of D13, which serves as the "first", upper-left cell in the range and so remains white). Note the expression—D13:H23. It means that *all* the cells from D13—the upper-left cell in the range—through H23—the lower-right cell in the range—have been designated for the range selection; and this upper-left/lower-right-cell nomenclature for range boundaries is indispensable to Excel formulas. Thus, by way of preview, if you see an expression that looks something like this:

=SUM(A34:C57)

You'll know it means that all the numbers in cells A34 through C57 are to be added (And by the way – this formula: =SUM(A:A) – would add all the cells in the A column).

One more point (for now) about ranges. Consider this possibility, shown in Figure 2–14:

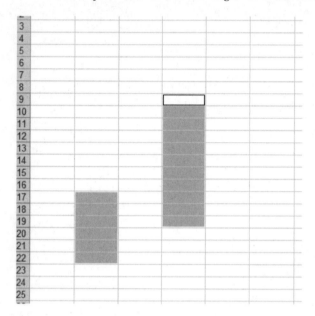

Figure 2–14. Two ranges selected at the same time

So what's going on here? In this case, *two* ranges seem to have been selected at the same time. How's that done? Truth to be told, rather easily. First, select one range as per the usual techniques. Then, keep the Ctrl key down, and with your mouse, drag across a second set of cells. You can even select three or more sets of cells with this approach—and if you're wondering why you would want to do such a thing, the answer is that you may wish to subject all these cells to the same change—you may want to alter the font size in just these selected cells, for example. Or you may want to delete the contents of a range or two of cells. If you do, select the range(s), and just press the Delete key. (And let's pass on the question about whether the screen shot above depicts two different ranges, or merely one range consisting of two non-adjacent sets of cells. In reality either answer could apply depending on your purposes, but in the great majority of cases you'd be regarding these as two distinct ranges.)

And if you want to try something a bit more exotic, you can also type something like this in the good old name box, followed by pressing Enter:

A3:D34,E6:H23

Note the comma. The above instruction will select cells A3 through D34, *as well as* E6 through H23.

And if you mess up—that is, if you select the wrong set of cells—the easiest thing to do is simply click anywhere on the worksheet. Doing so "turns off" the blue color scheme for the selected range, and you can start range-selecting again. And in any case, you're going to need to turn off the range sooner or later if you plan on doing work anywhere else on the worksheet.

Now if you *really* need to change the font for 50 million or so cells—or something even more global—try this. It's easy to overlook, but observe the button wedged between the A column and row 1 headings…Click it and *all* 17 billion cells turn blue (excepting A1 above. You can also press Ctrl-A to select all the worksheet cells). You've thereby selected the entire worksheet, and you might opt for this mass procedure if, for example, you wanted to change the color of *all* the text in your worksheet to say, green. Once you're finished, just click anywhere on the sheet, and the blue selection color disappears, as in Figure 2–15:

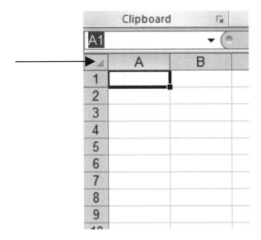

Figure 2–15. *Click here to select all the worksheet cells*

A last introductory point about ranges. Like amoeba, ranges can be single-celled, and if you're at a loss to understand why—after all, how in the world is selecting a one-celled range different from simply referring to a single cell?—stay tuned. There are sometimes very good and productive reasons for working this way. (Note: See the appendix on range names for a discussion of this and other range-related tips.)

Data Entry: Getting Started

But now that we've learned how to get where we want to go on the worksheet, let's learn the things we can do once we arrive. There are a few billion cells out there craving our attention, and we want to fill at least some of them with data. Here's how.

Unlike typing in Microsoft Word, data entry in Excel is a two-step, but still elementary, affair. Type the number 48 in Word, for example, and you're done. But enter 48 in a worksheet cell and you need to complete the process by *installing* the value in the cell. And that second step is carried out either by any navigational move away from the cell (e.g., pressing Enter or Page Down, or clicking a different cell) in which you've just typed, or by entering the value and then clicking the check box alongside the formula bar, as shown in Figure 2–16:

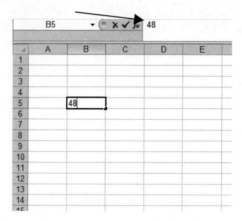

Figure 2 16. *Click the check to place the value in its cell.*

Here's the simplest-case scenario. Type 48 in cell A3 and then press Enter. You've just done two things:

1) installed the number 48 in A3, and

2) moved down a row into cell A4.

Remember you need to execute two steps in order to enter data: Type the value, and then finalize the entry with some navigational move (including Ctrl-Enter, which actually leaves you in the cell), or by clicking the check mark.

But if you have second thoughts about entering that value, you need only press the Esc key before you install it in the cell, or click the X you see above alongside the check mark. Do either of these things and the value simply won't make its way in the cell. Note also you'll only see the X and the check mark on screen when you start to type in a cell.

(Note that for our purposes, we'll always tell you to press Enter in order to enter data in their cells simply as a matter of explanatory convenience. But remember that you can use the other options, too, unless I state otherwise.)

It's rather easy, and it should be—so don't wait for the other shoe to drop. There are no hidden complexities here. Still, a number of classic data entry features and issues need to be explained, just the same.

Entering Text: Trespassing Allowed

For one thing, note that when you enter a number it's pushed by default to the cell's right border, or aligned right, as they say in the trade. That's because our number system is Arabic, and proceeds from right to left. Enter text, however—and text are *data*, too—and the results align left, as per our left-to-right, Roman alphabet.

Now if I type something a bit more extensive—say, the phrase "Microsoft Excel"—in A3, the result looks like Figure 2–17:

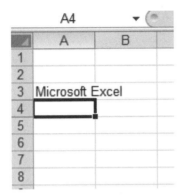

Figure 2–17. Run out of space?

thereby raising an ancient spreadsheet question. You'll note that our phrase appears to overrun cell A3 and invade the neighboring B3, implying in turn that the text occupies two different cells—but that isn't the case. In fact the entire phrase is still positioned in A3, appearances notwithstanding; but apart from the fact that I've done this a few thousand times, how do I know that?

I know it because I can direct my attention to that long strip to the right of the name box, called the *formula bar* (and again, we'll need to explain that name). Click cell A3 again and check out the formula bar—you'll see Figure 2–18:

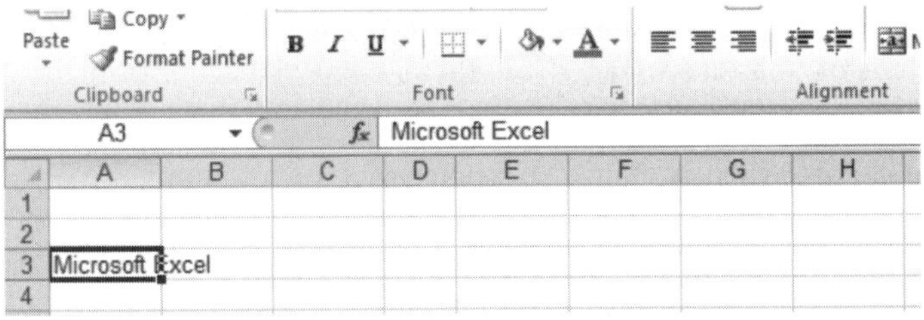

Figure 2–18. The Formula Bar: recording the actual contents of a cell

Note the visual relationship in force here. I've clicked on cell A3. The formula bar records what I've typed there, confirming that the phrase in A3 indeed occupies that cell, and *only* that cell. If you need additional proof, click cell B3 and turn to the formula bar—which now shows…nothing.

Yeah, this is another have-to-know, actually a few of them. First, we've learned that whatever you type in a cell is wholly confined to that cell, no matter what optical illusions are perpetrated on the worksheet. Second, we've learned that the formula bar tells you exactly what's going on in the cell you click, a point that will acquire additional importance as we proceed.

But there's more to this. If I go ahead and actually type something in cell B3—say, "Thursday"—the worksheet reports what you see in Figure 2–19:

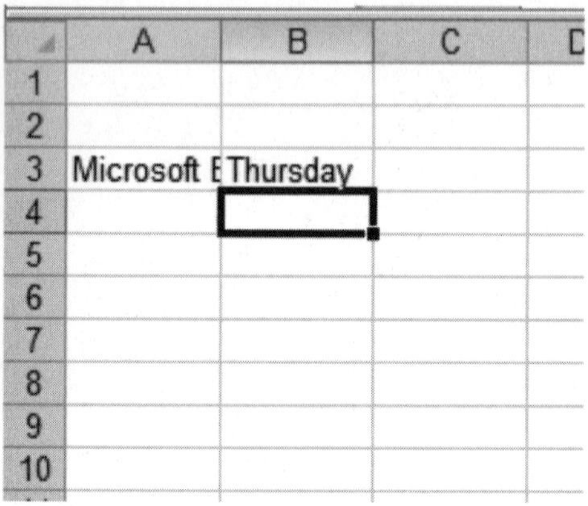

◢	A	B	C	D
1				
2				
3	Microsoft E	Thursday		
4				
5				
6				
7				
8				
9				
10				

Figure 2–19. The case of the disappearing word

Now, Houston, we have a problem—a rather obvious one. We have seen that as long as the adjoining cells to the right remain empty, it's perfectly permissible to enter a lengthy phrase (at least one comprising text—more on this soon) in a cell, even if its contents encroach on the nearby cells. But type anything—even one character—in one of the adjoining, empty-till-now cells, and the cell reclaims its own turf, barring any excess text from other cells to its left. As a result, you'll have two obvious questions: Has the clipped text in cell A3 been somehow deleted, and, whatever the answer to that question, what do we do next?

The answer to the first question is: No. Click back on cell A3 and scan the formula bar. You'll see that the phrase "Microsoft Excel" is intact. None of it has been deleted, but rather some of it—that segment which had spilled into B3—has been *obscured* by the text entered in that latter cell. And that's what happens to text if it exceeds its column boundary: it continues untouched across empty, adjoining cells—until one of those cells is empty no longer. It's then visually restricted to its own column.

And as for question two: If we delete the entry in cell B3, then *all* the text in A3 reappears on screen. But if we want to keep "Thursday" in its place, we need to *widen* the column in which "Microsoft Excel" resides—in this case—the column A. Doing so should make room for all the text in both cells.

There is, as is usual with the Office programs, more than one way to do this. The two easiest and fastest are carried out as follows:

With your mouse, move up to the *right* boundary of the column you wish to widen (and *not* row 1). What started out as Excel's familiar thick white cross—the one you see when you move about the worksheet proper—should now appear as the slender, black, double-arrowed object seen in Figure 2–20:

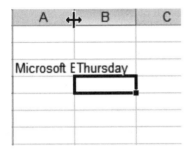

Figure 2–20. The A column, selected for widening

You *must* bring about that double-arrowed pointer in order to widen the column; but it should appear automatically as soon as your mouse arrives atop the right boundary. Then click the boundary, and drag to the right (don't release the left mouse button). As you do so, the column should expand, revealing ever more of the text. And as you drag, a caption accompanies the action, tallying the current column width both in units of text characters and pixels (this bit of information is usually of little more than academic importance most of the time; just bear in mind that the *default* width of an Excel column is set at 8.43 characters, for historical reasons). When you've achieved the desired width—presumably after all the hidden text has been brought to light—you can release the mouse. Nothing stops you from widening—or narrowing—the column again, by dragging it again to the right or even to the left. If you've accidentally clicked on the left boundary of the column you want—which is, after all, the right boundary of the column to its left—then *that* column will be widened instead.

Bring your mouse to that same right column boundary, make sure the double-arrowed cross is in view, and this time double-click. The column will automatically resize itself to reveal all the data in the column. Known as Autofit, this rather efficient device is a time-honored means for solving the hidden-text problem. Note that Autofit modulates the column to make sure to reveal what is *currently* its widest entry, fitting itself snugly to that entry's width; and so if you delete that item from the column and perform another Autofit, the column may *narrow*, as it hugs what is *now* the widest entry.

Now for an important variation on the Autofit theme, here's a scenario you might very well have to confront. Suppose you've entered the months of the year, and your data look like Figure 2–21:

January	February	March	April	May	June	July	August	Septemb	October	Novemb	December

Figure 2–21. Columns in need of widening—or narrowing

The problem is clear: some of the longer month names have barged into the cells to their right, and these happen to be occupied by months of their own. Thus the same column-width issue emerges; but what's new here is that we can conduct an Autofit on *several* columns at the same time.

To make this happen, click the first of the column headings—A—hold the mouse button down, and drag across the remaining headings (again, *don't* drag across row 1 on the worksheet; you need to select the headings). Your worksheet would look something like this, as shown in Figure 2–22:

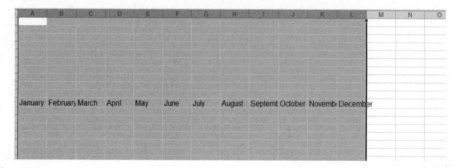

Figure 2–22. Columns selected and prepared for autofitting

That blanket of blue cells teaches us incidentally that when you click a column heading, all the cells in that column are selected; but what interests us *here* is the column width question; so now double-click *any* one of the boundaries separating any of the selected columns, e.g., the one separating B and C, or J and K (again, you'll need to see that double-arrow cross). All the columns should now be resized, with each new width reflecting the *respective* widths of the months. See Figure 2–23:

Figure 2–23. Autofit: one size doesn't fit all

It's a nifty way of Autofitting lots of columns in one go; but now you may have to contend with another possible problem. Thanks to Autofit we can now see all the text, but since each of the months exhibits a different width, so then do the columns housing them—and presentationally speaking, that may not look very nice. You may want uniformly widened columns instead, but you can't get there from here using Autofit. What to do?

The answer is to select all the column headings as described above, but this time, instead of double-clicking any boundary, we click the right column boundary of the *longest* month—in this case "September," given the font being used—and drag a bit to the right. Then release the mouse. This technique—really a variation on the first column-widening approach we cited earlier—*equalizes* the width of all the selected columns; and because we dragged on the widest month's column, naturally all the other months should be visible as well. And if you drag and release the mouse too soon and fail to reveal the word "September" in its entirety, note that all the columns remain selected, so you can resume dragging until the word is completely exposed.

You'll also want to know about another data entry option, one you'll have difficulty ignoring in any case. If you enter text down consecutive cells in a column and have occasion to enter the same datum (that's the singular, believe it or not) twice in different cells, Excel will automatically enter it for you the second (and every subsequent) time in the cell in which you're typing, as soon as it recognizes it. That is, if you enter "John" in cell D2 and "Bill" in D3, and then begin to enter "John" in D4, Excel will complete the name "John" as soon as you type the letter J (this will happen even if you type a lower-case j. See Figure 2–24:

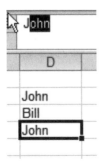

Figure 2–24. *AutoComplete in action; note the formula bar*

That is, Excel will *try* to AutoComplete the name. If you approve of the suggestion, simply press Enter. But if you really want to type "Jerry" in D4, just keep on typing. Note that if you've already entered "Mary" and "May" in different cells, you'll need to type the third letter in either of these names, as Excel won't otherwise know which name you wanted to AutoComplete. But again, if you want "Martin" instead, keep on typing.

But what *is* entirely possible to ignore is another, related feature. Once you've typed even one name with the intention of continuing to type down a column, you can right-click the next cell, and take note of this option in Figure 2–25:

Figure 2–25. *Your on-the-fly drop-down list in the making…*

If I click here, the menu shown in Figure 2–26 appears:

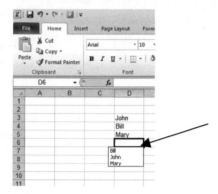

Figure 2–26. *...and here it is*

It's a mini-drop-down, grabbing its data from the current list of names you've typed in the list to date—and the list incorporates any new names as you type them. Just click one. Cool, and little known.

Numbers are (a little) Different

Now let's return to the business of data entry proper, because to date we've omitted a rather essential form of data from the discussion—numbers. The mechanics of numerical data entry are identical to those governing text: Just type the number, and then execute one of those moves away from the cell. Don't worry about typing commas and dollar signs for now; just type the number. Note by way of introduction that if you type:

56.2

for example, the number will appear just as you've typed it. But if you enter:

56.00

you'll see 56 only, because by default Excel sheds those meaningless zeros—until you format it differently (but if you reformat the number, remember it really remains nothing but 56. A glance at the formula bar will provide that confirmation). Note in addition that a number less than 1, say .78, will appear by default as:

0.78

that leading zero can be removed by a customized format, about which we'll have more to say later.

And you'll soon discover a couple of other issues that apply to numbers only.

For one thing, and unlike with text entry, Excel will *never* permit a number to advance into an adjoining column, even if that column is vacant. The reasons are fairly clear. Because our numbers move right-to-left, allowing a number to break into the column to its right would hopelessly misalign a set of numbers streaming down one column. If, for example, a 12–digit number in A4 were to take over some of the space in cell B4 because of its extreme width, and a merely 3-digit number were to populate A5 just beneath it, the "ones" column in the two numbers would be out of whack. The "ones" in A4 would be shunted into B4, even as the "ones" in A5 would remain in A5.

Moreover, if that long number in A4 *were* allowed to ooze into B4—as happens with text—and a number were then entered directly into B4, you'd find it difficult to know A4's true value—because some of its columns would be clipped from view, again as with text. The whole thing is just too messy, and as a result, numbers do *not* enter adjacent columns.

So what *does* happen, then? That depends. If you type a 12–digit number in a column with the start-off, default column width in effect, say

$$123456789123$$

You'll see this instead:

$$1.23457E+11$$

If you haven't seen a number like that lately, it means you graduated high school a long time ago. The long number is rewritten in scientific notation, a kind of shorthand that hems the number into its existing column width, thus keeping in it view, though the number as you typed it *is* displayed that way in the formula bar. But you can reformat the number into the original value you typed—as you almost surely will—and when you do reformat it, Excel then accompanies the process with an Autofit on its own to display the number in its entirety, as you originally entered it (and we'll see how to apply this and various other number formats in Chapter 4).

If, on the other hand, you type a long number and then for whatever reason *narrow* its column substantially, you'll see this:

$$\#\#\#$$

—another classic spreadsheet indicator. Seeing those pound (or hash, or number sign, if you live in the UK and other distant locales) signs in a cell means the cell contains a number that is too long for its current width—and you see pound signs there instead of the scientific notation when you *actively* narrow the cell. The solution: do an Autofit.

Relocating the Data: Copying and Moving

Now here's another indispensible form of data entry you need to know about, though it isn't generally characterized in those terms—copying and moving data.

After all, when you copy data you're reproducing, or entering, more of it, and Excel's copying options are several, and don't always resemble the sorts of things you'd do in Word. Let's explore some of the permutations.

We'll start of course with the basics. Say I want to copy *values* or *text*—and let's begin with one cell's worth of data:

- Click the cell whose data you want to copy.

- Click the Copy button in the Clipboard group in the Home tab (or its time-honored keyboard equivalent, Ctrl-C. Ignore the button's drop-down arrow for now). Note how the cell border is suddenly enlivened by what are called marching ants (I'm not kidding), as seen in Figure 2–27:

Figure 2–27. Text, as copied

- Click the destination cell—the cell *to* which you want to copy, and

- Click the Paste button to the left of the Copy button in the Clipboard group, or Ctrl-V (yes, there are other paste options, but we're in introductory mode). Or—and this option is exceedingly easy to overlook—press Enter. The item is duplicated.

Note as well, however, that even though you've done your job, the marching ants continue to troop around the cell border—at least if you click Copy or press Ctrl-V (but not if you press Enter). That's not a cue for an exterminator, but rather an indicator to the effect that you can paste the cell *again* to other cells, with repeated pastes. When you want to turn the process off, just click the Esc key, and the ants recede. Note that if you paste with Enter, the ants *immediately* disappear. How about copying a *range* of cells? This time:

1. Select the range and release the mouse (or keys, if you're pressing).

2. Click Copy.

3. Click the *first* of the destination cells only. That is, if for example you want to copy cells H2:H5 to say, J6:J9, click J6 *only*. Excel is smart enough to know that if you're copying four cells you're pasting four, and it merely needs you to tell it where the new destination *starts*.

4. Execute one of the Paste options described above.

Note that when you paste a copied range Excel preserves the orientation of the cells in question. That is, if you copy a column of cells, Paste will always paste these in columnar fashion, and a copied *row* will always paste as a row (yes, you can paste a column into a row orientation and vice versa if you want to, but that's for a bit later).

And what of *moving* data? That's what we really mean by cutting and pasting, and the process is rather easy:

1. Select the cell or cells you want to move.

2. Click the Cut button directly above the Copy button, or its equivalent, Ctrl-X. The marching ants do their thing, but note that the cell contents *don't* disappear, even though you've apparently cut them

3. Again, select the first destination cell.

4. Click Paste, or one of its equivalents, including Enter. You're done. (Note: moving a cell containing a formula will *not* change any of its cell references, a point to remember when we discuss relative cell addressing in a later chapter.)

Note that with Cut and Paste the marching ants retreat after one Paste. That's because, well, what's the alternative? The data have been cut and moved elsewhere; granting users another Paste means they'd want to move the data again immediately—a not terribly likely prospect.

There's an alternative way to move (and copy) data in cells, though this one requires a bit of delicacy. Select the range you want to move and rest your mouse *anywhere* along the range's perimeter, until you see a pair of double-sided arrows. Then click and drag the range to its new destination, and release the mouse. If you do the same thing while holding the Ctrl key down, you can *copy* the range. These techniques are fairly easy to mess up, though; releasing the mouse too soon will let the data down in the wrong place.

Now there's still another way to copy cell contents, this one also mouse-powered, and it works like this: We'll start with a number in one cell. Click the cell and slide your mouse atop the lower-right corner of the cell pointer border, where you'll notice a small square lodged in the corner, like a dimple. When you roll the mouse over that little shape, your indicator should remake itself into a slender black cross, as shown in Figure 2–28, not to be confused with the black double-arrow variety you generate when you widen columns:

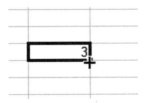

Figure 2–28. The fill handle

When that cross appears, click and hold the mouse button down. Drag as far as you wish, either across a row or down a column, depending on the direction in which you want to copy. Release the mouse when you've dragged the desired distance; you'll see the original number has been copied down or across the range you've dragged. You'll also doubtless take note of the caption that escorts you down/across the range as you drag; it tells you what value will appear in each cell in the copied-to, destination range as you drag. But because, in this case, you're simply copying the same number to each cell again and again, you may think that the caption tells you something you already know—and you're right—this time.

We've just demonstrated an application of what's called Auto-fill, a device that can serve you most productively once you learn its capabilities. And that square dimple we dragged is called the *fill handle*, and you'll want to handle it with care.

And you'll notice something else. When you've completed dragging, Excel caps the process by appending to the lower-right corner of the new, copied range what's called an Auto Fill Options button. Click it and four selections place themselves at your service. We'll discuss the first two here, because the latter two carry out formatting options, which aren't our concern here. Take a look at Figure 2–29:

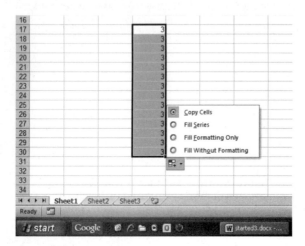

Figure 2–29. *Auto-fill options*

The default selection, Copy Cells, really characterizes what we've just done. But assuming we've copied the number 3 as per the screen shot, from the D17 source cell down through D30, look then what happens when we click selection number two, Fill Series, as shown in Figure 2–30:

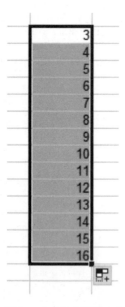

Figure 2–30. *A Fill Series*

I'll bet *that* one got you to look up and stop texting. What Excel has done here is add an increment of one to each of the cells in the range to which we copied the original value, 3. That's a rather cool capability (and it hasn't debuted in Excel 2010, either—this option goes way back), and we're just getting started with it.

Now try this: type the numbers 3 and 5 in cells G3 and G4. Then select both cells and release the mouse. Next, Click and drag the fill handle down the G column to G10. You should see this (Figure 2–31):

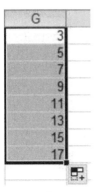

Figure 2–31. Getting a handle on the process: A fill series displaying an interval of 2

Here, Excel works with *two* starting cells, containing the numbers 3 and 5; these alert the worksheet about the *interval* that will pump up all the numbers in the range. As per the Auto Options button command, we've generated what's called a Fill Series, and we could have dragged the fill handle down thousands of cells had we wished, with each successive cell displaying a value 2 higher than the preceding one. And if you start with 5 and 3 instead of 3 and 5 and drag the handle, the numbers will *descend* in decrements of two, e.g., 5, 3, 1, -1, -3, etc. Nor is Excel intimated by exotic intervals: if you enter starting numbers of say 1.36 and 2.43, Auto-fill is perfectly happy to roll out 3.5, 4.57, 5.64, and the like. Just keep this caution in mind: in order to carry out an Auto-fill properly and avoid a common mistake, don't, for example, type 3 and 5 and return to the 3 and begin dragging. Rather, you must select 3 *and* 5, *release* the mouse, and *then* return to that selection and drag the fill handle. That is, you must see this, shown in Figure 2–32, *before* you start the fill process:

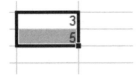

Figure 2–32. Learning to let go: release the mouse before you drag here.

Having Your Fill

Now get this. If I type any day of the week in any cell and drag on the fill handle (it's always there; you just may not have paid it any mind till now), this is what happens (Figure 2–33):

Figure 2—33. Cells-by dates

Rather economical, isn't it? I started here with Tuesday and dragged horizontally, and could have dragged as far as I wanted. (Yes, the column widths may need tweaking, but you know how to do that now.)

And if I type any month and drag on the handle, I bet you know what's going to happen (Figure 2–34):

| July | August | September | October | November | December | January | February | March | April | May | June |

Figure 2–34. 30-day guarantee…filling the months

Moreover, I can do the same with three-letter day or month abbreviations. Type Wed, drag the fill handle, and you get Thu, Fri, Sat, etc. Type Jul and Aug, Sept, Oct, etc. emerge.

These four Auto-fill routines—day, month, and respective three-letter abbreviations—are built into Excel. But you can construct your own lists, too, such that when you type any one of its names and drag the fill handle, all the other names streak onto the screen. How?

Like this. Click the File tab, and then Options (in the left column), and click again on Advanced. Scroll down the window—pretty far down, until you approach the end and see the Edit Custom Lists button (Figure 2–35):

Figure 2–35. Try this at home…where to start making your custom list

Click and you'll see (Figure 2–36):

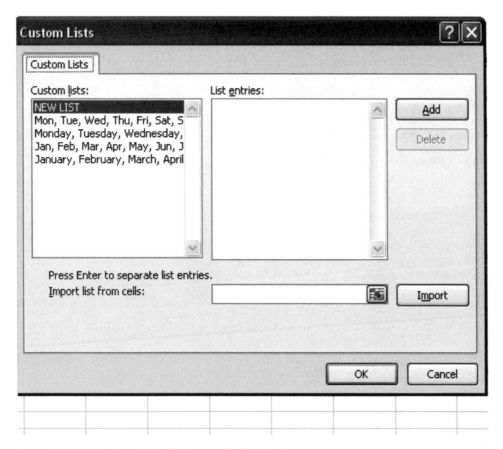

Figure 2–36. *Note the existing lists, supplied by Excel.*

Click in the List entries area and type each name you want to appear in your list, and in the desired sequence, following each entry with Enter, as shown in Figure 2–37:

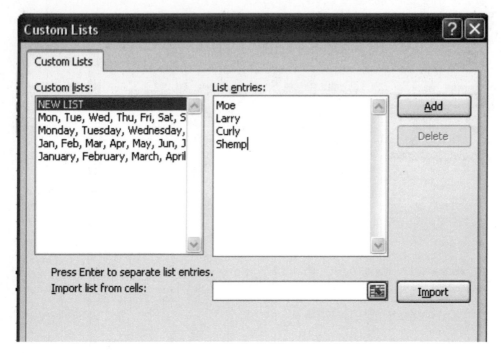

Figure 2–37. *Where the list takes shape*

When you're done, click Add, and your list is swung into the Custom Lists column, where it now shares a zip code with Excel's built-in, default lists.

Then just type *any* one of your custom names in a cell, drag the fill handle, and your list plays down or across the range.

Just bear in mind that we haven't exhausted all the possibilities for copying and moving data. That's because a different kind of cell content—a *cell reference*—can also be copied or cut, with some new implications. That one is coming soon.

Now on to some concluding observations about basic data entry. Note that this expression:

123 Main Street

is considered *text*. Indeed, for starters, *any* data entry containing a non-numerical element, such as:

(212) 555-1212

or say, a social security number:

123-45-6789

is to be treated as text, as opposed to a number. You can't add a social security number; and Excel won't treat the number above as a case of subtraction, either. You'll soon see why.

Now there's one other basic data entry principle you'll want to know that will at last shed some light on that pristine white cell you'll always see topping a range selection. Again, if I go ahead and drag my mouse across a range of cells:

There's that ever-present white cell. And what purpose does that cell serve? It marks the cell that will receive the next bit of data you type. Select a range, begin to type, and then press Enter. The entry ends up in the white cell.

And if you need any corroboration, select any range, observe the address of the white cell, and glance in turn at the name box. You'll see that very address recorded in the box.

And the white-cell/range selection does something else. If you select any range and begin to type, the first entry stakes the white cell—and if you press Enter, the cell pointer plunges down one row, of course—but the blue range color remains in force. Try this: select cells D12 through D21, type the number 51, and press Enter. This is what you'll see (Figure 2–38):

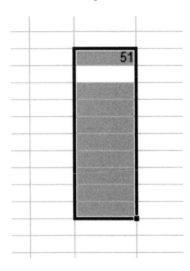

Figure 2–38. Within range—data entry inside the selection

Type a number in the current cell—D13—and press Enter, and the number is once again registered in its cell—and the pointer again descends one row, to D14. And so forth.

But of course you'll have a question about all this: Entering data in a cell and pressing Enter *always* does exactly what I've described above—even if you *don't* select a range. So what are we gaining here?

Here's the answer: Select this range instead: D12:E21. Start typing and press Enter. The data locks into D12 and proceeds to D13, etc. But when you reach cell D21—the last cell in the D column—and press Enter, this time the cell pointer *won't* drop down to D22—it'll pop up to *E12* instead, which is after all the next cell in the selected range (Figure 2–39):

| 51 |
| 23 |
| 46 |
| 76 |
| 45 |
| 88 |
| 12 |
| 567 |
| 72 |
| 59 |

Figure 2–39. Knowing its place: the white cell remains within the range

And when you reach cell E21—the last cell in the range—and enter data there and press Enter, you'll be taken back to D12.

This, then, is the data-entry advantage of selecting a range, if you need to: the range selection confines your data entry to precisely that area of the spreadsheet and nowhere else. But note, however, that if you follow up each data entry in the range by carrying out some of the *other* navigational moves instead of Enter, such as pressing the various keyboard arrows, or clicking your mouse, the blue range selection will turn off and the method we've just described will likewise be voided—unless you select the range again, of course. If you do want to conduct your data entry within a specified range, these keystrokes work:

- Enter—takes you down one row within the range.

- Shift-Enter—takes you up one row within the range.

- Tab—takes you one cell to the right in the range, or back to the first column and down one row if you're already in the last column of a range.

- Shift-Tab—takes you one column to the left in the range, or one row up and into the last column if you're already in the first column of the range.

That concludes our discussion of the basics of data entry—but not to worry; we need to return to the subject. There's all that formatting to do, after all!

But in any case, once you nail down the basics we still need to remind ourselves that no one's perfect, and in the course of imparting their data to worksheets users make mistakes, change their minds, and have to enter new numbers as events warrant. So once the data is squirreled into their respective cells, we still need to ask: how do you edit all this?

There'll Be Some Changes Made—Editing Cells

As you'd expect, there's more than one way to modify the contents of cells, all of which are pretty easy to master. The most straightforward approach is to simply overwrite any existing cell contents; that is, just click or key your way into the cell you want to overwrite, and type something new. That's all.

Another rather obvious and decisive editing tack of course is to simply delete the contents of the cell(s) in question, if that's what's called for. Just select the cell in question—or a range of cells—and click Delete on your keyboard.

But these appealingly lucid approaches aren't always the most efficient. For example—click any cell and type:

this is how to edit cells in Excel

You'll note that the *t* in *this* isn't capitalized, but you want it to appear in upper case. Sure, you could retype the whole phrase, but if you're as lazy as I am you'll be searching for a less demanding workaround. Remember that any given Excel cell can hold up to 32,767 characters, and while you're not likely to ever exhaust that capacity, some Excel formulas can be rather dense and ornate, and rewriting them from scratch is an invitation to error. So we need a Plan B to edit this kind of data—and here are three very standard, textbook techniques:

First, click the cell you want to edit and press the F2 key, an ancient command that dates back to the last century (it's been carbon dated). You'll see (Figure 2–40):

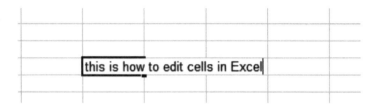

Figure 2–40. *Inside the cell*

Look closely on your screen and you'll see the ***cursor***—that's what it's called—flickering to the immediate right of the last letter of the phrase. You're now "in" the cell, and once you've gained this kind of entree you can carry out word processing-like actions in order to edit whatever you want. Thus here you can press the Home key that, as it does in Word, will take to you the beginning of a line of text. Once there, simply press the Delete key, remove the lowercase *t*, and replace it with *T*. Press Enter and you're done. You can edit any character in the cell by pressing the Left or Right arrow keys until you reach the character you want, and then pressing either Backspace or Delete, depending on which side of the character you've positioned yourself. Once in the cell you can also double-click any word, thus selecting it (as you do in Word); you can then either press Delete, thereby eliminating it from the cell, or type something else over it—again, just as you would in Word.

(**Note:** By clicking off the File ➤ Options ➤ Advanced ➤ Allow editing directly in cells checkbox, you won't be able to avail yourself of the above option. But by doing so you'll be able to double-click any cell containing a formula, and thus automatically highlight, or select, all the cells contributing to the formula. As result, you can change the values in those cells easily.)

Textbook method #2 reacquaints us with the formula bar, that band of space stretching to the right of the name box, as shown in Figure 2–41:

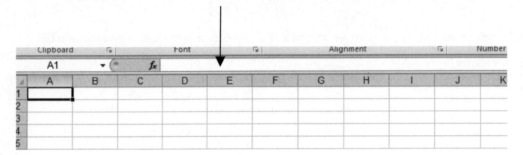

Figure 2–41. The formula bar revisited

To edit our text via this method, just click the cell containing our text. As usual, you'll see it displayed in the formula bar, as shown in Figure 2–42:

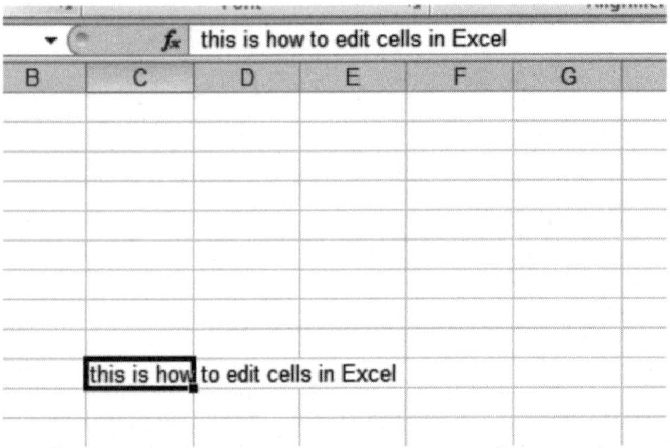

Figure 2–42. What you type is what you get in the formula bar

Then click *inside* the formula bar, right alongside the lower-case *t*. Note that when your mouse enters the formula bar area, it acquires a Word-like I-bar appearance, exactly what you see in Word when you move your mouse around text in a document.

And when you click in the bar, the cursor reappears (along with that check mark and X), as you can see in Figure 2–43:

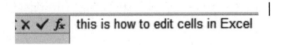

Figure 2–43. Editing a cell inside the formula bar

Then just make any changes as per standard word-processing steps; when you're done, press Enter *or* click the checkmark. And if in the course of your editing labors you click alongside the wrong character in the formula bar, just click again wherever you want and start to edit.

This last technique is also easy, but requires a measure of care. Let's return to that recalcitrant lower-case *t*. We can place our mouse over that letter—back in the cell this time, and not the formula bar—and simply double-click. The standard Excel white cross remakes itself into the cursor, at which point you can begin to edit. The caution is this: you can't directly double-click any letter that by appearances has run into adjoining columns. Thus you can't double-click the *E* in Excel (Figure 2–44):

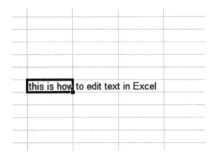

Figure 2–44. Double-click to edit? That depends.

even though, as previously noted, all the text is lodged in but one cell. Thus, in order to edit the E this way, you need to double-click anywhere within the span of the source cell—in this case somewhere between the words "this is how" and *then* press your arrow keys or click upon the *E* and edit. Quirky, but that's how it works. And remember, as per our discussion earlier, you can cancel an edit by pressing the Esc key or clicking the *X*.

And now that we've found a place for our data, what do we *do* with all of it? It's time to learn some of the ways you can crunch all those numbers that beckon in your newly entered cells. So just turn the page.

CHAPTER 3

■ ■ ■

From data entry to data creation: formula basics and beyond

Now that we've gotten this far, we need to remind ourselves of the obvious: Excel is all about *doing* something with the data once it's been nestled into its cells—analyzing it, presenting it, and synergizing something new from all those static numbers and text entries; and that reminder takes us to a new domain of have-to-knows—the world of ***formulas*** and ***functions***. It's here, once you learn the fundamentals, that you begin to sense the nearly infinite potential of the application—starting of course with the how-tos for adding those rows and columns.

The very first thing you need to know about formulas is that by that term I'm referring to *any* expression you can write in a cell which conjures something new from the existing data—and it doesn't have to work with numbers, either. Learning which, or how many, students in a lecture class have a last name starting with the letter L or how many major league baseball players were born in Nevada may not be what's keeping you up at night, but if you need to know these things and the basic data are there, there's a formula-based way to find out.

The second indispensible thing to know about formulas is that they *always* begin with the equal sign. This, then, is a formula:

=3+5

And this isn't:

3+5

That latter expression is pure *text*, and won't "do" anything more than appear in the cell in which you inscribed it. The voice of experience is speaking: if you write a formula, no matter how ingenious and complex, and you leave out the equal sign, what you get is text.

And since I seem to have written a formula just a few lines ago, let's take a second look at it while it's on hand. Entering =3+5 in a cell will indeed yield the answer you've been looking for: 8, but we need to learn a bit more about the relationship between that answer and the formula that gave rise to it.

Go to any cell, say B6, and type =3+5, followed as usual by Enter or any other navigational optionl such as the checkmark. First, of course, the number 8 stations itself in the cell. Then click back on B6, and take a look at the *Formula Bar*, shown in Figure 3–1:

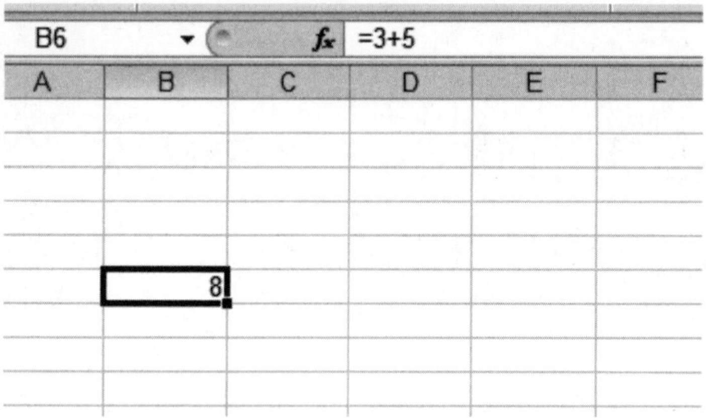

Figure 3–1. Comparing the Formula Bar and its current cell

Now we know why the Formula Bar is so named. It opens a window on what is *really* going on in the cell beneath the surface, and in this case of course what you see in the bar doesn't correspond to what you see in the cell. If you print the spreadsheet you'll see the number 8 (by default, anyway), and that's nearly always want you *want* to see. But you also may need to know that the number was brought about by a formula, and not a simple act of data entry. To glean that bit of information, click on the cell and view the Formula Bar.

Now, nothing at all prevents you from writing a more protracted formula, such as

=3+5+6+78+91+5+12+45+1

Press Enter and you'll get your answer. Remember, after all—you have 32,767 characters per cell to work with. But for a variety of reasons, spreadsheet users don't like to enter numbers directly into a formula; it's inefficient and a pain to edit, and if you content yourself with this approach you're treating Excel as little more than a PC-based calculator. The far superior way of proceeding is to enter the data you're going to work with in cells, and to work with **cell references**.

Cell references explained

What's a cell reference? It's an expression that, as its name suggests, refers to, or **returns,** the contents of another cell. Thus if you type the number 45 in cell C6 and proceed to type =C6 in cell C7, that latter cell will display 45 onscreen. If I type Excel in C6, cell C7 will now naturally display Excel. What it *won't* display onscreen is =C6, even though that's what you've actually typed in the cell.

Now back to our addition example. If I type the same numbers I added above in separate cells, as in Figure 3–2:

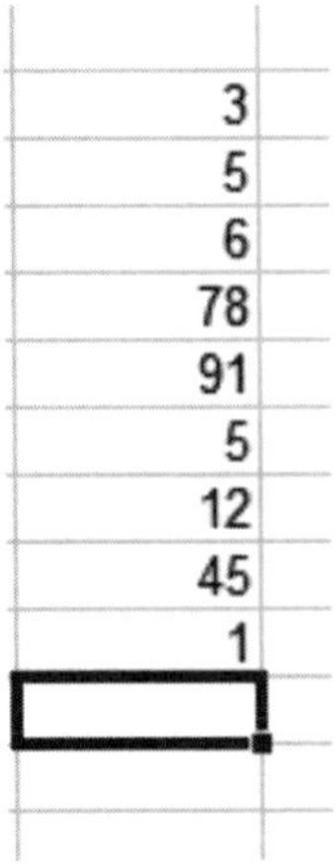

3
5
6
78
91
5
12
45
1

Figure 3–2. Each value assigned its own cell

and then subject these to a formula instead, we'll achieve the same result—246—but we'll also realize some very important spreadsheet advantages (note that the numbers *don't* have to be lined up in one column or row in order to be able to add them; they can be strewn anywhere on the worksheet, but we're starting simple).

So let's try to add those numbers. Say you type the numbers above in cells B6 through B14. Then do the following:

- Click in cell B15 and type the equal sign =

- Click on cell B6 and type +. You should see the result shown in Figure 3–3:

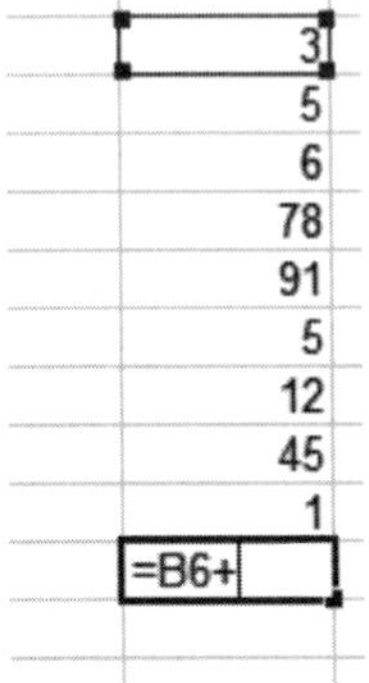

3
5
6
78
91
5
12
45
1
=B6+

Figure 3–3. Plan B: Adding the values with cell references instead

- Click on each of the remaining cells to be added, followed in each case by +.

- When you're finished, tap Enter. Your formula:
=B6+B7+B8+B9+B10+B11+B12+B13+B14

Your answer should once again come to 246—but once you achieve that result we need to review the process more closely, because you're asking the obvious rhetorical question: That's a lot of clicking, isn't it? And what if we wanted to add 90,000 numbers instead of 9? Stay tuned…but back to the formula itself.

First, and as stressed earlier, the formula must begin with =. We then clicked on each cell to be added, following each click with +, simply because we're *adding* the numbers. Had we wanted to subtract some or all of these we would have typed a minus sign instead.

Once we're satisfied we've clicked on the right numbers, we press Enter—or Shift-Enter, Tab, or Shift-Tab, or Ctrl-Enter (or click the checkmark, which in this case actually advances the cell pointer down). And that's how it works. Type =, click each of the cells you want to include in the calculation, followed in each case by a mathematical operator such as + or - (more on this soon), and wind it all up by tapping Enter, or one of the other possibilities cited above. And remember that you can click on cells dispersed *anywhere* across the worksheet.

And if we've realized our result and then discover we'd made an error in data entry, say, the number in cell B7 is really 15, not 5—all we need do is type the corrected number in that cell, and our formula in cell B15 *automatically recalculates* to read 256. That's because formulas don't work with particular values as such—rather, they work with *whatever* values have been entered in the cells to which they refer. And this capacity of spreadsheets – —their ability to recalculate a change in data entry without having to redesign the formula which does the calculation – —may stand as their single greatest contribution to Western Civilization.

Now time for a couple of quick but necessary digressions. First, Table 3–1 shows a list of the basic mathematical operators you can apply to formulas:

Table 3–1 *List of Operators*

Symbol	Operation
+	Addition
-	Subtraction
*	Multiplication
/	Division
^	Exponentiation, e.g., =4^2 equals 16

Ordering Up Your Results

Digression number 2. There's another tricky set of rules you will need to understand—or review, as the case may be—because you probably had to put up with some of these in school: the order of operation. For example, what's the answer to this formula?

$$=4*5+7$$

It could be 27—that is, 4x5 plus 7—or 48—4x12. Which is it? In this particular case you can resolve the problem by surrounding the relevant numbers with parentheses, e.g.,

$$=(4*5)+7$$

Or

$$=4*(5+7)$$

You get the idea. Excel resolves this kind of ambiguity with a set of orders of operation—a kind of priority listing which declares which operation takes precedence—that is, is calculated first—in a formula. (In the cases above, the values flanked by parentheses are treated as a unit.) The order reads like this:

Parentheses

Exponents

Multiplication

Division

Subtraction

Addition

Let's illustrate this hierarchy with a few cases. This formula:

$$=4+5/2$$

results in an answer of 6.5. It divides 5 by 2 and *then* adds 4—because priority goes to division over addition.

This formula:

$$=4*5/2$$

results in 10, because the *multiplication*—4 times 5—is carried out *first*. That result—20—is then divided by 2.

This formula, however:

$$=4*(5/2)$$

also yields 10, but this time because the parenthetical expression—(5/2) that is, 2.5—has priority over any other operation.

Now let's get back to our regularly scheduled program—this matter of adding numbers via a formula. While the method we recounted above surely works, it conceals a problem. What if you need to add 20,000, or even 200, numbers? You won't want to click on each and every one of those cells as per our initial method—and, given Excel's cell character limit, you may not be able to do it anyway. So what's the alternative?

Good question. The answer takes us to the first and most important of Excel's built-in operations, or *functions*, called *SUM*. How does SUM work? For introductory purposes, we'll demonstrate the standard way to implement SUM in a worksheet—with the **AutoSum** command, which is actually stored in two different tabs (remember that term?) in slightly different guises—**Home** and **Formulas**, shown in Figures 3–4 and 3–5:

Figure 3–4. *The location of AutoSum in the Home tab*

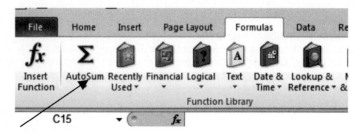

Figure 3–5. *AutoSum in the Formulas tab*

And once you appreciate how AutoSum works—and it's rather simple—you'll go a long way toward firming your grasp of the whole function genre.

So let's try the following: click on the Home tab, if you're not already there. Delete your answer in cell B15, stay in that cell, and click AutoSum. You should see Figure 3–6:

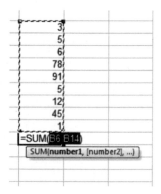

Figure 3–6. *A more efficient way to add all those cells*

Then press Enter, and presto—your answer should materialize.

You see what's happened. AutoSum installed a function—SUM—into the cell in which you clicked, a cell that happens to be positioned directly below the *range* of numbers we wanted to add; and that's a range SUM *automatically* identified. That's why it's called AutoSum.

But before we return to the workings of SUM in particular, note some very basic principles of Excel functions. First, apart form the equals sign (=), an open parenthesis *always* follows the name of the function—here, SUM. Then some additional information—which could be a range and/or some other entries, as you'll see—follows, after which the expression is concluded with a close parenthesis. To summarize the basic syntax for any function:

=NAME(various data in here)

Remember that the equals sign always appears at the outset of *any* formula, e.g, =67+SUM(B6:B15000). (Here we're describing the basic syntax of a function considered alone.) What kind of data gets interposed between the parentheses depends on the function, as you'll see; here, in our current case, SUM identifies the *range* to be added.

Now back to AutoSum. We see that AutoSum indeed correctly identified the range we wanted to add—and had that range, for example, been B6:B15000 instead, we could have clicked on cell B15001, and proceeded to click AutoSum. We'd then see this in B15001:

$$=SUM(B6:B15000)$$

We'd go on to press Enter, and the numbers in all those cells would be added.

Thus we're beginning to infer what exactly it is that AutoSum does. It's programmed to automatically identify a range of *consecutive* numbers to be added in the *column or row in which you've clicked*. And you needn't click in the cell *immediately* below the column or immediately to the right of the row containing the numbers—just somewhere in that column or row. Thus AutoSum will work in the example shown in Figure 3–7, too:

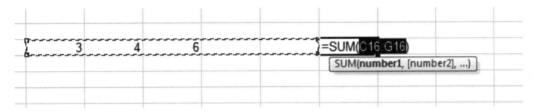

Figure 3–7. This time it's a row being added

Starting to get the point? Here we're adding a row of numbers, even as we've spaced the AutoSum cell two columns away from the last number—and Excel doesn't mind. And look at the range SUM identified—it's included the two empty cells to the left of AutoSum, as the formula itself appears in H16.

In sum (pun intended) and by default, AutoSum will begin to total all consecutive numbers in the column or row in which it's been positioned. But what if you see something like Figure 3–8 in cells C18 through C24?

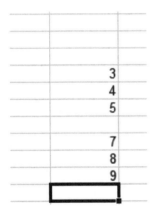

Figure 3–8. Mind the gap...what about that blank cell?

If you click on cell C25 and turn to AutoSum, the resulting formula will read (Figure 3–9):

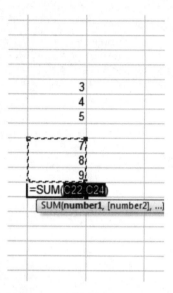

Figure 3–9. The blank cell interrupts the range to be added

What's wrong with this picture? You want to add C18 through C24—and what you get is C22 through C24.

But you may now understand why. AutoSum designates ranges consisting only of *consecutive* number-bearing cells; and in the case before us there's an empty cell—C21—which breaks the continuity. And so AutoSum frames a range that extends only as far as the consecutive string of number-bearing cells closest to it. That's why we see C22:C24.

But we want to add cells C18 through C24. When I've presented students with this problem, many have replied that a zero could be entered in the vacant cell—a worthy suggestion, because a zero naturally won't alter the sum we want to compute, and because it contributes a longer, gap-free range to the formula—C18 through C24. But I strongly advise against this tack—even though the answer it proposes is correct. Because if you go ahead and also compute the *average* of the numbers in C18 through C24, the zero will heavily skew the result—because zero is a number, and a blank cell isn't (as we'll soon see).

The by-the-book way to solve the puzzle, then, is to click in cell C25, click AutoSum, and *then drag* cells C18 through C24—in effect, overriding AutoSum's original (C22:C24) recommendation, as seen in Figure 3–10:

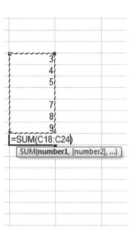

Figure 3–10. Drawing a blank: or rather, drawing your range over a blank cell separating two sets of numbers

As an alternative, nothing prevents you from *typing* the correct expression in the Formula Bar; but dragging the desired cells may be visually easier to track. *Then* press Enter, and all the desired cells are added. (Don't, by the way, accidentally over-drag into cell C25—because that cell contains the formula itself, and you can't incorporate it into its own result. That kind of miscue is called a *circular reference* (and Excel will deliver an onscreen error message to you to that effect), whereby the cell adds itself, as it were—and that causes way too many problems).

Thus we see that the initial range drawn up by AutoSum is merely a friendly suggestion, yours to accept or reject, and one you can replace with a different range if events warrant.

And along these lines, suppose you wanted to add the numbers in Figure 3–11, deposited in cells C14:C16 and E14:E16 respectively:

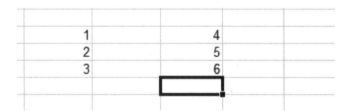

Figure 3–11. Adding multiple ranges

First, we need to decide the cell in which we want our answer to appear. In the interests of simplicity, let's choose cell C17. We click AutoSum, and are presented with the range selection seen in Figure 3–12, of course:

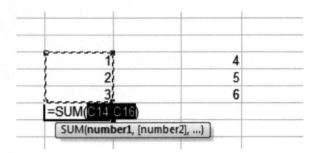

Figure 3–12. Feeling left out: we want to add 4, 5, and 6 too

Now we have a decision to make. Because we want to add both ranges, we could next drag across *all* the cells in question, as in Figure 3–13:

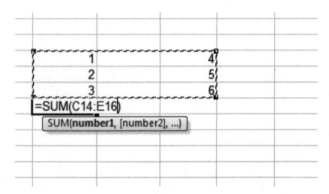

Figure 3–13. Kind of a drag: spanning two ranges to be added in one SUM. Note, however, that the function treats these values as one range for formula purposes: C14:E16

And that's what you probably *would* do, after which you'd press Enter and return your answer. But suppose there were an additional set of numbers in those in-between cells D14:D16—and you *don't* want these incorporated in your answer. If we proceed with the range selection we've just named—C14:E16—the numbers in D14:D16 *will* be brought along, because they too inhabit the selected range. So how do we exclude these unwanted cells?

We can do the following:

Click AutoSum, yielding the initial C14:C16 range selection. Then type a *comma* (don't add a space) and drag range E14:E16 (you can also hold down the Ctrl key after selecting the first range, and then select E14:E16 (Figure 3–14):

60

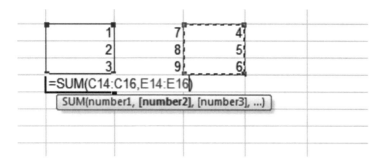

Figure 3–14. Adding two ranges-here the two sets of values are treated as two distinct ranges.

Then press Enter.

You get the picture. The comma splices our cell selections into two distinct ranges, thus leapfrogging the D14:D16 cells.

We've now learned a deeper truth about SUM, one that can be projected to all functions: you can identify *any* cell or range(s) you want in *any* formula, and place your formulas in *any* cell in the worksheet (so long as the formula isn't dropped into the very range you're referencing in the formula). Remember that AutoSum was devised in order to execute a simplest-case scenario, the spreadsheet equivalent of a hanging curveball—that classic, add-one-row-or-one-column chore, where the row or column to be added consists of a range, all of whose cells are filled with numbers. But your formula requirements may be more nuanced, and the reality is that you can recruit cells and ranges from all across the worksheet—and even beyond it, as remains to be seen.

Note as well that nothing whatever stops you from *typing* SUM if you're so moved, or any other function in Excel, for that matter. As long as you know the syntax, you're free to tickle the keys as wish; and as we'll see, Excel offers you a number of ways to see to it that whatever you're writing turns out correct.

And here are some AutoSum shortcuts: The keyboard equivalent for calling up the command is Alt+=. And if you're working conventionally, and you know you want to add a standard range of consecutive numbers in a column: just click in an empty cell at the foot of the column and *double-click* the AutoSum button (as it appears in either the Home or Formulas groups). Double-clicking cuts immediately to the answer, without requiring you to make any additional range decisions.

And one more observation about AutoSum: if you rest your mouse over either of its buttons, the resulting caption tells you that AutoSum helps you "Display the sum of the selected cells directly after the selected cells". But we know that isn't quite true; as we saw earlier you can leave some space *between* the numbers (as long as these are consecutive) and the formula itself in that column or row and *still* get AutoSum to work for you, though those empty cells will also be referenced in the formula.

Now, you'll note that both AutoSum buttons on either tab are accompanied by one of those drop-down arrows we alerted you to a good many pages ago (Figure 3–15):

Figure 3–15. What you see when you click that arrow

Click the arrow and you'll see a small list of additional functions, and pretty important ones, ones I've used a million times:

Sum
Average
Count Numbers
Max
Min

How do these work and what do they do? To answer those questions in order—these functions behave virtually identically to SUM, in the sense that they're written in the same manner, with the same kinds of range references and issues as described above. Moreover, each of these has an "Auto" character—meaning that if you click beneath a column or to the right of a row of numbers, you can click on their names and install them in the desired cell—just as with AutoSum.

Now let's explain what these functions actually do.

Not Just Your Average Function

AVERAGE is a spreadsheet staple that performs as advertised—it computes the average of a range, or a set of selected cells. Again, its structure is a virtual clone of SUM, so for example:

=AVERAGE(D23:D42)

returns the average of that range. As implied earlier in our discussion of SUM, AVERAGE *ignores* any blank cell in a range, refusing to treat it as the mathematical equivalent of zero. Thus AVERAGE yields a result of 8 for the range below, and not the 6.4 you'd compile if the blank cell were assigned an ad hoc value of zero.

5

7

8

(blank cell)

12

And once again, if your data are arrayed conventionally in one column or row, you can click on Average in the AutoSum drop down menu, press Enter, and AVERAGE will be posted in the cell you've selected (Figure 3–16):

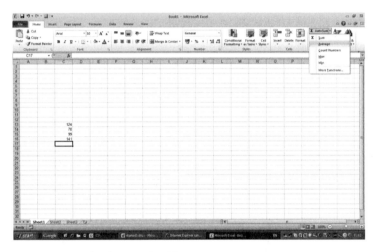

Figure 3–16. *Selecting AVERAGE*

You can incorporate multiple ranges in AVERAGE as well. (Your decimal point questions will be taken up in the next chapter).

Making Range Values COUNT

And what about the third entry in the AutoSum drop-down menu, **Count Numbers**? Here Excel's menu description doesn't quite match the actual name of the function it generates —*COUNT*—and for a reason, which we'll explain right after we let you know what COUNT actually does. (Figure 3–17):

Figure 3–17. *Counting numbers—only*

COUNT simply *counts* all the cells in a range (or ranges) which contain *numbers*—nothing more mathematical then that. Thus in the above screen shot, if I click cell C17 and select COUNT—and the method for doing this is identical to AVERAGE and SUM—I'll drum up a result of 4. But substitute a *text* entry for any the cells in Figure 3–16 and my formula result now reports 3.

You may want to ask rather compelling question about COUNT: namely, why would I need to use it? By way of illustration—if you're a teacher, you may need to tally the number of tests the students in your class have taken, for example. Consider the scenario below, in Figure 3187:

Student	Test 1	Test 2	Test 3
Bill	67	88	65
Jack	77		81

Figure 3–18. Jack needs to see the dean

COUNT will thus tell you that Bill has taken 3 exams and Jack has attempted 2, and so needs to make one up. Or, by way of additional example: if you've entered a list of potential donors to a charity on your sheet and key in the amount of each contribution when it's received, you'd use SUM to learn how much money you've taken in to date, and COUNT to let you know *how many* individuals have donated, by counting each donation. And while you're at it, you could compute the average size of the donations, couldn't you?

But why does Excel advertise COUNT as Count Numbers on its drop-down menu? It does so in order to distinguish COUNT from another function—*COUNTA*—which counts all the cells in a range that contain *any* kind of data. Thus for the range shown in (Figure 3–19):

3
56
Cell
67

Figure 3–19. COUNT or COUNTA—Different results this for range

COUNT will return 3, COUNTA 4. (COUNTA, by the way, is written in the same way as COUNT, though it's not included in the above drop-down menu.)

MAX and MIN—Recording Highs and Lows

But let's return to the entries in the AutoSum menu. MAX and MIN are almost self-evident; they identify the highest and lowest cells in a range while ignoring blank cells (and text entries), an important omission in these regards. After all, treating blanks as zero could erroneously yield a MIN of zero among a range of other cells—and if you're working with a range consisting entirely of negative numbers, counting a blank cell as zero could yield a MAX of...zero!

And you'll doubtless be able to find a broad niche for MAX and MIN in your spreadsheet doings.

And by way of recapitulation—all the functions assigned a place on the AutoSum drop-down menu are written the same way:

=NAME (range, or ranges)

I'm harping on this point because a great many of the other functions in the Excel repertoire display a different syntax, as you'll see.

And while we're talking about SUM, COUNT, AVERAGE and the like, here's another handy but easy-to-miss, hidden-in-plain-sight take on these operations and some more. If you select any set of cells containing numbers (at least two cells, to be exact) and train your gaze on the lower right of the worksheet screen, on what's called the **Status Bar**, you'll suddenly see a see a mini-report about the data you've highlighted (Figure 3–20):

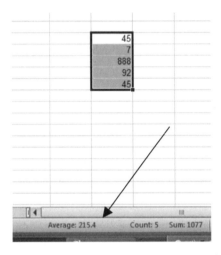

Figure 3–20. A range's status report on the Status Bar

There it is—the Average, Count, and Sum of the range you've selected. Just know that the Count here is really COUNTA; that is, it will count *any* data in the cell—values, text, and even formulas. What we're presented with here is an on-the-fly summary of the data in the selected range. None of this information will actually appear in the worksheet—and once you move elsewhere to other cells, those figures will change. Still, if you need a quick improvised read on certain data, select that range and take a look.

And what you see there can be customized, at least within limits. If you right-click anywhere on the status bar, you'll trigger a towering short-cut menu, which, among other things, allows you to add three more calculations to the bar (Figure 3–21):

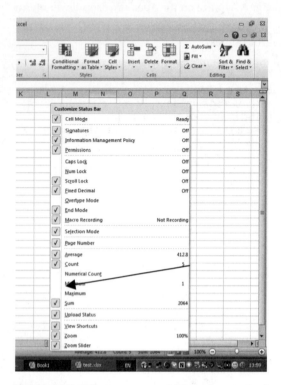

Figure 3–21. Where you can add functions to the Status Bar

Thus Numerical Count (that is, COUNT), Max, and Min can take their place on the Status Bar too if you need them; simply click them on.

But now that we've gotten our feet wet in the Olympic-sized pool of functions, grab a towel and sit back, because we've some more copying and moving to do, of a different and most important kind.

And in this connection, let's go all the way back to that sample grade-average worksheet I served up in Chapter 1, the one festooned with red highest-score cells and those Sparklines. Don't remember it? I'm not taking it personally—look at Figure 3–22 for a refresher:

	Exams						
Student	1	2	3	4	5	Average	
Alice	67	96	67	100	85	83.0	
Derek	82	89	45	93	67	75.2	
Dorothy	73	70	93	65	93	78.8	
Edith	81	48	52	75	76	66.4	
George	90	67	84	59	77	75.4	
Gordon	90	86	89	77	94	87.2	
John	83	96	60	63	70	74.4	
Mary	77	78	80	90	100	85.0	
Paul	61	91	68	61	99	76.0	
Ringo	56	80	79	82	77	74.8	
Class Averages	76.0	80.1	71.7	76.5	83.8		

Figure 3–22. Grade averages by student

Now look at the Formula Bar. I've clicked cell I10, the one bearing Alice's exam average, and its means of calculation—using AVERAGE, of course—-is recorded up there in that bar. By way of review, we see that Alice's grades occupy range D10:H10 and, by inserting that range reference between AVERAGE's parentheses, we determined her average grade was 83.0.

The point is this: What if I have 150 students in the class (and I've had more than that on occasion), and I need to figure the test average for each and every one of them? Do I have to click the AutoSum button 150 times in order to carry out that disagreeable task?

Yes, that sounds like a rhetorical question, and it is. The answer to it is no, because what we can do instead is *copy* Alice's AVERAGE formula down the I column for as many rows of students as I need.

Yes, this is a have-to-know, because copying a formula—which entails in essence copying *cell references*— is something new—and vital—to the your understanding of how Excel works.

But in fact the *ways* of actually copying cell references are identical to the ones we described earlier (and we're going to learn an additional one soon); what's different is what happens when you copy them. And that preamble raises a larger point. *All* the cell copying we've discussed to date and will continue to discuss in this chapter entail copying whatever we *enter* in a cell—as opposed to what we *see* in the cell. If I copy Alice's AVERAGE elsewhere, I am most assuredly *not* copying her average of 83. Rather, I'm copying what I typed in cell I10—the formula that calculated her 83.

The following table enumerates the relationship between the kinds of data I could enter in a cell and what I would see in that cell. In every case, what I would *copy* is posted in the left column of Table 3–2 below:

Table 3–2. Cell Entries and Cell Displays

Data Example (what you've typed in the cell, which is what gets copied)	What you see in the cell
3	3
=4+5	9
=T3/7	The result of whatever number you enter in T3 divided by 7
=AVERAGE(A4:G4)	The average of all the numbers you've entered in A4 through G4.

Again, what gets copied is what you've actually typed in the cell. And if you copy any expression which contains a cell reference, what will happen is that the cell references in the destination cells—the cells *to* which you've copied—will change, corresponding to the distance in either rows or columns from the original cell you've copied.

If I copy the number 1, either 1 or a 100 times, I'll see nothing but 1's in the range to which I've copied. But if I copy this:

$$=C7$$

what I'll see depends on *where* I've copied it. If that =C7 was positioned in cell A2 and I copy it to cell A3, I'll see this in that destination cell:

$$=C8$$

By way of a more pertinent example, if I go to cell I10 in our grading worksheet and copy Alice's formula:

$$=AVERAGE(D10:H10)$$

down one row to I11—Derek's row—we'll see:

$$=AVERAGE(D11:H11)$$

You're probably starting to get the idea. If I were to copy Alice's formula all the way down to say, cell I20000—and there's no reason why I couldn't—I'd see:

$$=AVERAGE(D20000:H20000)$$

See what's changed, and what's remained the same? Remember that a cell address comprises a lettered column reference and a number row reference—and when you copy cell references down a column, *only* the original *row* references change, commensurate with the distance you've traveled from the original cell. That's because you've moved down rows, and haven't shifted any columns—and the destination results reflect the amount of movement from the source cell reference.

If on the other hand, were I to copy Alice's formula to cell L10, I'd see:

$$=AVERAGE(G10:K10)$$

And see why? In this case, I've copied Alice's original formula three *columns* to the right, such that only the column parts of its cell references—that is, the *letters*—have changed, again corresponding to the degree of movement from I10. Thus G is three column letters "away" from D, and K is three columns removed from H. And this time there's been no change in the row references—the numbers, because we've copied across columns only, remaining on the same row as Alice's average. We're still on row 10 in this case.

A quick, acronymic way for nailing this row/column movement question is **CARD**, which stands for: Columns Across, Rows Down. Copy a cell reference across, and the column letters change; copy it down—or up—and the rows numbers change.

In any event, we've encountered a foundational spreadsheet feature—***relative references***—which describes what happens by default when you copy a cell reference to any other cell. We can see now that if I click on Alice's original AVERAGE formula, I should be able to copy it down the I column for as many rows as I need, confident in the knowledge that, as long as the original formula is correct, I should be able to compute *all* the other students' averages correctly. Put another way, I need only write AVERAGE *once*—and then copy it; and so you can see why this tool is so potent.

And note, by the way, that cells can certainly team cell references with simple numeric values; just keep in mind that copying such a cell will only change the cell reference. Thus if I write this:

$$=D5+7$$

in cell H2 and copy it down one row, I'll get:

=D6+7

We see, then, that the 7 won't change—only the original D5 will.

And when you need to copy a formula containing cell references down a column or across a row, there's a most expeditious way to do so, by finding a novel use for a tool we already know—the fill handle. To illustrate:

Let's take a few steps back in the design of our grading sheet, and for the sake of clarity, we'll scrub away all the fancy formatting, too. We've written Alice's AVERAGE formula, and now want to copy it down the column, as in Figure 3–23:

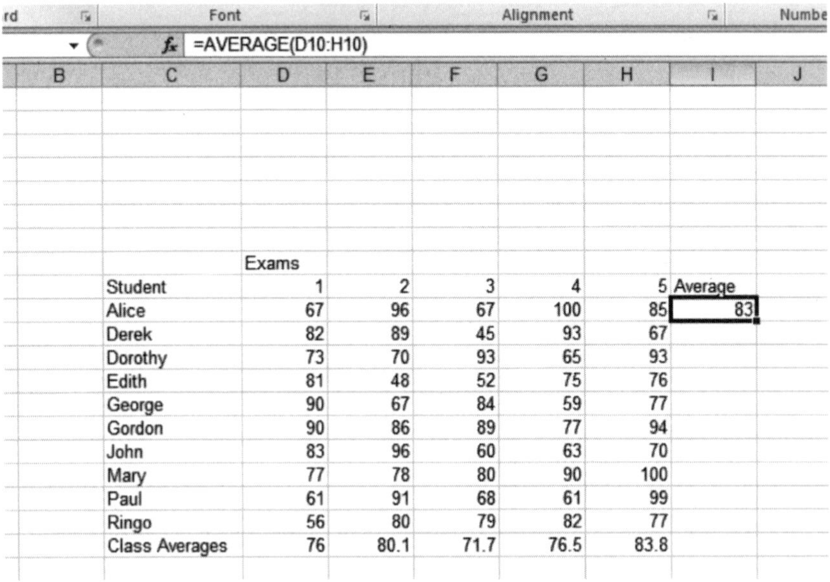
rd
Font
Alignment
Numbe
=AVERAGE(D10:H10)
B C D E F G H I J
Exams
Student 1 2 3 4 5 Average
Alice 67 96 67 100 85 83
Derek 82 89 45 93 67
Dorothy 73 70 93 65 93
Edith 81 48 52 75 76
George 90 67 84 59 77
Gordon 90 86 89 77 94
John 83 96 60 63 70
Mary 77 78 80 90 100
Paul 61 91 68 61 99
Ringo 56 80 79 82 77
Class Averages 76 80.1 71.7 76.5 83.8

***Figure 3–23.** Alice's average will serve as the formula to be copied*

If I station my mouse over the fill handle in cell I10—Alice's test average—and then click the handle, don't release the mouse, and drag down the column through Ringo's cell in cell I19 and then release the mouse, I will have copied all the student AVERAGE formulas, as in Figure 3–24:

	Exams					
Student	1	2	3	4	5	Average
Alice	67	96	67	100	85	83
Derek	82	89	45	93	67	75.2
Dorothy	73	70	93	65	93	78.8
Edith	81	48	52	75	76	66.4
George	90	67	84	59	77	75.4
Gordon	90	86	89	77	94	87.2
John	83	96	60	63	70	74.4
Mary	77	78	80	90	100	85
Paul	61	91	68	61	99	76
Ringo	56	80	79	82	77	74.8
Class Averages	76	80.1	71.7	76.5	83.8	

Figure 3–24. Copying allowed, here: Dragging to copy Alice's formula gives me the averages for all the students

Then click anywhere to turn off the blue selection color. Here, the fill handle—that same device we earlier put to the task of producing series of data—e.g., 1,3,5,7, days of the week, etc.—is used to *copy formulas.* Just click on the first (which at the moment is the *only*) formula, and drag the fill handle as far as you need to go—either down a column or across a row. The copy procedure collaborates with relative referencing to install the proper cell references in each cell, and what this means is that if you need to copy a formula to many cells, you only need to actually write the formula *once*—the formula that will serve as the model to be copied to all other cells.

And once you learn how that capability works, there's an even easier and cooler means to carry out this kind of copying task. Once you write that first, model formula, click back on that cell (in this case Alice's average in I10), and *double-click* the fill handle. All the other student cells running down the I column receive the formula, without you needing to drag the fill handle. The double-click *automatically* copies the original formula down *all* the cells that also have data in the immediately adjoining column to its left or right.

To summarize this tip—if you need to copy a formula down a column—and this only works when you copy down a column, not across a row—click on the cell storing the original formula and then double-click its fill handle. As long as there are data in the *adjoining* column (either to the left or right; and that means in our example if the H column were empty this wouldn't work), the formula copies down for as many rows as there are data. And this will work as surely for 20,000 rows as it will for 20. I use this shortcut all time; I *told* you I was lazy.

Now there is one more permutation of this cell-reference copying business that you need to know. Consider this case:

Suppose I've given my students a rather challenging exam, and, after having canvassed the sobering results, decide to grant them an extra three points in order to curve the scores upward. My simple grade book looks like Figure 3–25, at the outset:

Student	Score
Gordon	64
April	49
Tony	70
May	63
John	58
June	61

Figure 3–25. Test scores, about to be boosted by three points each

So how do I go about padding these pause-giving scores by those three points? Gordon's score is in cell D11, and so I could write the following in E11, couldn't I:

=D11+3

Sure I could. Then I'd return to cell E11, and utilize my newfound double-click-on the fill-handle trick. I'll bring about this revised grade distribution (Figure 3 - 26):

Student	Score	With Bonus
Gordon	64	67
April	49	52
Tony	70	73
May	63	66
John	58	61
June	61	64

Figure 3–26. Nice guy: the three-point curve, now in effect

Are my calculations correct? Absolutely; but still I wouldn't recommend this approach. That's because if I conclude that I need to award my charges say, 5 points instead, I'd need to edit the formula in E11 to read:

=D11+5

and then copy that rewritten expression down the column again, so that all the students will enjoy my 5-point largesse. Not an enormously big deal, but not an elegant way in which to proceed. As a rule, one wants to avoid editing cells if one can; it can get messy, and a preferable alternative would be to enter the 5-point bonus figure in a cell—say in this case, A11, and rewrite Gordon's formula thusly:

=D11+A11

and copy it down the column. And exactly why is this approach recommended? Because if I change my mind again and issue a 7-point curve, all I need do is type 7 in cell A11, and all the scores should change automatically—with no additional cell editing required.

Absolute References: Absolutely Important

But if I go ahead and enter =D11+A11 in Gordon's E11 cell, and once again copy down the E column, I'll see this (Figure 3 - 27):

		Student	Score	With Bonus	
5		Gordon	64	69	
		April	49	49	
		Tony	70	70	
		May	63	63	
		John	58	58	
		June	61	61	

Figure 3–27. Nice try, but wrong answers. We'll explain why.

Hmmm. That doesn't look quite right, does it? Gordon's score surely exhibits the 5-point increment, but his colleagues seem to have come away with nothing extra at all. What's happened?

What's happened is this: Gordon's bonus-conferring =D11+A11 is correctly written; it references both his test score—64, in D11—and the 5-point give-away, stashed in cell A11. But when I copy this spot-on formula down to April's cell in E12, her formula states:

=D12+A12

and therein lies the problem. Because relative referencing has done its thing, both row numbers in April's formula have pumped to 12, up one from Gordon's 11. And even though cell E12 *correctly* cites Alice's original test score, cell A12 contains…nothing. And 49 plus nothing... is 49. And that also means that Tony's cell bonus formula—=D13+A13—has to be wrong, too, because A13 is likewise blank, and so on. So apart from Gordon's original bonus calculation all the other students report the *wrong* bonus result, because they don't reference the cell—A11—in which the bonus is entered. So how is this puzzlement resolved?

Like this. Return to Gordon's cell E11—which remember, contains the *correct* grade bonus formula —and edit the cell to read:

=D11+A$11

Then copy this revised version down the E column to all the other students. You should now be viewing the correct, bonus-bearing grades for each student. So what's going on? Obviously the dollar sign has something to do with it.

First, we need to understand that the dollar sign has nothing at all to do with currency formatting. Rather, the sign is a programming convention, which *freezes* the part of the cell address to its immediate right. Installing the dollar sign where we did—alongside the 11 in A11—means that no matter where we copy Gordon's =D11+A$11, that 11 will *never* change. Thus April's formula now states:

$$=D12+A\$11$$

and Tony's declares:

$$=D13+A\$11$$

and so on. Now every student formula reads correctly, because each refers to the *same* cell containing the grade bonus—A11.

This exercise exemplifies what's called **absolute cell referencing**, a spreadsheet option in which part of a cell address is held *constant*, for the kinds of reasons we've just described. It's also certainly possible to place that dollar sign before a *column letter*, too, if you need to, e.g.:

$$=\$A11$$

Here the A, or column-referencing segment of the cell address, will never change when it's copied. And if you need to, you can also type:

$$=\$A\$11$$

in which case *neither* the A nor the 11 will ever change, irrespective of the destination(s) to which they're copied.

Here, then, we've witnessed the potential downside of relative cell referencing. Precisely because relative referencing shifts cell addresses according to their distance from the original, source cell, a series of errant references has crept into our grading process, distorting all our grades save the original, source formula.

And if all these relatives and absolutes are leaving you feeling slightly groggy, you're not alone. This topic is also an acquired taste, and in the early going it takes some doing to acquire it. But give it some thought, play around with it with some mock formulas, and your taste buds should acclimate. With practice they should become second nature to you.

To recapitulate:

You use relative referencing when the *same kind* of formula needs to be copied down (or across) similar rows or columns of data—such as our grade book example. But of course, the copied formulas can't be *identical*, because each one needs to calculate a different set of cell references—e.g., Gordon's grades on row 11, April's on row 12, etc.

You'll want—or need—to use an absolute cell reference when *different* formulas need to reference the *same* cell repeatedly, e.g., our grade bonus example, where each student's grade adds the point bonus stored in A11.

More of the Same

And what about all those other functions? Excel has hundreds of them; and while you'll be pleased to learn that we don't have room to expound them all, it may be time to recall that bit of unasked-for advice I issued to you about 30 pages ago: namely that it really pays to learn about as many functions as you can.

When I first encountered spreadsheets—in the Paleolithic late 80s, pioneer days when Lotus 1-2-3 ruled the roost and the Undo button was merely a gleam in Bill Gates' eye—my then-boss handed me a rather copious 1-2-3 manual, and wrapped it with one laconic instruction: Learn it. And when I came upon the chapter describing functions—and many of the ones we still use date back to that time—I was incredulous that anyone could actually find a place for these arcane concoctions. But as I learned more about spreadsheets I came to see the wisdom—and the potential value—of a good many of them. In fact, we already know five functions; let's learn some more. Not all of them, mind you, but some important ones—after we learn a few preliminaries.

First, you'll want to know that all the Excel functions are neatly catalogued and warehoused inside the buttons shelved in the **Function Library** group in the Formulas tab (Figure 3 - 28):

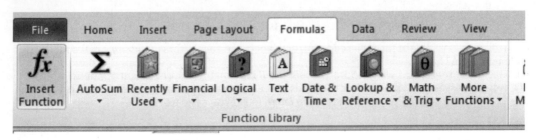

Figure 3 – 28. *The Function Library: must reading*

Click one of the buttons, and a directory of functions belonging to the category you clicked drops down, as in Figure 3–28:

Figure 3–29. *The Lookup & Reference drop-down menu*

Click one of the entries, and you'll be brought to a dialog box whose contents vary by function, but it looks more or less like this (Figure 3–30):

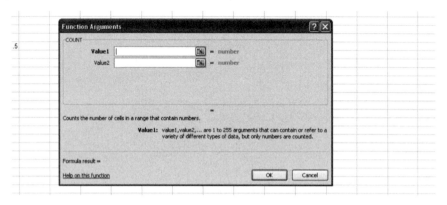

Figure 3 – 30. Friendly arguments: a function-writing dialog box

These dialog boxes afford the users a fill-in-the-blanks motif, requesting them to enter essential bits of information, technically called **arguments** (note the name of the dialog box in Figure 3–28), which when entered enable Excel to calculate the answer you're looking for. Let's look at one such dialog box of a function you already know: see Figure 3–28 for the dialog box for the COUNT function.

What sort of blanks are we asked to fill in here? In this case, *ranges*. I can type a range in the Value 1 field, or even drag that range on the worksheet itself. Either way the range is recorded in Value 1. If I need to introduce a second range to COUNT, I can identify it in Value 2. And if I need even a third or more ranges, a Value 3, etc., field appears. When I click OK, the COUNT function and result is instated in whichever cell I had clicked before I called up the dialog box.

Remember, though, that the kinds of blanks you'll see in the dialog box will depend on the function you've selected, and you will need to have a pretty good idea what's going on before you can proceed. So if you remain daunted at this point, you can click the Help on this function link in the box's lower left corner; you'll be whisked to a discussion of the function in Excel's Help facility, which is usually pretty clear.

While the buttons in the Function Library afford the most up-front way in which to access functions, Excel makes other ways available, too. You can also click the *fx* button flanking the Formula Bar to its left and call up this dialog box (Figure 3–31):

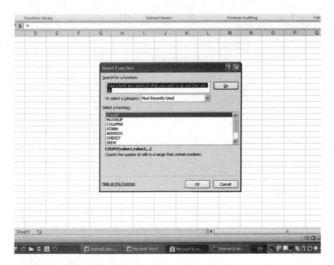

Figure 3–31. The Insert Function dialog box

In fact, this Insert Function box does nothing more than enumerate the same contents of the respective Library buttons. Click the Or select a category drop-down arrow and you'll see the identical categories by which the Library buttons are classified. Then click a category and any of the function names that appear next, and you'll be returned to exactly the same function Arguments dialog box we witnessed a few screen shots back..

And take note of the Formulas tab's Insert Function button. Click it and, well, you've done nothing more than tap a giant-sized twin of the *fx* button. Is this button redundant? Probably.

But there *is* another, decidedly different way to requisition the function you want. Click the cell in which you're working, type =, and begin to enter the function name. As you type, an AutoComplete mechanism activates, presenting and narrowing a list of functions beginning with the letters you've typed. Type more letters and the list shrinks, as shown in Figure 3–32:

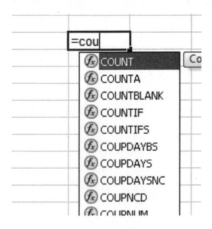

Figure 3–32. AutoComplete at work here, too

When you see the one you want, you can either double-click its name, or scroll down to the function in question with the Down arrow key and press Tab (but not Enter). You'll see, for example (Figure 3 - 33):

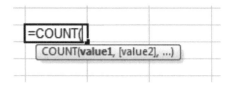

Figure 3–33. Function writing assistance on tap—the tap of the Tab key

Then start to type the remainder of the functions. True, you'll have to *know* what to type next, but that's going to come with repetition. (Note the small caption that offers a kind of running commentary about which argument you're currently entering between the parentheses, e.g., which number range you're now identifying in COUNT. But don't worry—more on arguments soon).

The first thing you want to know about functions and formulas (remember that functions are built-in Excel formulas) is that they can be mixed and matched in innumerable ways. They needn't be composed and applied in isolation, and can be related to each other in the same formula, and for a myriad of purposes. So start priming that spreadsheet imagination.

For example, consider this formula:

$$=AVERAGE(B3:E3)+5$$

This could, for example, be used to calculate a student's average for four exams (spanning columns B through E), to which 5 points are added—as a kind of bonus.

Now how about this?

$$=MIN(B3:E3)*1.05$$

We're working with same four tests. Here our beneficent instructor is adding 5 percent to a student's lowest—that is, minimum—score. Not five *points*, mind you, but 5 *percent*. Thus if our student bombed test number 3 with a 58, the above formula will take that score and multiply it by 1.05, coming up with 60.9. Of course, if our teacher is as beneficent as we say, she'll round it up to 61.

Note, by the way, that both of these formulas factor in *both* a function and an actual, garden-variety number. That's part of Excel's mix-and-match capability.

Now think about this one:

$$=(SUM(B3:E3)-MIN(B3:E3))/(COUNT(B3:E3)-1)$$

True, this one looks scary—at least at first, and perhaps even second perusal. But in reality, it doesn't introduce any feature that we haven't already learned. What this formula does is add the scores of all four exams, and subtracts from that total the *lowest* score. It then divides this new result by the number of remaining exams, that is, 3. In effect the formula calculates the average of the three highest exam scores, having dropped the lowest score.

Let's look at this one more closely—and I'll submit the hope that, upon reflection, you'll agree the formula isn't quite as daunting as you may suppose.

Let's assume our student has scored 76, 82, 58, and 91 on the quartet of exams. Note the entire formula as usual begins with an = sign. But then note that a pair of parentheses surrounds *both* the SUM and MIN parts of the formula together, this in addition to the parentheses surrounding the individual ranges identified in SUM and MIN. Thus observe the two consecutive parentheses following the B3:E3 range reference in MIN. One simply serves as the closing parenthesis in MIN's own range; the other bounds off the combined SUM-MIN expression, thus letting us compute this total:

$$76+82+58+91-58$$

Or 307-58, which equals 249. And why then do we need this pair of global parentheses around SUM and MIN? Because of the *order of operations*, which assigns priority to expressions surrounded by those parentheses, allowing us to treat the activity going in between them as one unit.

And once we derive it, that 249 is ultimately to be divided by 3—that is, the number of exams minus 1. Now take a look at our divisor:

$$(COUNT(B3:E3)-1)$$

And guess what—this expression is *also* surrounded by parentheses, and for exactly the same reason—the order of operations. Remove those outside parentheses and our divisior would read, formulaically:

$$COUNT(B3:E3)-1$$

and numerically:

$$249/4, \text{ then minus 1.}$$

The result: 61.25.

But bring back those outer parentheses and you get:

$$249/(4-1)$$

or 83, the number we want.

As a matter of fact, if we peeled off the global parentheses on both sides of the divisor, our formula would stand as:

$$=SUM(B3:D3)-MIN(B3:D3)/COUNT(B3:D3)-1$$

And that would yield us 291.5, not *even close* to the number we want. Try it and you'll see.

Thus writing formulas involves thinking your objectives through, fooling around with practice formulas, making mistakes, and learning from them—and lining up those parentheses when you need them (and Excel will be sure to notify you with an error message when the count of your open parentheses doesn't equal that of your closed ones, something like "Microsoft Excel found an error in the formula you entered," and will offer you a corrected suggestion. Click No to the suggestion and you'll be sent another message, observing that your expression as it stands is missing a parenthesis).

A final note on the above exercise. Even though our formula made important use of the SUM function, we'd probably be advised not to write it and not to click the AutoSum button in order to post it to its cell. And that's because SUM deoesn't stand alone in its cell this time; we needed to continue to *type* additional characters (incuding that first global parenthesis before the word SUM, which you won't get by clicking AutoSum) in order to combine SUM with the additional formula elements. Just remember, though, that you can always type any function if you need or want to; and in this case, you could type:

$$=(SUM($$

and at that point *drag* the range B3:E3, continue to type:

$$)-MIN($$

and then drag B3:E3 in order to identify that range for MIN, and continue to type. (And remember that when you begin to type a function name, the Auto Complete menu will appear.)

Now thus far we've confined our discussion of functions to the ones that are presented to us on the AutoSum drop-down menu. But as we stated earlier, there are hundreds more. Time and space will restrict our treatment here to just a few of them, but once you get the general hang of these things, learning additional ones will get that much easier.

You Could Look It Up

Let's start with **VLOOKUP**, a function I've used countless times to do countless things. The V in VLOOKUP stands for *vertical* and points to what's called a lookup table, a collection of data in which a value is....looked up.

But that's terribly abstract. Let's look at a VLOOKUP example, turning once again to the real-world domain of exam grading. Suppose I've been entrusted with one more batch of grades, to which I assign numerical scores which must be converted into letter grades. In cells K10 through L14, establish the scale shown in Figure 3–34:

0	F
65	D
75	C
85	B
92	A

Figure 3–34. Another lookup table, featuring a grading scale

It's a rather simple affair, but notice what the table seems to require, and *not* to require. The table reads vertically, naturally, and in our case consists of two columns, the first of which records a series of grade intervals which are arrayed in ascending order and *aren't* evenly spaced in equal numeric intervals—that isn't required.

The second column enumerates the alphabetic grade equivalents, each one of which represents a grade **threshold**. For example, in order to earn a B you need to achieve a minimum score of 85. Score an 84, and you get a C. Score an 84.9, and you get a C. Tough teacher.

Now we'll enter the scores to be looked up and assigned those alphabet grades. We'll just work with five students, so in cells A10:B14 enter (Figure 3–35):

0	John	66
1	Cynthia	71
2	Arlene	82
3	Walter	93
4	Carl	62
5		
6		

Figure 3–35. A typical lookup table, organized by student name

And it's in the C column, alongside each student grade, in which we'll compose our VLOOKUPs. Click in cell C10 and type:

=VLOOKUP(B10,K$10:L$14,2,TRUE)

Don't worry—we're going to explain all this. First note the constant elements we've spoken about earlier: the equal sign, followed by the function name and an open parenthesis. Second, we see that, unlike say, COUNT or AVERAGE, something more than just a range is fitted in between the parentheses. Here *four* different elements—or *arguments*, and we've spoken about them, too—have creeped in there. The first—in this case B10—names the cell whose grade is going to be *looked up* and assessed. That's John's 66. The second argument—K$10:L$14—pinpoints our lookup range itself, and yes, it's accompanied by those dollar signs, slipped in before the 10 and the 14—the row segments of two cell addresses. And why? Because we want to look up *all* our students' grades in the same lookup table again and again, and we intend to copy K$10:L$14 down the column of students without its cell references changing.

The third argument—2—refers to the column in the lookup table containing the "answer"—that is, John's alphabetic grade; and so what VLOOKUP does next is this: it takes John's 66 (in B10) and compares it to the numeric grades in the *first* column of the lookup table—that is, the K column. John's 66 falls between the 65 and the 75 in that column, whereupon VLOOKUP treats it as the *lower* of these two values (remember—these are grade thresholds, and John hasn't reached 75), and it then looks to see which grade has lined up with 65 in the lookup table's *second* column—in this case, D. That's the 2 in the third argument. John gets a D, and we can now copy this formula down the C column (using that nifty fill-handle double-click if we wish, because all the cells in the adjoining B column have data in them). The fourth argument—TRUE, which would have been assumed by default anyway even if you hadn't written it—provides for what's called an **approximate match**. It's this argument which allows VLOOKUP to assess each numeric grade and find its grade niche, e.g., a 78 falls between the lookup table's 75 and 85.

Once done, the student grades should read (Figure 3–36):

John	66	D
Cynthia	71	D
Arlene	82	C
Walter	93	A
Carl	62	F

Figure 3–36. Tough exam!

and of course this process would enable us to assign the grades of 5000 students, too, not just 5.

And note importantly that the lowest grade we're able to look up in this table is 0 (the entry in K10). Even if it's unlikely that any student will score that poorly, you want your table to be able to handle all contingencies—because had I entered a lowest-possible test score of say, 30, in K10 instead and the hard-partying John crashes and burns with a 25, that score would yield an error message in his VLOOKUP. You can't look up a score *below* the lowest value in the lookup table.

Let's demonstrate another instance of VLOOKUP, and then review. Suppose we want to calculate some income tax obligations (purely hypothetical, you understand). We can draw up this tax lookup table in cells B8:C18 (Figure 3–37):

0	0.06		
10000	0.1		
20000	0.12		
30000	0.15		
40000	0.2		
50000	0.24		
60000	0.27		
70000	0.3		
80000	0.35		
90000	0.4		
100000	0.46		

Figure 3–37. A lookup table for calculating tax obligation by income level

The table presents a tax schedule, which assesses income in dollars, and the values in the second column are really percentages. I haven't formatted either column as currency and percent, respectively, simply because we haven't gotten to formatting yet. Thus an income of $32,567 would be assessed at a rate of .15, or 15%, because that income falls between 30000 and 40000, and again VLOOKUP falls back to the *lower* of the two and "looks up" the matching figure for 30000 in the *second* column : .15.

In H8 we can enter any income total, say 62789, and in I8 we can write:

=VLOOKUP(A8,B8:C18,2,TRUE)

Our answer: .27, or 27%.

There's nothing conceptually new in this second case—it's pure review. VLOOKUP takes the number in cell H8-62789—and compares it to the values in the first column of the lookup table in B8:C18. Because the income falls between 60000 and 70000, it's treated as the former, whereupon 60000 is measured against the same row in the second column—namely, .27.

And where are the dollar signs, you ask? You *could* enter them, and you *would*, if you had a string of incomes to assess down the H column starting with H8. You'd then copy the original VLOOKUP in I8 down the I column, and yes—here the dollar signs would be most handy indeed, because we'd want all the incomes to be looked up on the same table.

As usual, there's more to say about VLOOKUP. For one thing, if you wanted to learn exactly how much tax a taxpayer actually owes, we could write in cell I8:

=VLOOKUP(A8,B8:C18,2,TRUE)*A8

See how that works? It looks up 62789, yields .27, and goes on to multiply 62789 by .27, returning:

$16,953.03

Once the formatting is applied.

Some other VLOOKUP thoughts: note that our lookup tables to date have comprised two columns. But nothing prevents us from adding a third and even more columns, which would enable us to achieve different sets of lookup outcomes.

For example, I could devise this lookup table, if we return to our grading chores (Figure 3 -38):

	0	F	Sit next to someone smart	
	65	D	Barely	
	75	C	OK	
	85	B	Good	
	92	A	Cool!	

Figure 3–38. A three-column lookup table

And we could rewrite John's VLOOKUP in C10 to read:

=VLOOKUP(B10,K$10:M$14,3,TRUE)

In which case we'd see Barely in that cell.

And what's different about this rewrite? Two things: the lookup table now spans three columns, and we're we're looking up our "answer"—the item which will appear in C10—in that third column.

One more VLOOKUP permutation: Suppose we wanted to be able to type a student's name in a selected cell and be able to immediately determine the numeric grade she earned. That is, if I type Cynthia I want to see 71 in the next cell, and so on. If so, we could treat our student name/grade list—A10:B14—as a lookup table. Why not?

And in D10 we could enter any student's name, and in E10 write:

=VLOOKUP(D10,A10:B14,2,FALSE)

I see I can't put anything by you. You've noticed a new, fourth argument in that formula, and here's why.

By default, VLOOKUP requires that the *first* lookup table coluum—the one containing the values to be looked up and assessed—be arrayed either in ascending numerical or alphabetical order (yes; that first column can display text). But we see that the first column in our current lookup table—the names of students—are assuredly *not* in such order. If we don't want to sort the list—and here we don't—we can enter FALSE in the VLOOKUP syntax, which instructs Excel to look for *exact* matches in the first column, irrespective their order—no more approximate matches. So if I type Cynthia in D10, I *should* see 71 in E10. If I omit the FALSE, I *won't* see 71 there. And if I type Barack in D10—a name which doesn't appear at all in the lookup table—I'll get an error message.

Again, project this scenario onto 500 or more students, and you'll appreciate how swiftly VLOOKUP can deliver information about any one of them. And before we move on, you'll want to know that VLOOKUP has a sibling named ***HLOOKUP***, which works in precisely the same way, except its lookup table runs horizontally, e.g., (Figure 3 - 39):

0	10000	20000	30000	40000	50000	60000	70000	80000	90000	100000	
0.06	0.1	0.12	0.15	0.2	0.24	0.27	0.3	0.35	0.4	0.46	

Figure 3–39. A horizontal lookup table, for use with HLOOKUP

If the table above has been written in say, E13:O24, an HLOOKUP might look like this:

=HLOOKUP(D3,E13:O14,2,TRUE)

Here a value in cell D3 is looked up in table E13:O14—and the tax percentage—the "answer"—is culled from the second *row*, not column.

If: Worth Knowing—No Ifs, Ands, or Buts

On to another function, one no less valuable—*IF*. As its name suggests, IF provides a way to sift between (at least) two data alternatives , and to act upon each accordingly. Again, that abstract introduction needs to be exemplified.

OK. Say I want to be able to award a bonus of $250 to any member of my sales team who exceeds $10,000 in sales in a given month. And suppose I start with this collection of data in cells A5:B8 (Figure 3–40):

Name	Sales	
Ted	9899	
Natalie	11034	
Jill	9934	
George	10342	

Figure 3–40. Sales data, to be analyzed with IF

Again, the size of the sales team doesn't really matter—we're just trying to prove the point. In cell C5—Ted's row—I could write:

=IF(B5>10000,250,0)

And there's your first IF statement. As with VLOOKUP's *default*, IF requires three arguments:

What's called a *logical test*—a condition which, if met, makes one thing happen, and if it isn't met, makes something else happen. In our case, the logical test is B5>10000 (note the greater than symbol) and it means, in effect: if the number in cell B5 exceeds 10,000, then…

Value if true. That is, what's going to happen If the condition is met. Again here, if B5 surpasses 10000, the value 250 will be posted in C5—the cell in which I've written the IF statement.

Value if false. What's going to happen if the condition is not met. Here, if the number in B5 falls below 10,000, a zero will be posted in C5—no bonus.

And we can copy this original formula down the C column for as many salespersons as we need—and no dollar signs, this time,—because we're assessing a *different* sales total for each salesperson. We'll see here, of course, that Natalie and George are in line for the $250.

And our Value if true/false consequences can be textual. For example, I could write our statement to read like this:

=IF(B5>10000,"Well Done!","We'll Get 'Em Next Month")

Written this way, one of these declarations will appear in the cells for each salesperson, once it's copied for all. I think they'd prefer the $250, but be that as it may, note that *textual* if true/false consequences require *quotes* around them.

And nothing stops you from incorporating other functions into IF, as long as you remember to keep your parentheses in line. Let's get back to Alice, and her 83 test average:

=IF(AVERAGE(D10:H10)>85,"Honor Roll","Nice Try")

If Alice's average were to exceed 85, Honor Roll appears in whatever cell the statement is written. In this case we see that AVERAGE is used here to establish the logical test—and once you've become practiced with nesting functions inside other ones, such as the example we're studying here, you can really start to rock 'n' roll. The data possibilities multiply exponentially.

There's one more function we can squeeze into into this sampler, and this one has real-world pertinence—*PMT*—short for Payment—a financial formula that can easily tell you how much money you can expect to pay for a mortgage—like it or not.

Stripped to its essentials, PMT has three arguments:

=PMT(rate,nper,pv)

Rate stands for your annual rate, one that will need to be *divided* by 12, or whatever the payment interval (example coming shortly). *Nper* signifies the number of payments you need to make across the life of the mortgage, and *Pv* denotes the present value of the mortgage.

Here's that example: you want to take out a 30-year, $200,000 mortgage at an interest rate of 5.2%. Let's enter these three values in cells B12, C12, and D12, shown in Figure 3–41:

(Again, we haven't formatted these values.)

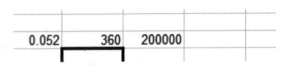

Figure 3–41. The basic three elements needed to write PMT: interest rate, number of payments, and current value of the loan

The .052 is, after all, 5.2%, and the 360 represents 360 monthly payments over 30 years. In E12, type:

=PMT(B12/12,C12,D12)

Note again: it's not obvious, but you need to divide the interest rate by 12 if you pay monthly, as we see above. (Were you to pay semi-monthly you'd have written B12/6—but you'd also be making 180 payments instead, and would have to enter that revised estimate in C12.)

When the smoke clears you should see this in E12:

$1,098.22

You'll note of course that Excel here has *automatically* formatted our result—by imparting currency features to the figure, as well as daubing the numbers red. Why red? To indicate that you're *debiting* your account whenever you incur this monthly charge.

Then you can go ahead and write *this* in any cell you choose:

=E12*C12

That little formula multiplies the monthly debit by 360, the number of times you'll actually have to pay out. Result: $395,359.83, for a $200,000 mortgage at 5.2%. Ouch!

But through the magic of automatic recalcuation, feel free to type in different numbers in any and all of the three cells—B12, C12, or D12. If you can nab a 4.9% rate, you'll pay $1,061,45 instead—37 bucks less a month. Don't spend it all in one place.

In Conclusion…

If you want to do more with your workbooks than compile data into lists, you need to know at least a bit about how to move your data to the next level—by writing formulas and utilizing Excel's numerous functions, and making something with the information that wasn't there before. In large measure, that's what spreadsheets are about.

As usual, these skills take practice—but again, the more you know about Excel's formula-writing capabilities, the more you can get the data to do what you want them to do, and to tell you what you need to know. And now that we've gotten that message across, let's take a look at the ways in which you can get *your* spreadsheet message across—by learning how to format your data.

■ ■ ■

CHAPTER 4

Keeping Up Appearances— Formatting the Worksheet

You've Got Designs on Your Worksheet

Ok—your data are in place, your scintillating, envy-stoking formulas are doing what you want them to do, and it's all over but the formatting. What do you do next? And how?

Obviously, that depends. After all, at the end of the day workbooks aren't meant to be things of beauty, at least not for their own sake. They're instruments of analysis and presentation, and the data you compile need to be as lucid and intelligible as possible—and indeed, should ideally make sense to someone who doesn't know terribly much about Excel.

Just the same, you want your workbook to look good—and to *enhance* your audience's comprehension of the data, even if that audience consists exclusively of the person who's designed the workbook. And in this connection Excel showcases a slew of ways in which you can engineer that enhancement. And we're going to explore quite a few of them. Not all, mind you, but a lot.

Of course, formatting a worksheet calls for a dollop of perspective, too. One mustn't give in to the it's-there-so-let's-use-it mindset that can entice the user into designing the worksheet equivalent of a polka dot blouse atop a plaid skirt. After all, does your boss *really* want to see her sales data in the Chiller font? You know the answer—and you'd probably *better* know it.

But aesthetic judgments aside, the first—and really integral—thing you need to know about formatting is this: apart from one obscure exception, formatting data on the worksheet changes the *appearance*, and not the *value,* of those data; and while you may hold that truth to be self-evident, it needs to be kept in mind, because the mind and the eye play tricks (as we'll see).

Thus if I enter the number 17 in a cell and tint it green, underline it, cast it into a boldface, enlarge it, center it in its cell, and angle it to a pitch of 48 degrees (and that's doable), that number remains exactly 17—and it remains a *number*, and so if I multiply it by 3 it'll still yields 51—no matter what it *looks* like. Formatting won't "*do*" anything to a number, other than change the way it looks. Coloring a negative number red or coupling it with a currency symbol may tweak the data informatively, but neither tweak will change the *value* that number represents. Coif your hair in dreadlocks or a Mohawk; either way, it's still you.

In the pre-2007 releases of Excel formatting options were assigned to their own, separate heading on the Menu bar, and as luck would have it, that command was called...Format. It's noteworthy, however, that that term has been banished from the Tab and Group names in 2010, although you *will* find a Format button in the Cells Group on the Home tab; instead, most of the standard formatting arsenal is now stockpiled in the Home tab groups, however its buttons are named. Indeed, the great majority of buttons in that tab can properly be called formatting in operation.

And as you proceed you'll also need to remind yourself that formatting in Excel 2010 avails itself of live previewing, meaning that when you rest your mouse over a formatting possibility—say, a change in font—the cells you've selected for that change will immediately display the change in preview form—*before* you actually click to implement the change. Decide against it? Just pull your mouse back or click elsewhere.

Bear in mind as well that the many of these formatting buttons perform commands that are *also* stored in a kind of catch-all dialog box called ***Format Cells***; and if you think back to Chapter 1 and that Dialog Launcher arrow (Figure 4–1):

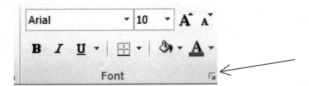

Figure 4–1. *The Dialog Box Launcher revisited*

you'll see that the Font, Alignment, and Number groups on the Home tab are all equipped with the arrow. Click *any* one of these and it'll take you to Format Cells, each one emphasizing a different one of its tabs, e g. (Figure 4–2):

Figure 4–2. *Golden oldie: the Format Cells dialog box*

But before we get to these buttons, we need to review what you'll encounter before you make any active formatting decisions.—namely, the worksheet defaults. Depending on your operating system, you will see a different default font. Windows XP brings back Arial 10-point as the default font in Excel 2010, whereas Windows 7 and Vista users will see the same Calibri 11-point font that was introduced in the 2007 version of Office. Points assay font heights, and so 72 points total an inch-high font.

The Font Button Group: A Closer Look

So let's turn more directly to the buttons in the Font Group in the Home tab. If you want to change the operative font in a cell, a range of cells, or the entire worksheet for that matter, you need to carry out what's called the select-then-do routine, a technique that really applies to *any* formatting change you wish to introduce anywhere. Very simply, select-then-do means you select those cells in which you want to implement the change, and *then* make the change.

Thus to change the font to, say, Chiller:

- Select the cells you want to change.

- If necessary, click on the Home tab, and then click on the down arrow alongside the Font box in the Font group (Figure 4–3):

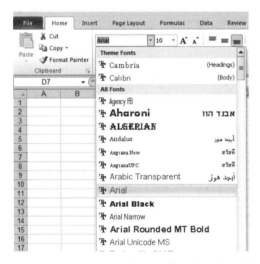

Figure 4–3. Your system's fonts, listed and previewed

- Click on the font you wish—in this case Chiller.

Note that the cells you've selected need *not* be currently populated with data. They can be blank, and so we see that formatting changes can be instituted prospectively or retroactively. You can format first, and enter data later—or vice versa.

Note in addition that after you complete your change the cells you've selected *remain* selected—because Excel wants you to be able to ascribe *additional* changes to the cell if you wish. Thus if I want to immediately follow the font change with a change in font *size*, I just click the down arrow alongside the Font Box, and click a size selection (Figure 4–4):

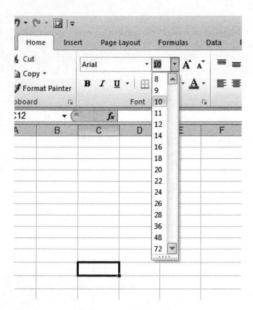

Figure 4–4. The Font Size drop-down menu

And information about these kinds of changes is cell-sensitive, meaning that the formatting characteristics of any cell you click are conveyed in the boxes and buttons in the ribbon. Thus if I click cell B7 on this worksheet I'll see (Figure 4–5):

Figure 4–5. Not a thing of beauty, but here's text in Showcard Gothic 26-point type, with boldface and italics added

I can immediately learn that the cell is set in a 26-point Showcard Gothic font, and is boldfaced and italicized besides (note the highlighted B and U). If I select a range of cells, it's the one in white—that is, the current cell—whose formatting info will appear on the ribbon.

If you're a Word user, these commands should be familiar to you—although in that application one changes fonts and font sizes of words and characters. Here the basic unit of currency is characters in *cells*.

Now note that the size intervals enumerated in the above menu leave gaps—there's no 17-point option there, for example. And so if you *do* need 17, 23, or 29-point characters, click in the Font Size box itself (Figure 4–6):

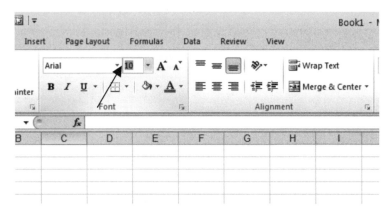

Figure 4–6. Click here in order to enter an unlisted font size

Type the desired size, and press Enter. Your font size is thereby changed. You can even shave your sizes in half-point increments, by typing 17.5, for instance.

To the immediate right of these boxes you'll see two disparately-sized A's. Click the larger of the two and your font enlarges by the next available interval in the Font Size drop-down menu—*for the cell(s) you've selected.* That means, for example, that if my selected cell has data in it set at 14 points, clicking the large A lifts its character size to 16—the next size interval you'll find in the Font Size drop-down menu. And if you've selected a range of cells with *different* current sizes—say some cells exhibit 12 points, and others 14—then *all* the font-changing methods work with the cell you've actively selected—that is, the cell in *white*—and will modulate the size of all the other cells to exactly match the font size of just the selected cell. For example, if I've selected this range (Figure 4–7):

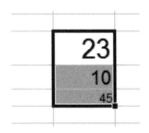

Figure 4–7. All these cells will match the font size of the white cell when they're changed collectively.

Clicking the large A will then treat the 23 as the *starting* font size, and resize *all* the cells as per whatever size you select for the 23. And, needless to say, clicking the smaller of the two A's does all of the above—in reverse, reducing font size with successive clicks. Thus the two A buttons really present you with a slightly swifter way of doing what the Font Size box does.

You'll also note the three formatting classics just beneath the font boxes—Bold, Italics, and Underline—B, I, and U—all of which submit to the same select-then-do technique. They also boast three classic keyboard equivalents—Ctrl-B, Ctrl-I, and Ctrl-U, respectively. Note in addition, however, the drop-down arrow accompanying the Underline button. Click it and you'll see this little drop-down menu (Figure 4–8):

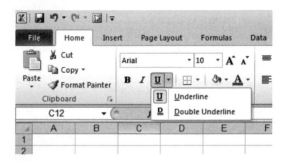

Figure 4–8. Two text underlining options

Click Underline and you'll wind up merely selecting the same single-underline option that was in force *before* you clicked the drop-down arrow. Select Double Underline, however, and you'll naturally inscribe a pair of lines beneath the *characters* in the cells you've selected (and not the entire cell width; this is the case with any underline). But this simple sequence illustrates a larger point: if you click Double Underline, you'll see this change in the Underline button (Figure 4–9):

Figure 4–9. The Double Underline selection

That is, Excel remembers the last selection you made with that button—at least for the duration of your session. Close Excel and the button reverts to its default appearance—in this case, the standard single underline. This last-selection-remembered feature applies to many formatting buttons, as you'll see. Note that the B, I, and U commands are toggles—that is, they have an alternating, on-off character. Click I, and your text is italicized. Click the I again, and the text is returned to its normal angle. The same idea applies to alternating clicks of Ctrl-B, Ctrl-I, and Ctrl-U—they turn the respective effects on and off.

And if you click the Dialog Box launcher in this group, you'll wind up here (Figure 4–10):

Figure 4–10. The Font tab in the Format Cells dialog box

You'll discover a couple of other underline options when you click the down arrow beneath Underline. And if you want to see what Strikethrough, Superscript, and Subscript do, just select a cell(s) with data, turn on the above dialog box, click the commands, and observe what happens in the preview pane. Strikethrough draws a line through the selected data in their cells, Superscript raises it (as per the 2 in $E=MC^2$), and Subscript sinks the data in a cell, as with the 2 in CO_2.

Borderline Command

Continuing our sweep across the formatting buttons gathered in the Font group, we've reached a button which, if you want to be technical about it, really doesn't impact fonts directly—the border button (Figure 4–11):

Figure 4–11. The cell Border option

But that doesn't detract from its usefulness, however. The border button draws lines, or borders, around *cells*, and not the *characters* entered in those cells. Borders are often applied around groups of numbers in order to call proper attention to them. You're viewing the default border setting above, called simply ***Bottom Border***, and simplicity notwithstanding, a bit of explanation is required. If you select a range of cells and click the Bottom Border setting you see above, a border will be drawn *only* along the bottom border of the *last*, or bottom cell; that is, all you'll see is *one* horizontal border lining the very lowest cell in the range—and not the bottom border of every cell you've selected. In other words, if you select nine cells and click the bottom border button you *won't* see this (Figure 4–12):

Figure 4–12. Don't expect to see this when you select the Bottom Border option down a range of cells

Instead, you'll see this (Figure 4–13):

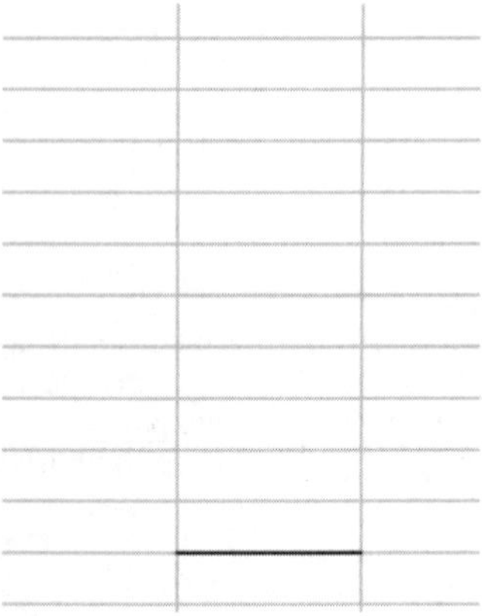

Figure 4–13. Surprise—only one bottom border, drawn at the bottom of all the nine selected cells

because the border options do their work by default on the *outer borders* of a selected *range*, that's all, not the internal borders of the cells (the ones *inside* the range). And if you click the drop-down arrow alongside the button (Figure 4–14):

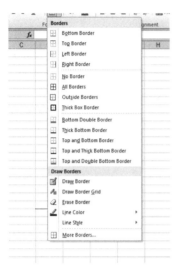

Figure 4–14. The Border drop-down menu

you'll discover that, with one exception, all the options subsumed under the Borders heading do their thing around a segment of the *outer border* of the range you've selected. The accompanying images clearly tell you what you can expect. The exception to the above: If you select All Borders, then *all* the borders around *all* the cells in a range will receive borders (Figure 4–15):

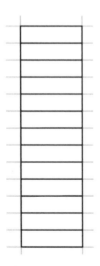

Figure 4–15. How the All Borders options looks over a range of selected cells

Note that the No Borders removes unwanted borders. Select a bordered range, click No Borders, and the borders disappear.

And what about the border commands shelved beneath the ***Draw Border*** heading? Here some very different options present themselves (Figure 4–16):

Figure 4–16. *Customize borders with the Draw Border option*

First, clicking Draw Border turns your mouse pointer into a pencil, enabling you to "draw" an *outside* border around any range of cells you wish (Figure 4–17):

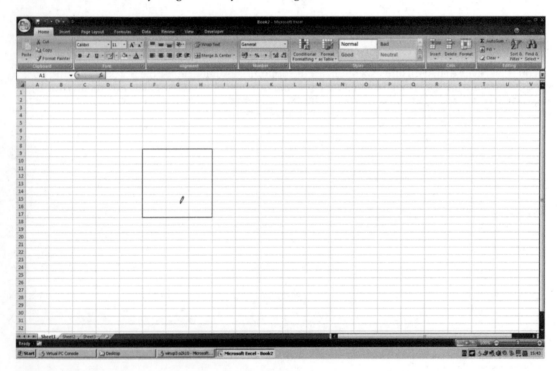

Figure 4–17. *Drawing a border with Excel's pencil tool*

And after you've drawn your range the pencil remains available, giving you the opportunity to draw other borders elsewhere if you wish. To turn the pencil off, just press the Esc key.

Selecting ***Draw Border Grid*** also calls up that pencil (duly sharpened) to the screen, and lets you draw lines around *all* the borders of any range of cells. And if you want, you can drag the pencil down only *one* column border, or only the lower border of cells. Thus, you can use Draw Border Grid to produce a border like this (Figure 4–18):

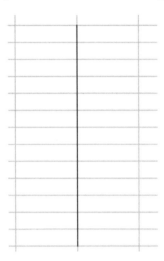

Figure 4–18. *Reading between the line: a single line, drawn with the pencil tool*

Erase Border will, when clicked, restyle the mouse pointer into an *eraser*. Once it's in view, you can click the eraser on any particular border line and the line will disappear. You can *click* on individual border lines or *drag* over a series of borders; either way, when the mouse is released the lines vanish. Again, to turn the eraser off, press Esc (Figure 4–19):

Figure 4–19. *The Eraser tool*

Line Color is really a subtle variation on Draw Border Grid. Click the command, select your color (Figure 4–20):

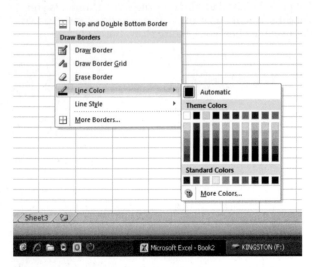

Figure 4–20. Where to find Line Color and Line Colors

There's that pencil again (Figure 4–21):

Figure 4–21. Drawing a line somehwere: the Line Color tool in action

Then, as with Draw Border Grid, drag the pencil over the desired cells. A border appears around all sides of the selected cells, in the desired color. You can apply this command to borders that currently don't display a line, or to existing, standard-black border lines, which means you can re-color borders.

Line Style allows you to modify the texture and weight (thickness) of the lines you draw (Figure 4–22):

Figure 4–22. Weighty matter: Line Style options

so that your borders can take on a different look, e.g., see Figure 4–23:

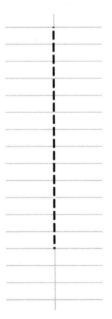

Figure 4–23. Not the same old line

The final line option, ***More Borders***, is, alas, the most confusing. It too allows you to draw lines around selected borders of selected cells, including diagonals running through cells. But you need to pay close attention to what the dialog box is trying to tell you. If you select just one cell on the worksheet, you'll be brought to the More Borders tab in the Format Cells dialog box, which looks like Figure 4–24 (note that here it's just titled "Border"):

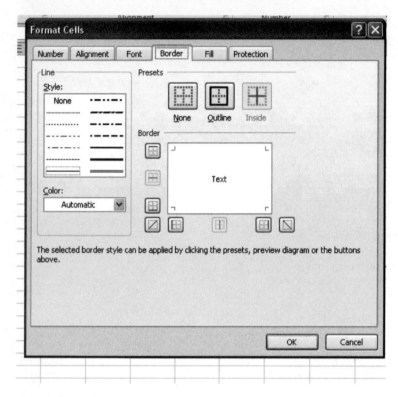

Figure 4–24. Where to add more borders

Select a **column** of cells and you'll see this (Figure 4–25)

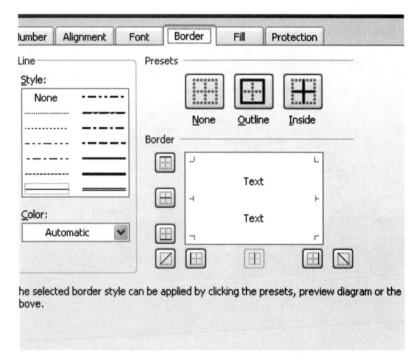

Figure 4–25. Subtle difference—Note the word "Text" appearing twice

Note the word "Text" appears here twice vertically, representing the columnar selection. Select a *row* of cells and you'll see this (Figure 4–26)

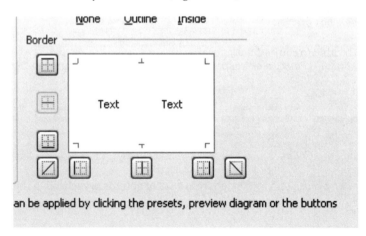

Figure 4–26. Text appearing horizontally, enabling borders to draw along that orientation

You're getting the idea. By then clicking the various line options surrounding the Text image you can border the selected cells; and while this option doesn't offer much more than what you're getting in the other border-drawing options, you do have those diagonals. If I click a diagonal, I'll see, by way of preview (Figure 4–27):

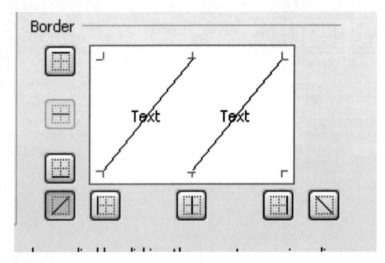

Figure 4–27. A new angle on borders

Click OK and you get this effect (Figure 4–28):

Figure 4–28. Angled lines, as per the dialog box preview

Odd but interesting, and you may be able to conjure a use for it.
The final two Font Group buttons, *Fill* and *Font Color*, respectively, are popular ones (Figure 4–29):

Figure 4–29. Two classic buttons: Fill and Font Color

When clicked, the Fill button colors any *cells* you've selected from a set of options presented in this drop-down menu (Figure 4–30)

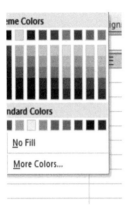

Figure 4–30. *Standard Fill color options*

It's very easy. Note you can remove any fill color by selecting the cells in question and clicking No Fill. You can also fill-color empty cells, that is, cells currently containing no data. Clicking ***More Colors*** yields a beehive of additional hues (Figure 4–31):

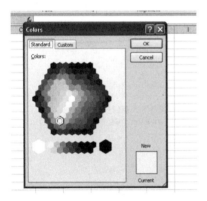

Figure 4–31. *A beehive of color activity*

Click the ***Custom Color*** tab and you can enter various numeric color values and add nuanced shadings to your tints. I'm still having trouble with ROYGBIV, though.

And befitting its name, Font Color serves up a nearly identical drop-down color menu, this time enabling you to change the color of the *data* you've entered in selected cells—*not* the color of the cells themselves (Figure 4–32):

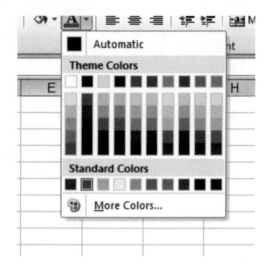

Figure 4–32. *Standard font colors*

Note, however, that the above menu also offers an Automatic color option; click it and you return the data to the default black font color. A More Colors option is likewise provided here, as well as a Custom color option.

Getting Oriented

The next group in the Home tab is called *Alignment*, and Alignment commands are likewise considered formatting. These enable you to position, and reposition, the data you've entered in their cells (Figure 4–33):

Figure 4–33. *The Alignment button group*

The lower-left buttons in the group are rather simple and commonly used, and bring about left, center, and right alignments of the data in the cells you click. That is, click the left alignment button and data will be shunted to the left border of the cell. (Of course, text is left-aligned by default.) Click the center button, and any data are situated in the middle of their respective cells (Figure 4–34):

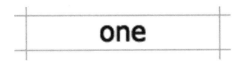

Figure 4–34. Centered text

Nothing prevents you from centering *numbers* in their cells, and this alignment decision seems to be a popular one. Users seem to like the symmetry it affords. Still, I wouldn't recommend it, and for an obvious reason (Figure 4–35):

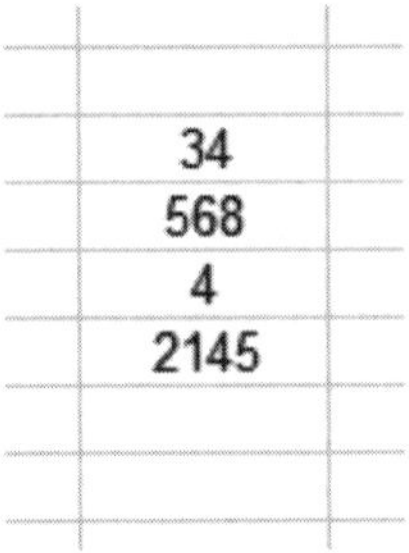

| 34 |
| 568 |
| 4 |
| 2145 |

Figure 4–35. It's your call: centered numbers...if you like this sort of thing

You see the problem. Enter numbers of varying widths in the same column, center them, and you'll thereby misalign the ones, tens, etc. But remember that alignments, no matter how ornate, *won't* change the quality of the data. Those numbers above are still numbers, and can be subject to exactly the same mathematical treatment as if they are right-aligned.

And while we're at it, the right-align button rams data to the right border of their cells—which is the default alignment for numbers, after all.

The upper tier of alignment buttons controls a far more exotic set of possibilities—*vertical* alignment in cells (Figure 4–36):

Figure 4–36. Where to control vertical cell alignment

If you need your data to look like this (Figure 4–37):

Figure 4–37. Centered data—centered vertically, that is

click one of the buttons shown in Figure 4–36. What these do is position data along a vertical axis in the cell—at the bottom of a cell (the default, when you think about it), in the center (as above), or even at the cell's ceiling (Figure 4–38):

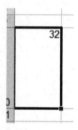

Figure 4–38. Hitting the heights. Cell data top-aligned

Just bear in mind that if you apply these formats to cells of normal heights, you won't see the above effects. That's because the default row height is too low to enable these to happen, and so you'll need to elevate the heights of the rows you want.

How do you do that? The technique is in many ways the right-angled equivalent of the column-widening methods we described in chapter 2. In order to raise a row height, click on the row's *lower* boundary and drag down (or up, if you want to shrink the row's height). And if I *select* several row boundaries at the same time by dragging along the row numbers, releasing the mouse and then dragging on *any* selected row boundary, I'll see something like this (Figure 4–39):

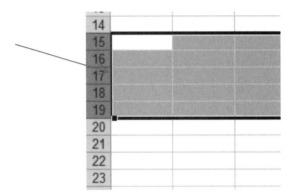

Figure 4–39. Modulating row heights

I can then modulate the height of all the selected rows at the same—and they'll all exhibit the same, new height.

So to achieve the row height you see in Figure 4–40—brought about in cell A10—I simply dragged down on the lower boundary by the 10 (Figure 4–40):

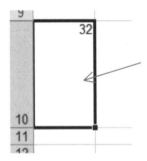

Figure 4–40. Cell A10, now heightened

And once I've engineered the desired height I then clicked the Top Align button—and you get your top-of-the-cell number. Of course as always I can heighten the row first, click Top Align, and *then* enter the number. The sequence of clicks doesn't matter here.

Now you'll recall my flippant aside about 48-degree text, the one I threw out on the opening page of this chapter. Well, if you need or want something like that, look here (Figure 4–41):

Figure 4–41. The Orientation Button

That's the Orientation button. Click its down arrow, and you'll see this (Figure 4–42):

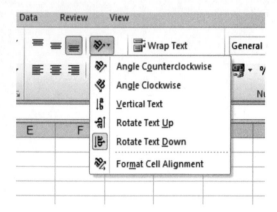

Figure 4–42. Orientation options

That's a pretty illustrative, what-you-see-is-what-you-get drop-down. Select a cell, then click Vertical Text, for example, and you get (Figure 4–43):

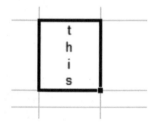

Figure 4–43. Vertical text: Like THIS

And so on. Note, though, that when you call upon these Orientation options they *automatically* raise the heights of rows (as also happens with font size changes|) in order to accommodate their effects, unlike the vertical alignment buttons, which require the *user* to heighten the rows.

When you click the last Orientation button, ***Format Cells: Alignment***, the aforementioned Format Cells dialog box appears, with the Alignment tab in view (Figure 4–44):

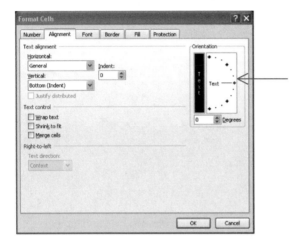

Figure 4–44. The Alignment tab of the Format Cells dialog box

If you type a number in the ***Degrees*** field on the box's right side and click OK, you can achieve that 48-degree angle, or any other tilt you want, at least between -90 and 90 degrees. You can also click on the red diamond referenced by the arrow above, and drag it along that Orientation half-circle to angle your text, too. Either way, you could get the example shown in Figure 4–45:

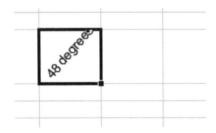

Figure 4–45. 48 degrees worth of text alignmnent

To turn this effect off—that is, to restore the data to a level orientation—return to the Degrees field and type "0."

And if you click that vertical ***Text*** field you see beneath the Orientation heading, that's what you'll get—vertical text in their cells, as per the Vertical Text options we saw in the Orientation drop-down menu in the Alignment Group.

On the left side of the Format Cells dialog are various Text alignment options. Now some of the options in those ***Horizontal*** and ***Vertical*** drop-down menus are obscure, but here goes:

General—Brings about standard data alignment defaults, e.g., text is left-aligned, numbers right-aligned. Obviously you'd only select this to *restore* realigned data to their original alignments.

Right and Left (Indent)—These simply push, or indent, data in their cells to the right or the left by the number of characters you type in the ***Indent*** field in the dialog box. But just remember that if you select a right indent, the text will move *left*, because it is the indent itself that pushes to the right.

Indents can bring about some rather unusual visual results. If I select a right indent and type 10 in the indent field, I can wind up with something like this (Figure 4–46):

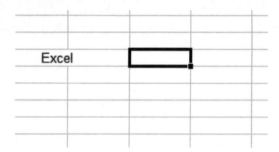

Figure 4–46. Cell-dom used: the indent option

Don't be fooled—the text is actually "in" the cell selected by the cell pointer. This *can't* happen with a number, however, and for a reason we've already discussed in the chapter on data entry; Excel won't allow a number to creep into another cell. Thus, if I type 43 in the very cell you see above with the same indent settings, this is what I'll get (Figure 4–47):

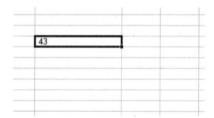

Figure 4–47. An indented number

Here the indent carries out what's tantamount to an Auto Fit. The number is indeed indented, but only within its own cell. Yeah—you're not likely to use this very often. The two indent buttons (Figure 4–48) found on the Alignment Group on the Home tab of the ribbon:

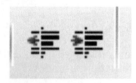

Figure 4–48. The Indent buttons

equate respectively with the Right and Left Indent options in the Alignment Dialog box—but look at the buttons. What I'm calling Right Indent features an arrow pointing *left,* **and** what I've called Left Indent bears an arrow pointing *right.* Nevertheless that's what they are. Moreover, the Alignment Group caption clinging to the first of the two buttons above (seen when you rest you mouse over it) calls it **Decrease Indent**, and not Right Indent; and the other button is labeled **Increase Indent**; and neither of these labels corresponds to what the *same* commands are called in the Alignment Dialog box.

   A couple other qualifications to what is again, not the sort of command you're likely to call upon daily: Click the left-pointing indent button arrow in the button group and nothing happens in the cell at the outset—the data stay put. But click either left or right setting in the *dialog* box and type a *number* in the indent field and the data *will* indent in the desired direction.
Sorry about that.

   Center—Really an equivalent of the Center alignment button. Typing a number in Indent here has no effect.

   Fill—Takes any data you've written in the cell and repeats it in the cell, until the cell's width is taken up with the data. For example, if I type the word "the" in a cell and select Fill, I'll see (Figure 4–49):

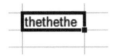

Figure 4–49. Filling the cell with data—repeatedly

And if I go on to widen the cell now, I'll get Figure 4–50:

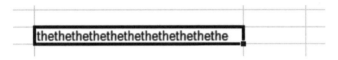

Figure 4–50. Same command, wider cell.

And yes, you can bring about the same effect with a number—though I can't imagine why you'd want to. That is, if I type 3 in a cell and invoke the Fill format I'll see

333333

   across the width of the cell—but its actual value is still….3. Don't ask questions, but remember—this is a *format*, and as such, it doesn't change the number's value.

   The *Justify* and *Distributed* options are similar, though not quite identical to one another. These commands represent a kind inverse of the column Auto Fit; instead of widening a column to accommodate its widest entry, Justify and Distributed treat the current column width as a fixed margin and stack the text in the cell so that it all fits. So for example, if I type (Figure 4–51):

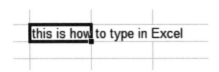

Figure 4–51. Before justifying the text…

And select Justify, the text is realigned like this (Figure 4–52):

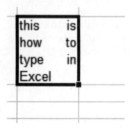

Figure 4–52. … and after

The text continues to use the *existing* column width, and so needs to raise its row height in order to pinch all the text within that width. The command is called Justify because it emulates a similar effect in Word, whereby text in a paragraph exhibits straight left *and* right margins—at least to the extent possible. Distribution differs only in that it *attempts* to distribute the text *equally* across each line in the cell, so that each line spans the current column width, including the last line—again, to the extent possible. Here's another instance of a justified cell (Figure 4–53):

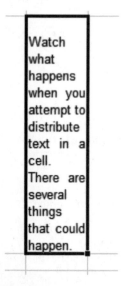

Figure 4–53. Justified vs. Distributed text

And here's the same test subject to the Distributed option (Figure 4–54):

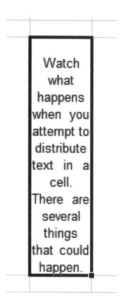

Figure 4–54. The text, Distributed

Note how the word "happen" is centered here. It's the closest Distribute could come to spanning the entire column width with that one word. Try typing the above phrase, applying the Justify and Distribute effects, and widening the column.

Center Across Selection centers a cell entry across a range of cells. That is, if I type this:

This is how to center data across a selection

in cell E28, and then select this range (Figure 4–55):

Figure 4–55. Data about to be centered across a range selection

And select Center Across Selection, I'll view this (Figure 4–56):

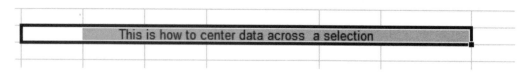

Figure 4–56. The data, now centered

The effect is clear. Excel treats the selected range as a single space—in essence as one big cell, even though each cell retains its own identity— and centers the data accordingly. You may want to contrast this with the Merge & Center command coming up soon.

Of the five Vertical Alignment drop-down options in our dialog box (Figure 4–57),

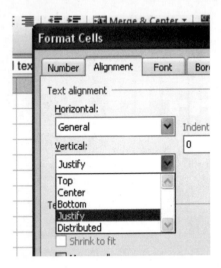

Figure 4–57. Vertical cell alignment options

the first three—***Top, Bottom*** and ***Center***—are clones of the Vertical Alignment buttons we've already seen in the Alignment Group. The other two—***Justify*** and ***Distributed***—attempt to realize the same effects as their similarly-named Horizontal options, but to appreciate how they work you need to tinker with column widths and text length. Here are two examples (Figures 4–58 and 4–59):

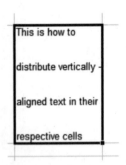

Figure 4–58. Vertically distributed text

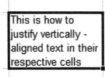

Figure 4–59. Text, vertically jusftified

The three **Text control** options in the Alignment dialog box are variations on themes we've previously sounded. As with Justify and Distribute, **Wrap text** regards a cell's current width as a margin, and wraps cell text accordingly. The difference here is that Wrap text doesn't try to flatten the right text margin, but rather lets text advance unevenly against cell's right boundary (Figure 4–60):

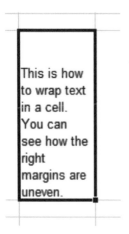

Figure 4–60. Wrapping and styling: text wrapped in its cell

Wrap text allows text to wrap naturally to the next line, and doesn't try the spacing heroics of Justify or Distribute; this command is represented by the Wrap Text button in the Alignment Group.

Those options—Wrap text, Justify, and Distribute—that realign text by raising row heights instead of stretching column widths do serve a real purpose. They're usefully applied to worksheets in which you want to present data in a series of columns and maintain the same width for all of them, even as the *data* in the columns exhibit various widths.

Shrink to fit is a curious flip side to the workings of Wrap text and column Auto Fit. Whereas Wrap text tries to pile text into a cell without changing its width by raising its row height instead, and Auto Fit tries to widen *columns* to accommodate all text in one cell, Shrink to fit changes *neither* column width *nor* row height; it shrinks *text* in order to gather it all into existing width and height. So if you start with this (Figure 4–61):

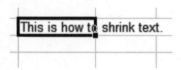

Figure 4–61. Text, normally sized

Shrink to Fit will recast the text to look like this (Figure 4–62):

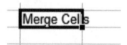

Figure 4–62. Look honey, I shrunk the text

Well, you get the idea.

Finally, the **Merge cells** option does as it says. It actually consolidates, or merges, selected contiguous cells into one mega cell. Thus if I start with this entry in cell J12 (Figure 4–63):

Figure 4–63. Text in cell J12

And I then select cells J12 through N12 and click the Merge cells command, I get (Figure 4–64):

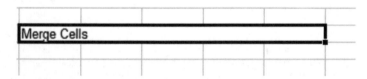

Figure 4–64. A merged cell

And what you're looking at now is *all* J12; all the selected cells have been absorbed by one cell—J12—in which I typed my data. All of which raises a fairly obvious question: what does that do for me? Answer: not much.

But what you really may want to do is merge these cells as we've demonstrated above, and *then* center the data in the new, super-sized cell. And indeed, there's an Alignment Group button—**Merge & Center**—which does exactly that (Figure 4–65):

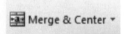

Figure 4–65. The Merge & Center button

By default, clicking Merge & Center on our selection of J12 through N12 brings about (Figure 4–66):

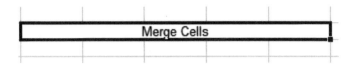

Figure 4–66. A mega, merged cell

This option resolves an old spreadsheet problem—the need to center a title over a collection of columns (Figure 4–67):

Figure 4–67. How to center that title over all those months?

In the old days, users had to resort to all manner of contortions in order to situate that title in the middle of the row above the month names, including trying to locate a "middle" column. But we're working with 12 columns here, aren't we? There *is no* middle column. Merge & Center will turn A1:L1 into one cell (of course that's the range you need to select), after which Monthly Sales will be precisely centered within the new super cell—which is still called A1.

The drop-down menu attaching to Merge & Center affords three additional options. *Merge Across* allows you to Merge & Center data in consecutive *rows*. Thus if you start with this (Figure 4–68):

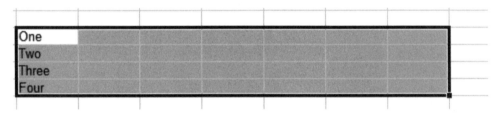

Figure 4–68. Text, one word per cell

You see that I've already selected the cells to be merged. Clicking Merge & Center: Merge Across results in this (Figure 4–69):

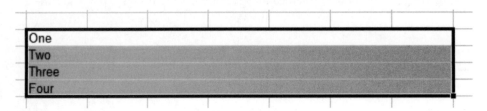

Figure 4–69. Each row, its selected cells merged

The respective rows are merged—but here, you see that the data in them are centered. At this point, you need to then click the standard Center button in the Alignment Group in order to center each bit of data in each new merged cell in each row. Inelegant, but it works.

Merge & Center: Merge Cells duplicates the Merge cells command we described above in the Alignment Dialog Box, and Merge & Center: Unmerge Cells returns all cells back to their original integrity.

An important additional note about the Merge Cells options: Be sure that *only* the *leftmost* of the cells you wish to merge has data in it. Thus if I want to merge cells J12 through N12, and any cells *other* than J12 have data in them, those data will be lost when you go ahead with the merge—though Excel will warn you about this prospect with an onscreen message.

Excel Has Got Your Number(s)

Now that we've gotten ourselves oriented and aligned, we can push on to a group whose modest bearing belies its importance—the *Number* group (Figure 4–70):

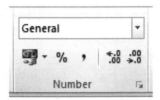

Figure 4–70. The Number button group

Needless to say, formatting numbers is a pretty essential Excel task, but with a couple of slightly pause-giving exceptions, the task is pretty easy. And the number formats you're *most* likely to need are a snap.

Let's start with the group's lower tier, moving left to right. That first button, picturing a pile of coins and a bank note of indeterminate origin, enables you to format numbers in *currency* mode—but unfortunately it's called, rather cryptically, *Accounting Number Format*, with its caption asking you to "Choose an alternate currency format for the selected cell" (of course you know that means *cells*, too). That term "alternate" is pretty cryptic, too—but what it means here simply is that clicking the button will impart a currency motif from one monetary system—Euro instead of Dollars, for example. (But as we'll see, there's a slightly different format out there called Currency, too—but we'll get to that.)

If you select a cell or a range of cells and click the Accounting Number Format, this is what happens by default:

- The number is now embellished by your indigenous currency symbol. If you're in the States, you'll see the dollar sign, in the UK the pound sign, and so on (how Excel knows what symbol to use is tied to your system setup in Control Panel).

- If the number exceeds 999, commas will punctuate where necessary, e.g., 1,234,582. (In France, the comma is replaced by a space. It's another country-specific, Control Panel thing).

- The number will exhibit two decimal points. Thus 27 will appear as 27.00, 678.1 as 678.10.

And why the term *Accounting*? Well, to repeat—this *is* a currency-specific format, but of a special type. What's special—or at least different—about it is that it lines up the currency symbol independent of the length of numbers. Consider this example: If I stack these numbers in a column (Figure 4–71):

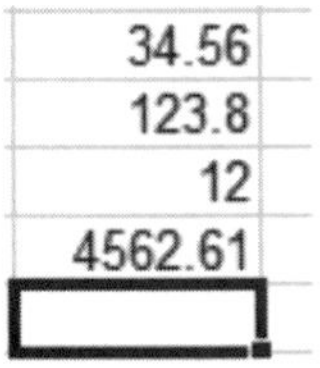

34.56
123.8
12
4562.61

Figure 4–71. Numbers, pre-formatted

And I click Accounting Number Format, I'll see (Figure 4–72):

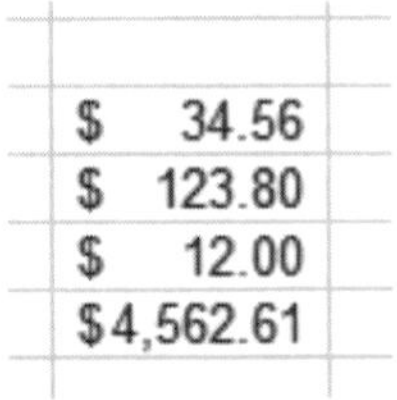

$	34.56
$	123.80
$	12.00
$4,562.61	

Figure 4–72. Numbers, as per the Accounting format

Note the position of the dollar signs—all positioned in the far left of their cells, even as the actual numbers describe various widths (note also how the 12 receives those two decimal points, as does 123.8).

Of course that's all for starters—and you can stop right there if you're happy with the defaults. But if you're in the US and require a different currency, click the down arrow and some standard, alternative currency options appear, e.g., the British pound and the Euro.

But if you need something else, click *More Accounting Formats* (Figure 4–73):

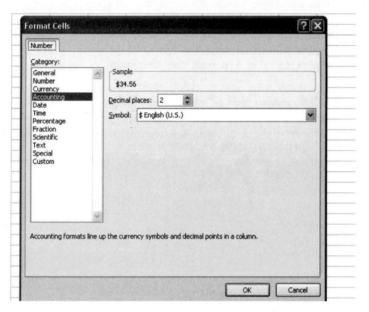

Figure 4–73. The Number tab, in an abridged Format Cells dialog box

We're back to the Format Cells dialog box, this time showing only one tab. Then click the down arrow by Symbol and click on any one of the long array of currency formats Excel makes available; your numbers will take on that denomination, and you'll note as well that you can add or diminish the number of decimal points your currency displays, either by typing a number in the Decimal places field or clicking one of those Spin Box arrows in either direction.

That's really all there is to the Accounting Number Format, but that's *not* all there is to currency formatting, as we'll see.

The next button in the Number lineup is ***Percent Style***, and while it's most easy to use (no drop-down menu, either!) you need to understand what the style will do to a number. If I type:

41

and select that cell, and click Percent Style, I'll see:

4100%

And *not* 41%. That's because percentages really express a number's percentage of the number 1—which is, after all, 100%. Thus our number above—which is 41 times the size of 1—has to turn out to be 4100%. If you were expecting 41%, you will need to have typed *.41.*

But there is an alternative way to institute the Percent Style. If I type:

41%

in a cell, complete with the percent sign, I *will* achieve exactly that figure—41 percent.

The next button, ***Comma Style***—symbolized, naturally enough, by the comma—imitates the Accounting Number Format, minus the currency symbol. Thus if I select a cell containing the number 3457, the comma button will make it look like this:

3,457.00

The following two buttons, *Increase Decimal* and *Decrease Decimal*, are simple, too, but a jot more thought-provoking. With each click, Increase Decimal will indeed add one decimal point to a number—and that includes numbers that have *already* received two such points under either of the Accounting Number Comma Style formats. Thus:

67

will appear as 67.0, 67.00, 67.000, etc., with each successive Increase Decimal click. If you write:

=4/7

your result will initially appear as:

0.571429

in a cell of default column width. If you execute an Auto Fit, you'll see:

.0571428571

a nine-digit rendition of this repeating decimal (note that the "9"—the last digit in the original six-digit version above—is replaced by 8571—adding additional precision to the number). But you can add still more decimal digits—up to 15 meaningful ones in total—to a number, after which 5 additional zeroes will then appear. But of course unless you're a currency-exchange high roller or a nuclear physicist, you're not likely to need all those extras.

Decrease Decimal works in the opposite direction, paring a decimal point with each click. And that means, for example, that if you click Decrease Decimal once on this number:

4.56

you'll see:

4.6

Click Decrease Decimal again and you'll see:

5

Now what's the numerical value of that figure? The answer: 4.56, and that's because—at the risk of repeating myself—we're formatting data, and formatting changes the *appearance* of the data *only, not* their value. And that means in turn that if I write the above number in cell A12, and write somewhere else:

=A12*2

I'll realize 9.12, not the 10 you might assume on the basis of appearances. And if you want proof of all this, type 4.56 in A12, click back in A12 and click Decrease Decimal twice, and grab a look at the Formula Bar. You'll see 4.56.

And what this could mean is that a printout of a worksheet containing the above activity would display a 5 in A12 and a calculation showing 9.12, when you multiply A12 by 2—and that could be rather misleading, to put it mildly. It's something you need to think about. (It should be added, by the way, that *text* entries in cells bearing any of the above number formats will be completely unaffected by any of this. It's only when you actually enter a numeric value in such cells that these changes matter.)

There's one other clarification to be made about the buttons we've examined thus far: that any one of the buttons overrules the effect of any other. Thus, if I've formatted 5457.67 to take on this appearance:

$5,457.67

and then click Comma Style, I'll see 5,457.67. If I click Percent Style, I'll see 545767%, and so on. The point is that the last format selected takes priority.

Now if you examine the broad strip—called *Number Format*—sitting atop all these buttons in the Number group, you'll view the default entry *General* (Figure 4–74):

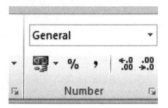

Figure 4–74. The General number format

Click the accompanying drop-down arrow and you'll see (Figure 4–75)

Figure 4–75. The Number Format drop-down menu

Each of those eleven options (you can't see that eleventh one—Text—in the screen shot, because you need to scroll down) introduces formatting variations, some of which you've already seen, others of which need to be explained. And note the More Number Format option at the base of the menu, too; that also requires a closer look. So let's move in sequence.

The default *General* format type is captioned No specific format—and that means General makes its own guess about what kind of data you've entered in a cell. If I type a number, General assumes that's exactly what I had in mind—an entry that possesses quantitative value. If I type a prose sentence in the cell instead, General deems it text in nature. If I type a formula, General treats it as such.

Now at this point you're probably itching to ask a rather pressing question, because I see a lot of raised hands out there. You want to know: Isn't this all completely obvious? Why do we need a format to make *any* decision about the data, when the nature of those data is so clear?

The answer is that the data types aren't always so clear. If I type this:

4/5

that sure looks like text, because it's missing the tell-tale = sign. But General treats the above expression as a *date*, namely:

05-Apr

And similarly, General treats:

4–5

the same way, as that same date. Yes—by rights, the General format *could* have assigned text status to these entries, but Excel assumes that users who write such expressions really want to enter dates. And dates, as we'll see, are really numbers.

In any case, the General format keeps an open mind about what it is you've written, whereas the other formats are a bit bossier, in the sense that they impose their expectations on the data to the extent they can.

Thus the *Number Format* option can't turn *text* into a number, but it can turn numerical data displaying a different format back into a garden-variety number—and it throws in *two* decimal points for free. Thus if a cell contains this entry:

34.5%

Clicking that cell and then clicking Number will yield:

.35

See why? Here, Number has really done two things: it's repealed the percent style, and rounded off the number to two decimal points—because that what Number does by default. But remember: the number is *really* .345. Check out the Formula Bar.

Currency is a cousin of the Accounting Number Format, and we've already alluded to it. It differs from Accounting in one respect: the currency symbol it imparts *hugs* each number's first digit, instead of assigning it to a fixed place in the far left of the cell. Thus our Accounting example of a few pages back looked like this (Figure 4–76):

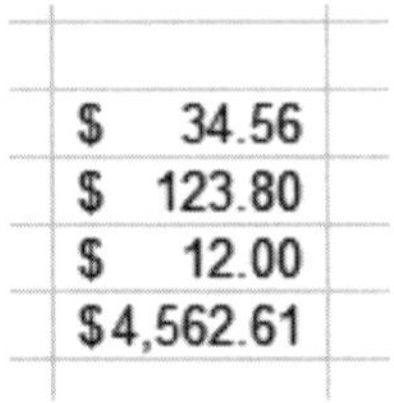

$	34.56
$	123.80
$	12.00
$4,562.61	

Figure 4–76. The Accounting format redux

Click Currency on the same range and you'll come away with this (Figure 4–77):

$34.56
$123.80
$12.00
$4,562.61

Figure 4–77. The Currency format

And you'll be happy to know we've already discussed *Accounting*.

Dates—The Long and the Short of It

But we've yet to discuss the next two formatting alternatives—***Short Date*** and ***Long Date***, which do require a bit of elaboration. In order to appreciate how Excel formats dates, you need to know that at bottom, a date is a sequenced *number*. And the sequence starts with January 1, 1900, a date to which Excel assigns the numerical value of 1. Any post-January 1, 1900 date you enter in any cell in effect supplies a count of the number of days that have elapsed between itself and that day 1. Thus May 4, 1972 superimposes a date *format* over the number 26423.00—the number of days stretching in time from the baseline January 1, 1900 to May 4, 1972. Put otherwise, May 4, 1972 *really is* 26423.

As a way of corroborating this point, you'll note that when you click on a cell containing numerical data—say 34567—and click the Number Format down arrow, you'll see something like this (Figure 4–78):

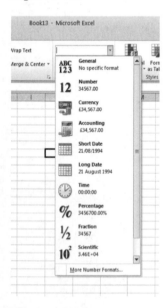

Figure 4–78. Mark that date

Look closely at the screen shot and you'll see that each format presents its proposed "version" of 34567, that is, how the number would look were you to select this or that format. And look in particular at Short and Long Date.

Understanding this formative concept (it probably qualifies as a have-to-know)—that dates are really numbers—helps you understand in turn that if you write April 6, 2001 in cell A1 (in any date format) and July 12, 1983 in cell A2, you can then write:

=A1-A2

and realize an answer of 6478, which signifies the number of days *between* the two dates you've entered—because what you've really done here is subtract 30509.00 from 36987.00.

Thus a date format—and again, that's what it is, a *format*—masks what's really a number in date terms. And so if I write say, 23786 in a cell, select it, and select Short Date, I'll see:

02/13/1965

That's the mode of date presentation that Excel calls Short Date. Select that same cell and click on Long Date, and I'll see:

February 13, 1965

And if write 7/8 in a cell and select Short Date, I'll see 07/08/2010. Choose Long Date, and July 08, 2010 emerges. Note in this case 7/8 omits the year; and when one does just that, Excel assumes you're referring to a date in the *current* year. But remember what I said earlier. If I type 7/8 under the *General* format—without earmarking *any* date format at all—I'll *still* see a date entry in the cell, because even the General format thinks you meant to type a date anyway. But this is what you'll see:

Jul-08

an even briefer format than Short Date. It's a *really* short date.

To sum up, Date formats paint a chronological veneer over what is really, when the smoke clears, just a number. And bear in mind that the inverse applies: if I type 7/8 and Jul-08, I can return to that cell, click the Number format, and see: 40367.00. But why the two decimal points?

Time Is On Your Side—Yes It Is

I was afraid you'd ask that question, and in order to answer it we need to bump down to the next formatting selection—*Time*. To Excel, any time or clock reading in a 24–hour span can be treated as a fraction of a 24–hour denominator. What does that mean? It means this: if I type .346 in a cell, and then apply the Time format to that cell, I'll see:

08:18:14

Yeah, I also found this baffling at first—and second—sight. But think about it: the above clock time actually represents .346 of a day in hourly terms; that is, 8:18:14 is the time of day which stands for 34.6% of an entire 24–hour span. And to trot out perhaps the simplest illustration, type .5 in that cell, and format it with Time. You'll see:

12:00

Get it? That's noon—exactly half, or .5, of a day.

Thus the Date formats provide a default number with two decimal points, e.g., 32456.00, in order to enable you to format a cell with *either* date *or time* readings. If you enter 31456.17 in a cell and opt for Short Date, you'll muster 02/13/1986. But if you select the Time format instead, you'll see 04:04:48, the time of day which stands for exactly .17 of an entire day. Choose a Date format, and the original number—31456.17—extracts and uses only the digits to the left of the decimal point. Choose Time and only the .17 is used.

And for putting up with all that, you get a break—because we've already discussed the next format—*Percentage* (even though Excel calls the equivalent button **Percentage Style**).

The next option, Fraction, is a wee bit tricky. It presents any less-than-whole number in fractional terms. This:

12.5

would be formatted by Fraction as 12 1/2.

That looks pretty simple, and it is; but by default Fraction rounds off if necessary. That is, the number:

34.32

will be treated by Fraction as 34 1/3 for starters, and that's not quite exact. As you'll see a bit later, however, there are ways of adjusting this discrepancy.

The penultimate option, *Scientific*, performs a scientific-notational makeover on a number. Type 567 for example and Scientific gives you:

5.67E+02

Thus 0.67 becomes:

6.70E-01

Notice the plus and minus exponent references.

And finally, *Text* imputes a text format to whatever you write in the cell. That sounds a bit gratuitous; after all, how else could you possibly format a prose sentence? True, but Text can also format *numbers* as text, although you're not likely to want to do such a thing—because doing so compromises the numbers' mathematical character. However, there are times when numerical data imported from the Internet assumes textual form, and some tinkering is required in order to restore their true quantitative status.

Now you'll also note that the last entry on the Number:General Format drop-down menu is entitled More Number Formats, and clicking it delivers you to the Number tab in the ubiquitous Format Cells dialog box (Figure 4–79):

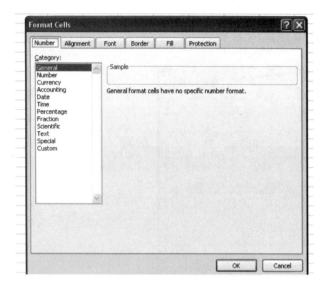

Figure 4–79. The Number tab in the Format Cells dialog box

The *Category* column simply reiterates the options on the Number Format drop-down menu (with two exceptions—*Special* and *Custom*). Clicking any of these often—but not always—presents the user with additional formatting variations available under that category. For example, if I click Number, I'll see this (Figure 4–80):

Figure 4–80. Accentuating the negative—negative number format options

Note here I can choose the way in which I want negative numbers to appear—in red, accompanied by a minus sign (the default), or featuring both elements. The ***Use 1000 Separator*** option simply allows you to decide if you want your numbers to utilize a comma when it tops 999. The ***Date*** category augments the Short Date and Long Date possibilities (Figure 4–81):

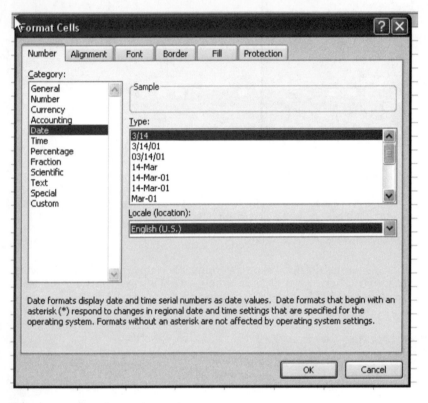

Figure 4–81. *Date formatting options*

(Note the discussion about asterisks, too. What it means is that *only* the asterisked formats are tied directly to the settings in your computer, meaning in turn that 3/14/2001 in the States would necessarily appear as 14/03/2001 in the UK. The other, asterisk-free options can be selected on any computer.)

And ***Time*** does the same—broadening the number of ways in which a time can appear in a cell (Figure 4–82):

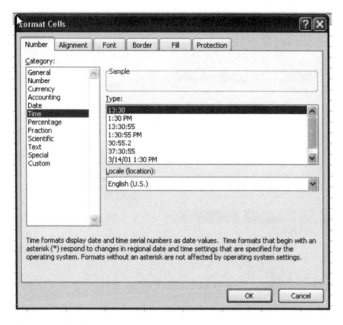

Figure 4–82. Time formatting options

A few words about the *Fraction* category may be in order. I earlier noted that when submitted to this format, the number 34.32 was rendered as 34 1/3—and that's not correct. 1/3 is .33, not .32, and that difference might matter—although again we need to remember that, because we're "only" formatting the cell, the value is *really* 34.32 in any case. But by default Fraction estimates the fractional equivalent of a decimal up to one digit. If we click on the cell containing 34.32 we'll see (Figure 4–83):

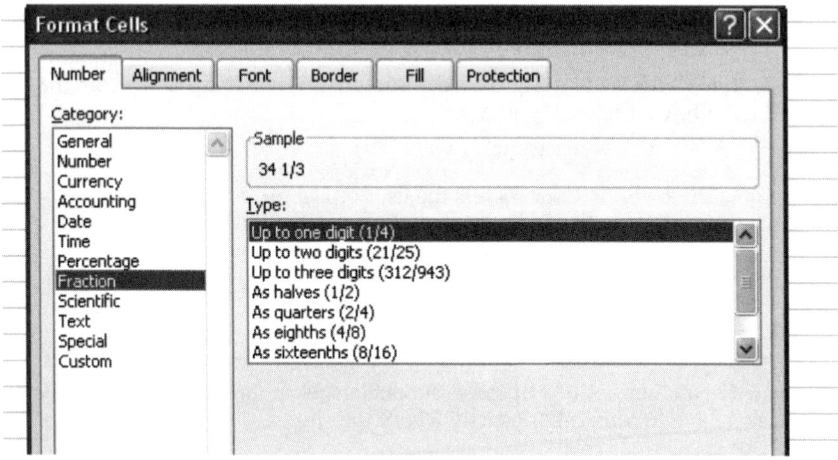

Figure 4–83. Fraction options

And note the sample captures the actual value in the cell we've selected. What's happening here is that Fraction starts by treating 34.32 as 34.3—one digit's worth of a decimal; but if we choose the next option, *Up to two digits*, we'll get (Figure 4–84):

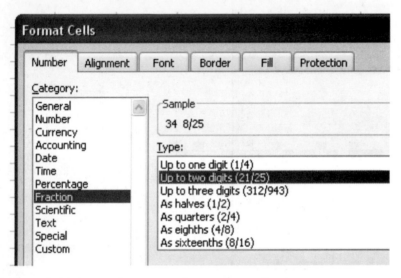

Figure 4–84. *Options for representing numbers as fractions*

The number is now regarded as the two-digit decimal it truly is, and the sample shows 34 8/25—or, exactly 34.32.

What about *Special*? This category automatically formats numbers in one of four motifs (at least for users in the US): *Zip Code, Zip Code+4, Phone Number*, and *Social Security Number*. Special imposes what is called in Access an input mask on a value, supplying punctuation in the cell that spares the user the need to do so. Some examples: normally typing a zip code in say, New England, where the codes begin with zero, poses a problem in Excel, because typing:

04567

is rendered by Excel initially as 4567, with the leading zero eliminated. But select Zip Code from the Special option, and you get all five digits. Indeed, if you type:

4567

Zip Code will automatically supply the zero. Zip Code +4 lets the user type a nine-digit number, whereupon Excel will insert the dash between the fifth and sixth digit. As a result, typing:

123456789

yields:

12345-6789

The Phone and Social Security Number options likewise supply dashes at the appropriate points in a number, so that the user doesn't have to remember exactly where they go.

The final option, *Custom*, entitles the user to adjust the appearance of numbers with *user-defined* embellishments. This option looks rather forbidding, but let's demonstrates just one Custom possibility. We've seen that a stand-alone decimal appears this way, by default:

0.28

If you want to excise the leading zero so that you'll see .28 in the cell (or any range of cells) instead, you can turn to Custom and adjust accordingly, like this, after you've entered 0.28 in any cell:

- Click Custom.

- Click this option in the Type field:

0.00

- The 0.00 appears as follows (Figure 4–85):

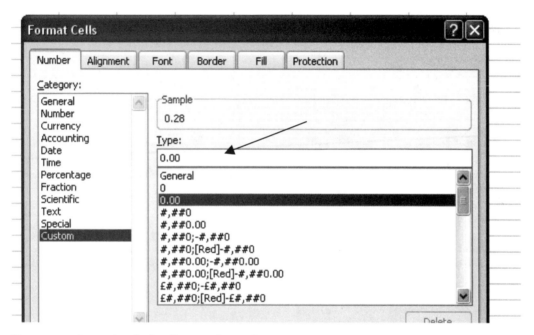

Figure 4–85. Removing the leading zero in a value

Delete the first zero, so you're seeing .00. The sample should display .28.
Click OK.

The cell is thus revised to exhibit decimals *without* the leading zero. Other customizations are more complex, but you get the idea.

A New Kind of Copy—and Paste

Formatting is portable. That is, if you copy a cell or a range of cells, all their associated formatting comes along for the ride to the destination cells. But there are times when you may want to copy *only* the formatting of a source cell, and leave the cell's data behind. You may be so taken by the *appearance* of a cell that you decide you want—or need—other cells to take on that same appearance. And if that's what you need to do—copy a set of formats in one cell to other cells—there's a handy way in which to do so.

But that very objective raises a question. Why bother to *copy* a format from one cell to another when I can simply click on the new cells and select any and all of the formatting options we've discussed so far? Why not format these new cells *directly*, without copying the formatting from somewhere else?

Good question; and the answer is that you may want to copy formats from a cell that contains *numerous* formatting changes, and you can't be bothered to reintroduce all of them to additional cells serially. For example—suppose cell B6 contains an 18-point, Bookman Old Style font, colored green and underlined, with a Center alignment to boot. If, for reasons best known to me, I admire this pastiche of cell adornments and want to impose them on other cells, it may be too much trouble to implement each adornment separately. But with a tool called the ***Format Painter*** I can copy *all* of B6's formatting features to other cells in *one* shot.

And to see how Format Painter works, we can swing back to the Home tab's Clipboard Group, a venue we visited a few chapters earlier when we introduced the Copy and Paste buttons (Figure 4–86):

Figure 4–86. Where to find the format painter

To use Format Painter:
- Click the cell whose formatting you wish to copy. Then click the Format Painter button, after which you'll see (Figure 4–87):

Figure 4 87. Giving your cells the brushoff: The Format Painter in action

■**Note** that the paintbrush icon makes its appearance onscreen, along with the marching ants buzzing around the border of the cell whose formatting you're copying (or "painting").

Then click the cell or drag over the cells to which you want to copy the source formatting. These destination cells immediately acquire the source formats, and the paintbrush and the ants disappear.

Thus if the above-mentioned B6 serves as the source cell, all its formats, but *only* its formats, will be exported to the destination cells, *overwriting* all their current formatting—while leaving *their* data alone. So if B6 contains the phrase "Have a Good Day," it *won't* be brought along for the ride; and the data residing in the destination cell(s) *will* now appear in the 18-point Bookman Old Style font, along with the green, underlined, centered attributes, too, all of which come from B6. Note that the Format Painter can work proactively, to copy formats to cells that are currently empty. What that means, of course, is that if you've executed a Format Painter command on a vacant cell, any data you enter from now on in the cell will display the new formats.

You also need to bear in mind that number formats are part of the deal. That is, if your source cell exhibits numbers with 2 decimal points, or displays a number as a Short Date, these elements will also be imposed on destination cells.

And if you double-click the Format Painter button, its paintbrush remains onscreen for as long as you need it. In this way you'll be able to apply the source cell formats to as many cells on your worksheet as you want, by repeatedly clicking or dragging cells across the sheet. And to eventually turn the Painter off, just press Esc.

What we're seeing here with Format Painter is a revelation of sorts: that copying and pasting can copy and paste *more* (or less) than just data. In fact, Excel stocks a broad array of Paste options that do a variety of things, some of which at first blush may seem bewilderingly similar.

In our initial discussion of Paste in Chapter 2 we looked at, among other pasting options, the Paste button in the Clipboard group. If you click its down arrow (you'll have to copy something first, though, in order to activate Paste), you'll see (Figure 4–88):

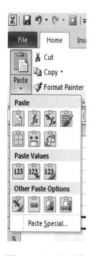

Figure 4–88. The various Paste options

Bewildered? Quite a variety of Paste options indeed. But here we want to examine only those Paste buttons that carry out various *formatting* actions.

These two buttons (Figure 4–89):

Figure 4–89. Two Paste options: Formulas & Number Formatting, and Keep Source Formatting

are called ***Formulas & Number Formatting***, and ***Keep Source Formatting***, respectively. The first button copies *only* a cell's formula (there has to *be* one in the cell, needless to say) and its *number* formatting. The button *won't* copy any other kind of formatting, etc., from the source cell. But the second button, Keep Source Formatting, *does* bring over *all* the formatting from the source cell, along with that cell's *contents*—and because it does, this button appears to do precisely the same things that the standard Paste button does.

The first button in the second row is called ***No Borders*** (Figure 4–90):

Figure 4–90. Cells without borders: the No Borders button

and it copies all the source cell's formats, *except* any borders that may be drawn around any or all sides of the cell. Thus if I copy a cell like this, one which features borders around all its sides (Figure 4–91):

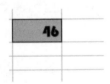

Figure 4–91. The cell with borders…

and paste it into another cell using No Borders, the paste will bring about this (Figure 4–92):

Figure 4–92. …can be pasted to another cell without the borders

Note the orange fill and altered font have been copied to the destination cell; but the borders have not. And this button (Figure 4–93):

Figure 4–93. Another route to the Format Painter

which is called simply **Formatting**, is nothing but an equivalent of the Format Painter button.

And check out a new feature of the Paste button collection, debuting with Excel 2010: when you copy a source cell and select your destination cells, and then rest your mouse over any of the Paste Special buttons (without yet clicking), the destination cells exhibit that button's formatting effects in *preview* fashion before you click, so you know what you're going to get.

And there's still *another* way to copy cell formats, one which we pointed to in chapter 2 but didn't discuss. When we execute a fill—the technique that allows us to copy a set of numbers in fixed intervals by dragging the fill handle, e.g., the interval shown in Figure 4–94:

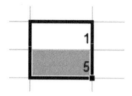

Figure 4–94. Selecting an interval of 4 to be filled down a range

it will yield this (Figure 4–95):

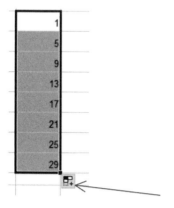

Figure 4–95. Note the Smart Tag

If you go on to click that **Smart Tag** (pointed to by the arrow above), the options include (Figure 4–96):

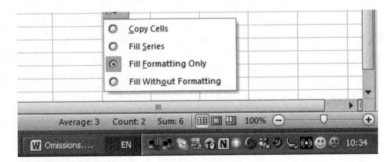

Figure 4–96. Tag, you're it: Smart Tag fill options

Fill Formatting Only, which means that if the initial interval you want to drag with the fill handle looks like this (Figure 4–97):

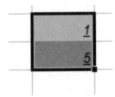

Figure 4–97. About to select Fill Formatting Only

Selecting Fill Formatting Only would generate this (Figure 4–98):

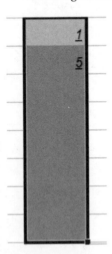

Figure 4–98. Again, only the source cell formats are copied

What we see here, then, is a Fill Series variation on the Format Painter. (Note: if you want to wipe cells clean of all new formatting and return them the original, default General format, select those cells and click Home ➤ the Editing button group ➤ Clear ➤ Clear Formats.)

Style Setter

Now if you're in need of a little cell format design inspiration, you can call upon the *Cell Styles* options waiting behind the drop-down arrow in the Styles button group (Figure 4—99):

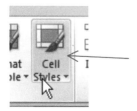

Figure 4–99. The Cell Styles Button

Select the cells you want to format and click Cell Styles, and you'll be ushered into this storehouse of pre-fab formats: (Figure 4–100):

Figure 4–100. Cell style options

Click any of the above formats and its style, as previewed above, will be transported to the selected cells. And note the *New Cell Style* option in the lower left of the dialog box. When clicked it enables you to format cells as you wish and *save* that format under a name, so that you can retrieve the customized style when you need it. Thus if I click on B6 and its garish, 18-point Bookman Old Style green, underlined, centered mix of formatting, and then click Cell Styles: New Cell Styles, I'll meet up with this dialog box (Figure 4–101):

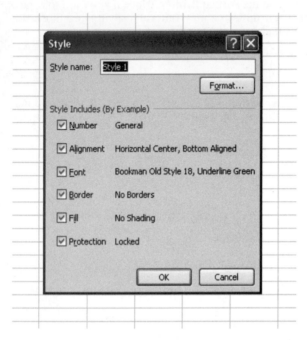

Figure 4–101. The Style dialog box: Where to design your own style

Type a name for your style in the *Style name* field. I'll type Tacky in there. Note that the characteristics of this imminent style—the Center alignment, Bookman Old Style, etc., are recorded in the *Style Includes* area. Click OK and the style is saved. Then when you want to use the style, select the desired cells, click Cell Styles, and you'll see (Figure 4–102):

Figure 4–102. Eye of the beholder: where your styles are saved

Click the name, and the style is brought to the cells.

Formatting—With Conditions

The next formatting option in the Styles group—really a whole warehouse of them—is an interesting and important one: *Conditional Formatting*. Conditional Formatting enables the user to define a condition that a cell must meet—and if the condition is met, the cell experiences a change in its *formatting*.

If that sounds abstract, here are some simple for instances. I can devise conditional formats which state the following: If any number in a range of cells exceeds 50, let those cell turn green, as a way of calling attention to that cell. Or, if I select a range of test scores, let those cells containing scores in the lowest 20 percent turn red.

Is any of this starting to sound—or look—vaguely familiar? It might, because if we go all the way back to Chapter 1 and that introductory grade sheet (shown in Figure 4–103):

Student	Exams 1	2	3	4	5	Average	
Alice	67	96	67	100	85	83.0	
Derek	82	89	45	93	67	75.2	
Dorothy	73	70	93	65	93	78.8	
Edith	81	48	52	75	76	66.4	
George	90	67	84	59	77	75.4	
Gordon	90	86	89	77	94	87.2	
John	83	96	60	63	70	74.4	
Mary	77	78	80	90	100	85.0	
Paul	61	91	68	61	99	76.0	
Ringo	56	80	79	82	77	74.8	
Class Averages	76.0	80.1	71.7	76.5	83.8		

Figure 4–103. The Gradebook, exhibiting conditional formats

You'll recall that the cells containing the highest scores in each exam were colored a conspicuous red—and that effect was brought about by a conditional format.

Excel has tried to make conditional formatting easy to apply—and for the most part, it's succeeded. Once you get a handle on the basic concept, you'll see that the wide array of Conditional Formatting options available to you work in similar ways, making the process pretty painless—and valuable.

Let's try a Conditional Format and you'll see what I mean. Instead of identifying the highest scorers on an exam, say you want to determine which students have scored below 65, which may represent the passing grade. On a blank spreadsheet, let's copy the above results for the exam 1 in cells B8:C18, minus the formatting (Figure 4–104):

Student	Score
Alice	67
Derek	82
Dorothy	73
Edith	81
George	90
Gordon	90
John	83
Mary	77
Paul	61
Ringo	56

Figure 4–104. Exam 1 grades , without the formatting

Next, select cells C9:C18, the range containing the test scores. Then click Conditional Formatting, revealing this sub-menu (Figure 4–105):

Figure 4–105. The Conditional Formatting drop-down menu

Then rest your mouse over the ***Highlight Cells Rules*** option, triggering this (Figure 4–106):

Figure 4–106. Highlighting the Highlight Cells Rules option

The route toward our objective—formatting all the sub-65 scores differently from all the other scores—should be a bit clearer now. We want to *highlight* those scores on the basis of a less-than-65 *rule*—and so we need to click the ***Less Than...*** option. And when we do we see (Figure 4–107):

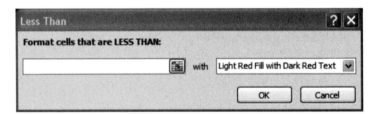

Figure 4–107. Low-grade format: highlighting test scores under 65

And this dialog box is pretty self-evident. Type 65 in the field to the left, and click the drop-down arrow on the right in order to view a set of pre-defined formatting selections. We'll choose Yellow Fill with Dark Yellow Text. That means that all the *cells* in the range we selected that contain scores dipping beneath 65 will be colored light yellow, and the *numbers* themselves will receive a dark yellow tint. And before I click OK, the cells *already* exhibit the format in preview mode. Then just click OK and the deed is done—and we see that Paul and Ringo—the two students whose score meet the condition we've established (that's why it's called Conditional Formatting) experience a change in their cells.

Moreover, conditional formats remain responsive to *changes* in the selected cells, and they format accordingly. If I type 85 in Paul's cell, the yellow will disappear, because 85 obviously doesn't meet our less-than-65 rule. But replace Edith's 81 with a 55, and her cell turns yellow.

And had I selected the Custom Format option from that drop-down, I would have been brought here: (Figure 4–108):

Figure 4–108. *Where to customize a conditional format*

to a modified Format Cells dialog box, which enables you to ascribe your own collection of formats to cells meeting your condition (note, however, that you can't change the font).

And once you understand how Less Than… works, you'll see that the ***Greater Than…***, ***Between…***, and ***Equal To…*** Conditional Formats work identically, with the obvious proviso that you specify a number Greater Than a particular value, or numbers *between* two selected values (*including* those two values), or a value Equal To one particular number, respectively. ***Text That Contains…*** works in a comparable way too, requiring that the user name a specific word or phrase that must appear in selected cells before the Conditional Formats kick in (and they're not case-sensitive). *A Date Occurring* when clicked yields this drop down (Figure 4–109):

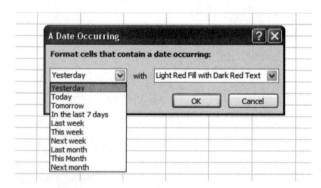

Figure 4–109. *Establishing a date-based rule*

Duplicate Values is a useful option that lets you format *either* all the values in a range that appear more than once, *or* all unique values—values that appear only once (Figure 4–110):

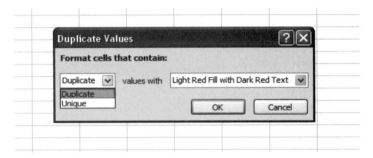

Figure 4–110. *Where to higlight duplicate values in a range*

But if you want to go ahead and *remove* those duplicate values once you track them down—well, no; you can't get there from here, because Conditional Formatting is, its bells and whistles notwithstanding, a *formatting* technique, and as such doesn't "do" anything to the data. If you really do need to winnow those duplicates, you'll have to resort to some other approach, one that actually impacts the data. (And yes—we've omitted the ***More Rules*** options—that one's coming up shortly).

The ***Top/Bottom Rules*** section (Figure 4—-):

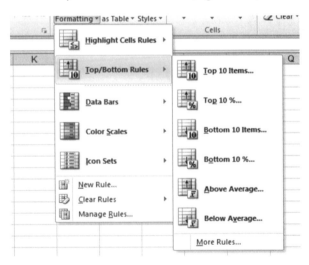

Figure 4–111. *Top/Bottom Rules*

is no less easy to master. ***Top 10 Items…*** allows you to format the top X items in your range, the choice of number vested with you (Figure 4–112):

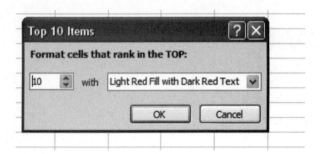

Figure 4–112. *Where to highlight the top—or bottom—tier of a range of values*

It goes without saying, then, that "Top 10" isn't literal; you can designate the top 20, etc.

Bottom 10 Items offers the opposite choice, enabling you to format the lowest X values in a range. The **Top and Bottom 10%** options ask you to format you highest/lowest values in *percentage* terms, e.g., the highest or lowest 15% of all test scores (Figure 4–113):

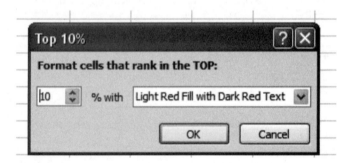

Figure 4–113. *Playing the percentages: Where to format highest or lowest values in percent terms*

Above and **Below Average** mean what they say—they format *all* scores that rise above or fall beneath the average of the numbers in the range you've selected (Figure 4–114):

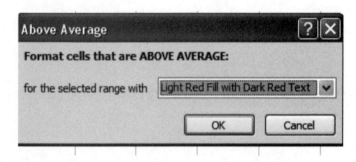

Figure 4–114. *Above and Below Average formatting options*

And to anticipate your next question: values that turn out to be exactly average are excluded from *both* Above or Below Average; that is, in neither case are average values subject to any Conditional Formatting.

The next collection of options—***Data Bars***—works differently (Figure 4–115):.

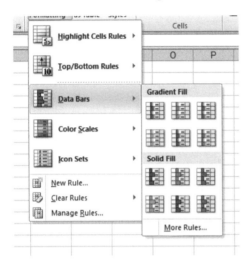

Figure 4–115. Data Bar options

Data Bars offers 12 options, but they all work in the same way, distinguished only by the colors and textures they use. Each Data Bar possibility draws a mini-bar chart in the cell of each value, capturing its magnitude relative to the other values in a range. It's easy to implement: just select a range, and click on one of the Data Bar options. I've clicked on the first option, and have come up with this (Figure 4–116):

67
82
73
81
90
90
83
77
61
56

Figure 4–116. Data Bars: a mini-chart in each formatted cell

Color Scales capture relative disparities in values by characterizing them with color gradations, either in two or three basic initial colors (Figure 4–117):

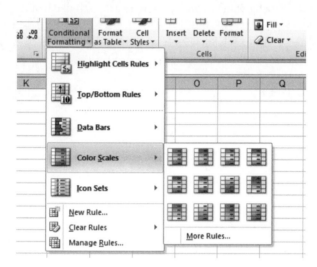

Figure 4–117. Chromatic scales: Color Scales options

By selecting the second option on the first row—called the ***Red-Yellow-Green Color Scale***, and applying it to our range of grades, I get this (Figure 4–118):

67
82
73
81
90
90
83
77
61
56

Figure 4–118. Grade values, colored by score group

In this color scheme, Red captures the highest values, Yellow the intermediate ones, and Green the lowest—all in shadings to reflect fine differences in values.

The final option—***Icon Sets***—supplies the user with a large assortment of symbols with which to format the relationship between values, and in a range of ways (Figure 4–119):

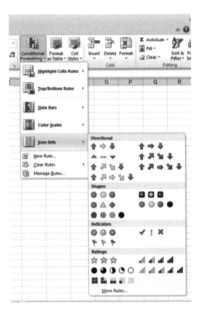

Figure 4–119. Icon Set options

Directional Icon Sets symbolize values by their position in a percentile scale via the designated icons. Thus if I select the first such option and apply it to the grade range, the conditional format looks like this (Figure 4–120):

⬇	67
⬆	82
⇨	73
⬆	81
⬆	90
⬆	90
⬆	83
⇨	77
⬇	61
⬇	56

Figure 4–120. An arrow icon set in action

Here we see that the highest scores sport an up arrow, the intermediates a flat one, and the lower scores a down arrow.

Shapes represent values with a trove of shapes. If I apply the second selection in the Shapes first column on the grade range, I'll see this (Figure 4–121):

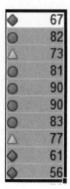

Figure 4–121. Shape of things to come: the same grades, formatted by shape icons

Here the red diamond captures the highest values, the green circles the intermediates, and the yellow triangles the lowest .

Ratings communicate value relationships through a potpourri of possibilities—stars, bars, pie charts, etc. Thus if I choose the pie chart option (the second selection, first column), we'll see (Figure 4–122):

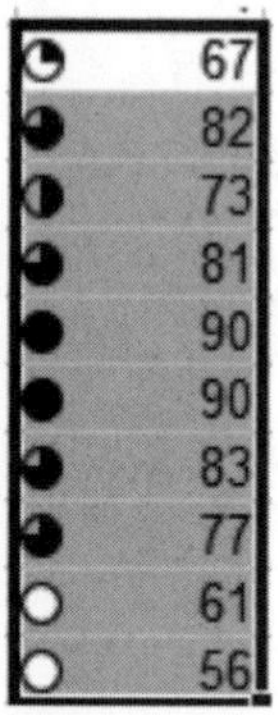

Figure 4–122. Bite-sized pie charts

You'll note, by the way, that the various icons *don't* portray values in precisely calibrated ways. Look at the screen shot above, and you'll see that the 82, 81, 83, and 77 all display a three-quarter-blackened pie. That's because by default Excel organizes the data by their *percentage* distribution. In the case of the pies above, Excel assigns a clear icon to those data that fall below 20% of the highest value in the data, the one-quarter-filled pie for data that occupy the 21-40% percents, and so on. But in addition to these initial distributions, Excel enables you to customize your own—first by clicking the *Manage Rules...*

Continuing with our grade book: If we leave the pie format in place, select these grades in C9:C18, and click Manage Rules..., we'll see this (Figure 4–123):

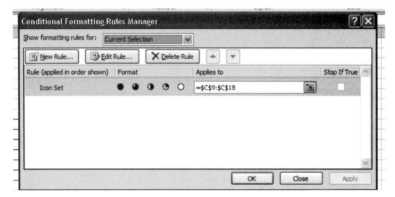

Figure 4–123. Changing the conditional formatting rules

Click **Edit Rule...** and observe the dialog box shown in Figure 4–124:

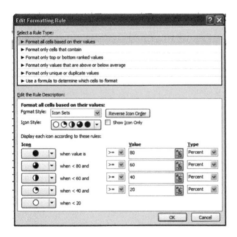

Figure 4–124. Rules are made to be…edited

This is a wide-ranging dialog box that contains numerous options, but for now we're interested in changing the icon *numbers*—the score thresholds at which the pies blacken more or less. Note the defaults about which we've already spoken.

Moreover, we see that the **Select a Rule Type** area in the **Edit Formatting Rule** dialog box lets you change your rule *completely;* if for example I select **Format only values that are above or below average,** I'll be brought here (Figure 4–125):

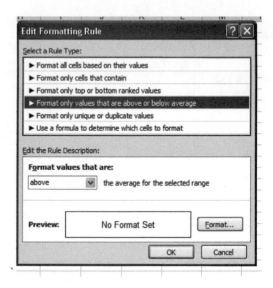

Figure 4–125. Selecting—and changing—a rule type

And if I click the drop-down arrow by ***Format values that are*** (Figure 4–126):

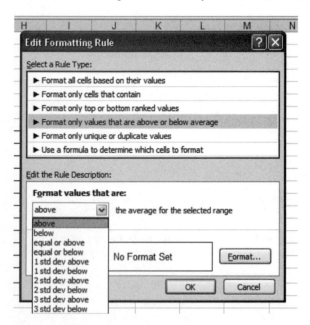

Figure 4–126. Additional rule options

I can select any of these choices, including values that fall within 1, 2, or 3 standard deviations from the range *average.* But the larger point is this: by selecting Edit Rule, you can basically *replace* your existing Conditional Format with any other sort of rule.

In addition, you can subject the *same* range to multiple rules. For example, I could compose a Conditional Format to color blue all the cells with test scores in our range that exceed 80, *and* to color red all cells with scores that fall below 60. That is, we could format our range with the **Highlight Cells Rules Greater Than… and Less Than…** options. If I went ahead with this plan, my range would take on this appearance (Figure 4–127):

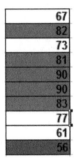

Figure 4–127. Note some cells meet neither criterion and remain white

And that's fine. But what if I wanted to color all the cells with scores topping 80 blue, and all the cells with scores over 85 *green*? Our wicket has just gotten stickier—because a score such as 90 meets *both* conditions. After all, 90 exceeds both 85 *and* 80—raising the obvious question: which format will I see in such a cell?

That's a question Excel wants *you* to answer—because you'll need to tell the application which of the rules will activate *first.* Once you execute both rules, you'll want to select the range and click Manage Rules. Note (Figure 4–128):

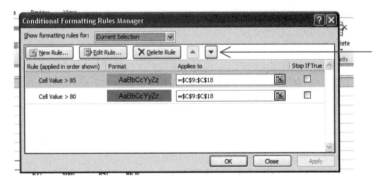

Figure 4–128. You need to decide which rule is listed first

The two rules impacting our range are recorded—and in the proper order, because Excel will simply carry out the rule *which appears first* in the above dialog box—and we want Excel to consider the >85 rule before >80, for a simple reason. If *>80* is listed first, then even the cell containing 90 will turn *blue*—and you'll never get to >85.

To allow you to arrange your rules in the proper order, you can click on any rule in the Rules Manager and then click the down arrow button (which the arrow in Figure 4–128 points to).

And if you've messed up or simply want to start over, you can purge your worksheet of all your Conditional Formats, either for particular ranges or the entire sheet, by clicking (Figure 4–129):

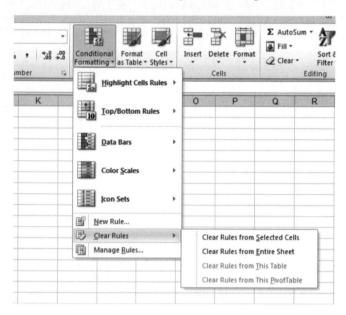

Figure 4–129. The Clear Rules option

And choose the appropriate option.

While there's a large set of permutations crowded into Conditional Formatting, we've introduced the important basics, and you'll find that with experimentation many of its other features will come to light.

Just a Bit More…

We can begin to wind down this rather exhaustive—and probably exhausting—résumé of formatting with a quick look at a curiously-titled button, one holed up in the Cells Group on the Home Tab. It's called, as luck would have it… *Format*, which doesn't tell you terribly much about what it does. But when you click its drop-down arrow, it presents a mixed-bag of commands, some of which you wouldn't be inclined to call Formatting, and some of which operate on worksheets in their entirety—and we'll reserve those for a later chapter. In fact only the upper half of its drop-down menu, shown in Figure 4–130, concerns us here, listing alternative ways to do some things you already know:

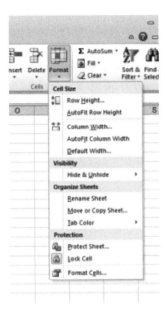

Figure 4–130. Still more formatting options

Clicking *Row Height* and/or *Column Width* allows you to modulate the height and/or width of selected rows and columns (note: unlike the techniques we described earlier, you *don't* have to select row or column headings in order to carry out this option here. If you click in any *cell* in the row or column, that will enable you to go ahead with these commands. And you can drag across a range of rows and columns if you want to change multiple row/column heights and widths. And as you see you can also execute an Auto Fit of selected columns—but here you *will* have to select the column headings before you proceed. Finally, the *Default Column Width* option doesn't necessarily do what you think it will. It doesn't *restore* the default width to changed columns; rather it lets you *change* the default column width on the worksheet. If you click the command, you'll see the dialog box shown in Figure 4–131:

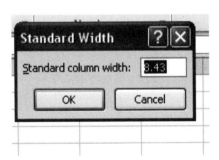

Figure 4–131. Establishing a new column width

that lets you type a new width, which will apply to all worksheet columns—except those whose widths you've already changed. And don't ask me why the dialog box is called *Standard*, and not Default, *Width*.

P. S.

And before we bring this chapter to a close, there's one slightly loose end we need to tie for neatness' sake. On the chapter's very first page, I declared that:

> *"...apart from one obscure exception, formatting data on the worksheet changes the* appearance, *and not the* value, *of those data.."*

You've politely refrained from asking the big question, so I'll do it for you: What's the exception?
It's this: if you click the File tab, click *Options*, then click *Advanced* and scoot down to the *When calculating this workbook* section, you'll take note of an unchecked command called *Set precision as displayed*. If you check it, any number you've formatted with X decimal points will *become* precisely that number. That is, if you've entered 5.76 in a cell and formatted that value to one decimal point, you'll see 5.8. But with Set precision as displayed, 5.8 becomes its *value,* too—and this is an all-or-nothing proposition. Turning this option on impacts all the values in the workbook—that is, all its worksheets. And when you click OK, a prompt on screen reminds of just that: you'll be told, "Data will permanently lose accuracy," meaning your values will take on new, rounded-off values.
And that's precisely what happens.

IN CONCLUSION…

Long chapter, long subject. That's because appearances matter. They can't substitute or cover for mistaken formulas, or worksheets that don't deliver the information that's been requested. You can't really fake a spreadsheet, but the ways in which data are *presented,* or formatted, are integral to the spreadsheet process too. Think of spreadsheet design as a kind of desktop publishing—and it is—and the issue becomes clearer. And the next chapter, on charting, picks up the baton and runs with the same theme. Charts: More than pretty pictures? You bet; just turn the page.

■■■

CHAPTER 5

The Stuff Of Legend – Charting in Excel

They say a picture is worth a 1,000 words—a remarkably durable exchange rate to be sure, given how long they've been saying it. But is it true?

As with most such pithy declarations, the answer depends. When it comes to spreadsheets, Excel jams a toolbox full of charting options for framing some very pretty—and meaningful—pictures of your data, but wealth needs to be managed wisely.

It makes sense to have the chapter on charts follow our discussion of formatting, because charting stands right atop the boundary between data manipulation and the *way* in which that data is presented. How charts are formatted, and indeed, the very choice of which chart to use, can exert a significant pull on readers' perception of what the data *mean*. It's one thing to color a number blue, but it can be quite something else to assign a chart's vertical axis a minimum value of zero—and if that sounds like Greek to you, don't worry, and keep reading.

The point is that, as with formatting in general, Excel's charting adornments mustn't get in the way of the story the chart is attempting to tell. As with comedy, the first rule of charting is: Know your audience. Think of the charts you see in newspapers and magazines, and ask yourself if they meet your standard of intelligibility. They probably do, because the chart-makers at these publications understand the tradeoff between beauty and truth, so to speak, and will likely opt for simplicity over bling. On the other hand, you may come upon a very different charting environment in a scientific journal, where the informational needs of readers can be very different.

In any case, Excel makes basic charting almost unnervingly easy, and if you have a few seconds to spare you'll have more than enough time to draw a chart up: click in a range of data, dick on a chart type, and—there it is. If you're happy with the results, you're done. Yet there's more to charting than those quick decisions, or at least there *can* be; and again, knowing more about how it all works beats knowing less. So, let's get started.

Starting Charting

First, a bit of terminology. Charts work with *data series,* which comprise *data points*. A data series is a collection of data assigned beneath a category. Thus in this set of data (source: Euromonitor.com) depicting visitor totals for the top ten tourist cities for 2006 and 2007 (in thousands—that is, the numbers you see should be multiplied by 1000, shown in Figure 5-1:

	2006	2007
London	15,637.10	15,340.00
Hong Kong	11,081.80	12,057.00
Bangkok	10,347.33	10,844.00
Singapore	9,757.12	10,284.00
Paris	9,757.24	8,762.00
New York City	6,216.26	7,646.00
Antalya	6,407.73	7,292.00
Toronto	6,874.48	6,627.00
Dubai	6,118.91	6,535.00
Istanbul	5,298.85	6,454.00

Figure 5–1. Tourist figures for popular cities—data ripe for charting

both 2006 and 2007 qualify as data series—but if we stand the data on their side, as we shall see, London, Hong Kong, and all the other city names *could* serve as series instead (and no, I've never been to Antalya, either). *Data points* are the individual data items belonging to a series. Thus 15,637.10 is a data point in the 2006 series.

To actually produce a chart:

1. Click *anywhere* among the data you want to chart (a point that needs to be explained),

2. Click the *Insert* tab, and select from this roster of chart types (Figure 5-2):

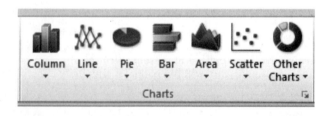

Figure 5–2. Chart options

3. Then click any chart type's down arrow and choose one of the chart variants in that type, and that's it, at least for starters. By carrying out the above sequence, my tourist data could come out looking like this—depending on the chart I choose, of course (Figure 5-3):

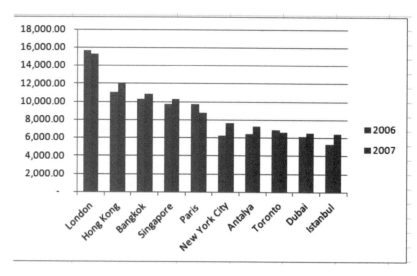

Figure 5–3. Those tourist data, brought to a column chart

Estimated time of chart construction: about 4 seconds. Bear in mind that we're looking at a first pass at the chart as it would present itself to us by default (note it appears on the same worksheet as the data that contributed to it), and before we've tried our hand at reformatting the result with Excel's bag of tricks. Still, 4 seconds is 4 seconds. And a batch of *3-D* chart selections is available, too (Figure 5-4):

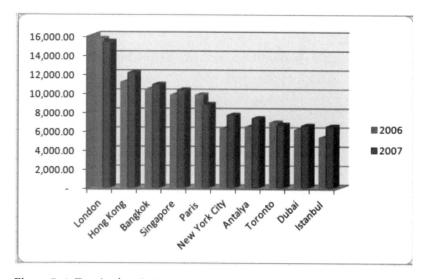

Figure 5–4. Tourist data in 3-D

And charts are dynamic—meaning that any change you make in the source data will *automatically* be reflected in the chart. Type a different number in any data cell contributing to the chart, and the column, or bar, or pie slice tied to that value will experience a change in its size.

Making a Chart of Our Own

But let's try to construct a chart of our own. In the interests of continuity, we'll turn back to our test-grade worksheet, which I've entered, sans formatting, in cells C8:I20 (if you have these data on hand already, you can use those. And you needn't actually calculate all those averages you see in the data, though it would be good practice—you can just enter these as numbers here, without writing any formulas (Figure 5-5):

Student	Exams 1	2	3	4	5	Average
Alice	67	96	67	100	85	83.0
Derek	82	89	45	93	67	75.2
Dorothy	73	70	93	65	93	78.8
Edith	81	48	52	75	76	66.4
George	90	67	84	59	77	75.4
Gordon	90	86	89	77	94	87.2
John	83	96	60	63	70	74.4
Mary	77	78	80	90	100	85.0
Paul	61	91	68	61	99	76.0
Ringo	56	80	79	82	77	74.8
Class Averages	76.0	80.1	71.7	76.5	83.8	

Figure 5–5. That gradebook

You'll see there are some important initial points to learn here, so let's look into them.

Excluding Data

As we indicated a few paragraphs above, you could simply click anywhere among the data and commence the charting process in earnest. But take a look at the screen shot above. Do you want to chart the scores of a student named Class Averages? Because you *will*, if you don't take steps to *exclude* that row of data from the chart. And the same question could be asked of the column entitled Average—do you want its data to be treated as the *sixth* test in the series of exam results above? Likely not; and so in order to present Excel with precisely the data we need to in order to complete the chart, we should *select* cells C9:H19 (but not the data in the I column—the test averages), as you see in Figure 5-6:

	1	2	3	4	5	Average
Alice	67	96	67	100	85	83.00
Derek	82	89	45	93	67	75.20
Dorothy	73	70	93	65	93	78.80
Edith	81	48	52	75	76	66.40
George	90	67	84	59	77	75.40
Gordon	90	86	89	77	94	87.20
John	83	96	60	63	70	74.40
Mary	77	78	80	90	100	85.00
Paul	61	91	68	61	99	76.00
Ringo	56	80	79	82	77	74.80
Class Averages	76	80.1	71.7	76.5	83.8	

Figure 5–6. Selecting gradebook data—averages omitted

Time, then, to modify the chart data selection rule we stated earlier: to start the chart-making process, you can click *anywhere* among the data, provided there are *no* adjoining columns or rows containing data you *don't* want to see in the chart. But in our case, where there *are* data we want to exclude, we need to go ahead and select exactly the range we need. And this can be a real-world scenario.

Once we put these understandings in place and select our range, then all we need do is click one of the buttons in the *Charts* group, which identify Excel's various chart possibilities. Let's click the *Column* button (Figure 5-7):

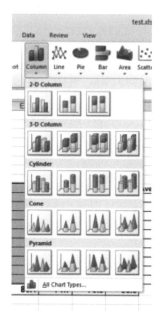

Figure 5–7. Column chart options

159

Note the array of column chart sub-types. For illustration's sake, I'll click the first option on the first row (titled *2-D Column*), yielding this chart (Figure 5-8):

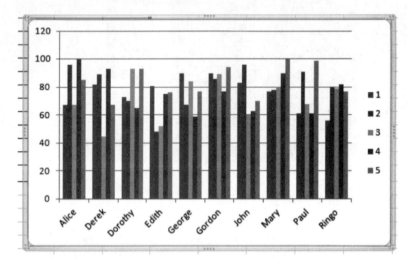

Figure 5–8. *Not bad—a first column chart*

There's your chart. Suitable for framing? Probably not, but it does communicate the data pretty clearly, even if a formatting tweak here and there would help it along. And if you need or want to, you can delete a chart by clicking on its chart area to select the entire chart, and pressing Delete.

Evaluating the Chart

But before we tweak, let's review some of the things the chart has done with the data. The chart portrays each student's scores for tests 1 through 5, with each test number comprising a data series. The *legend*—that column of numbered cubes on the chart's far right—color-codes each exam series, while the *vertical (value) axis* (also known as the *Y axis*) constructs the scale of values against which each test can be measured. That scale—here spanning 0 to 120 and subdivided into intervals of 20—is improvised from the data. Devise a new chart based on a different set of values and the scale could look radically different. The *Horizontal (Category) Axis* (also called the *X axis*) enumerates each student name, placing these beneath each set of their five scores. It requires a bit of delicacy in view of the thinness of the columns, but if you position your mouse atop any column in the chart (don't click) a caption detailing the value of that score along with the name of the student in question appears (Figure 5-9):

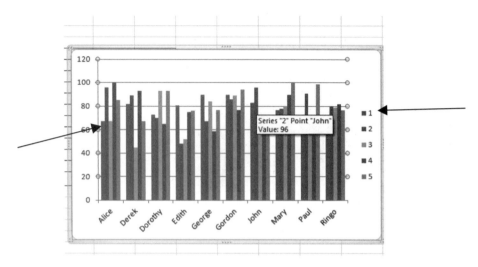

Figure 5–9. *Captioned information about the data represented by each column*

A couple of other definitions need to be introduced here. The **Chart Area** is the larger background of the chart, indicated by the arrow at the right of the screen shot above, in Figure 5-9. The **Plot Area** is the smaller, rectangular space in which the chart *itself* is actually positioned, evidenced by the gridlines above and the left arrow. And you can easily move the chart by clicking the chart arrow, and dragging the chart wherever you wish on the worksheet. You'll know you're in the Chart Area—or any other segment of the chart, for that matter—by simply resting your mouse over that element and viewing the identifying caption.

Resizing the Chart

You can also *resize* the chart by clicking on any one of the chart's eight resize handles, represented on the chart's border by these dots (Figure 5-10):

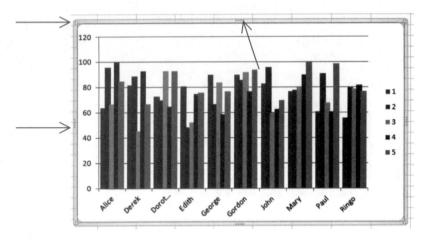

Figure 5–10. Dot's right—where you can click to resize the chart

Click a handle and drag in the desired direction—left, right, or, on a corner handle, in a diagonal direction. Dragging diagonally resizes the chart while maintaining the chart's original aspect *ratio,* or the ratio between the chart's height and width. Dragging a resize handle, left, right, up, or down, on the other hand, will distort the height-width ratio in one direction or another (Figure 5-11):

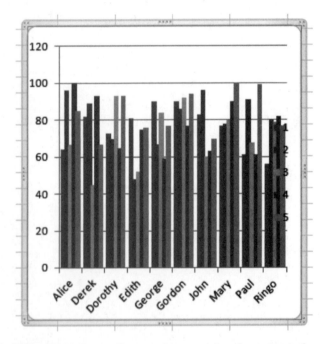

Figure 5–11. Sense of proportion—resizing charts is a judgment call

These kinds of distortions raise classic questions about the ways in which chart data are presented. Pinching the chart, as we see above, makes the column bars seem higher than they "really" are.

Flipping the Data Series

Now back to an earlier point about data series. If you click anywhere on the chart, the ribbon takes on this appearance, showing you the *Chart Tools* (Figure 5-12):

Figure 5–12. The Chart Tools tab

Each of the *Design, Layout,* and *Format* tabs are lined with a set of chart-related button groups. Click Design, and click the *Switch Row/Column* button in the *Data* group, and the chart undergoes this transformation (Figure 5-13):

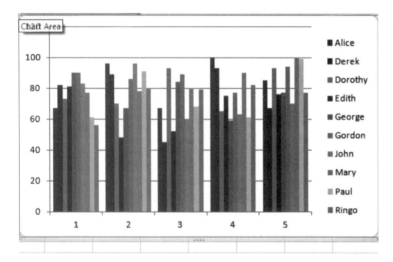

Figure 5–13. Same data, different angle

What's happened? What we're seeing is a flipping of data series. Whereas our initial chart designated each of the five *tests* as a series, here the data have been right-angled, so that the *student names* now serve as the series and the *tests* occupy the Horizontal Axis (tip: the legend will identify the data series). Our revised chart clusters the student grades by each *exam*, so that each *student* is represented once in each series. In the original chart version, however, the grades are clustered by each *student*, so that each *exam* is represented once in each series. Just keep in mind that the data with which we're working in both cases are *identical;* it's the data *series* that have traded places.

This ability to switch and re-designate data series—even as the data used in the switch remain *precisely the same*—is an important presentational option, and you need to decide which works for you.

Changing The Chart—It's Your Call

In any case, if you decide the column chart motif isn't quite what you want, you can readily select a new chart with by clicking on the chart and then clicking the ***Change Chart Type*** in the ***Type Group***, on that same Design Tab. You'll trigger this dialog box (Figure 5-14):

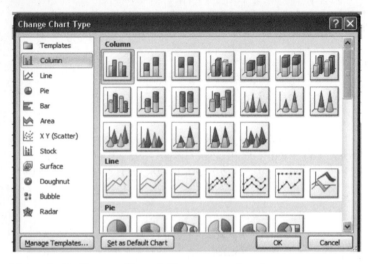

Figure 5–14. *Change of heart? Change your chart!*

The gamut of chart types and sub-types are placed before you for you to select as you see fit—provided the chart works with your data. And that friendly word of caution serves as a lead-in to a brief cataloging of the basic chart types, and what they can and can't do. Some chart usage decisions are judgment calls, but the fact is that certain sets of data simply *can't* be captured by certain kinds of charts, a point that will become clearer as we proceed.

The Column Chart

Column—perhaps the most commonly deployed chart, and probably the most straightforward. That's probably why it's listed first among the chart types (the order isn't alphabetical). Column charts, according to Excel's own accompanying caption, "are used to compare values across categories." Granted, that's a fairly innocuous description at best, but as we've seen, these charts do compare different categories in an easy-to-understand mode of presentation. Look back at the tourist chart we composed at the outset of the chapter; both the city and year dimensions are crisply, if not daringly, portrayed. To mix metaphors, this ***Clustered Column*** *chart* is a garden-variety, vanilla chart, at least until you jazz it up.

Note, however, that a popular column variant, the ***Stacked Column***, is a touch more subtle, and Excel offers two kinds of these. The Stacked Column chart piles, or stacks, the values in all chart series atop one another, for each point on the Horizontal Axis. If that sounds murky, here's what a Stacked Column rendering of our grade data looks like (Figure 5-15):

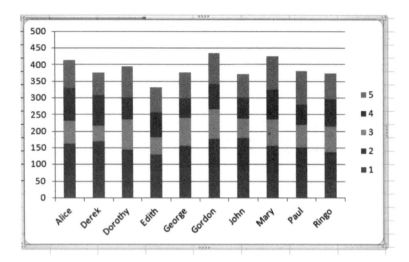

Figure 5–15. *The Stacked Column chart*

Here, and unlike in the standard Clustered Column chart, each student is represented by *one* column, which combines all his/her test scores into one aggregate stack. Note the values on the Vertical axis; they're far higher than the original, because this chart is adding all the students' scores.

The *100% Stacked Column* is far rarer, and in our illustration treats every student's total test score as an individual baseline totaling 100%. Each individual student grade is then stacked to represent the proportion it contributes to *that student's* total (Figure 5-16):

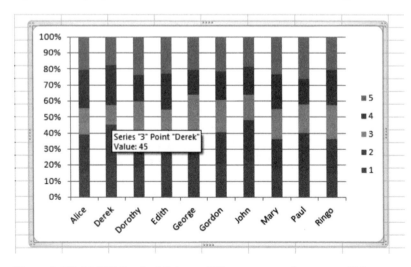

Figure 5–16. *A 100% Stacked Column: Where every student scores 100*

Note the Vertical Axis; every student "scores" 100%, because his/her particular set of scores is regarded as a whole. We see here that Derek's low grade of 45 on exam 3 contributes a small green bar to his total, but all his grades "add up" to 100%. Exotic it is, but the 100% Stacked Chart could be well applied to a look at the proportions of various types of household expenses contributing to various families' budgets.

The Line Chart

The *Line* chart type is a best seller, too, and is particularly adept at conveying change in a category, e.g., a ballplayer's batting averages across his career or a person's weight across a series of scale measurements. While in theory this type would be well applied to our test data, there are too many students in the mix, and thus our line chart presents itself with this tangle (Figure 5-17):

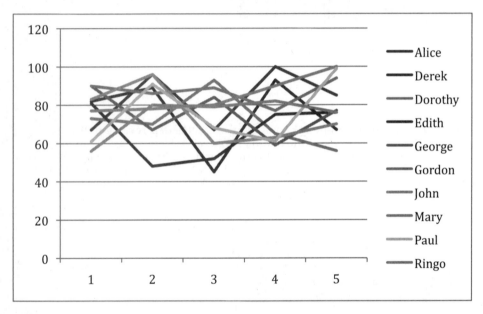

Figure 5–17. Lining up students' grades: Not a pretty picture

Ready to slap that one on your boss's desk? Only you can answer that question.

On the other hand, because it features only two data series, the tourist data might be a more suitable candidate for a Line chart (Figure 5-18):

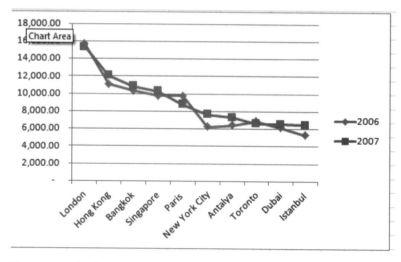

Figure 5–18. *Lining up tourist data*

Note here I've chosen the **Line with Markers** chart type, which highlights each data point with a small symbol.

The Line options also offer Stacked line charts, including a **100% Stacked Line**, but these are much harder to interpret. Here's our test data in Stacked Line mode (Figure 5-19):

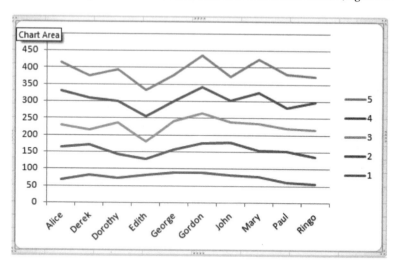

Figure 5–19. *How the tests stack up: Test scores via a **100% Stacked Line** chart*

Here each student's grades are stacked atop one another in a series of points on the respective lines, with each line representing each exam. Use with care. You might more profitably apply such a chart to compare, say, the number of home runs hit by the players on different baseball teams, broken out by the positions they play.

The Pie Chart

The next chart category, *Pie*, won't work with our grade data—because pie charts can only capture the data from *one data series at a time*. Pie charts treat the data as a single whole, with each data point contributing one "slice" to the recipe. Thus a purely hypothetical monthly budget that exhibits these expenses (Figure 5-20):

Housing	$1,100.00
Food	$ 280.00
Transportation	$ 573.00
Clothes	$ 122.00
Health Care	$ 159.00
Insurance	$ 303.00

Figure 5-20. Piece of the pie: One data series—eligible for pie charting

would be eligible for a pie chart, because it consists of merely one series (Figure 5-21):

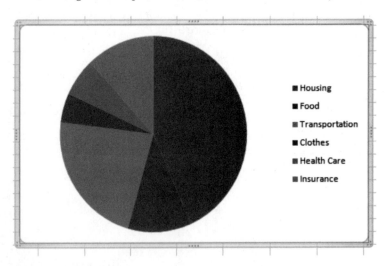

Figure 5–21. The above data, realized in a pie chart

Now that's a pretty attractive 4-second chart; but yes, you can add descriptive numbers to the chart (the actual values or percentages associated with each slice) and other elements, as we'll see when we get to chart formatting. (You can't fashion a pie chart if any of your data points contain a negative number, by the way; try to imagine how a negative slice could be portrayed.)

Pie charts also offer several "exploded" options; e.g., Figure 5-22:

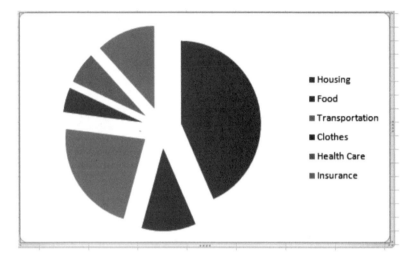

Figure 5–22. Don't stand too close: An exploded pie chart

Another option enables you to explode just *one* slice for the sake of emphasizing any one data point (Figure 5-23):

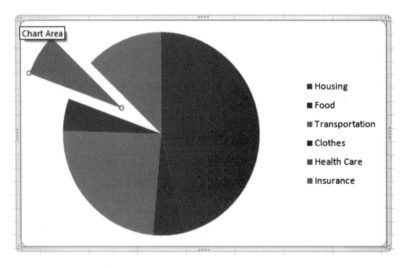

Figure 5–23. One slice to go

and still another allows you to break out a *group* of slices on the basis of a criterion you define:

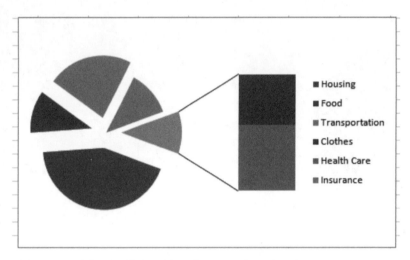

Figure 5–24. *Selective slicing: identifying pie chart data by a criterion*

This customized "explosion" singles out all budget expenses less than $200, for example. (*Note*: to select one slice for formatting, click the pie, and *then* click on the particular slice.)

The Bar Chart

Bar charts are really column charts pitched horizontally (Figure 5-25):

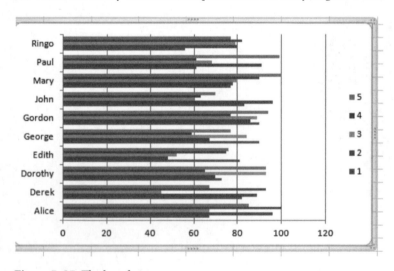

Figure 5–25. *The bar chart*

and come with the same stacking options.

The Area Chart

Area charts, according to Excel, "emphasize differences between different sets of data over a period of time." Of course that description could be applied to any number of chart types, but area charts draw the same data *trajectories* as line charts—but they fill in the space between the line and Horizontal axis. Here's the tourist data, committed to an Area chart (Figure 5-26):

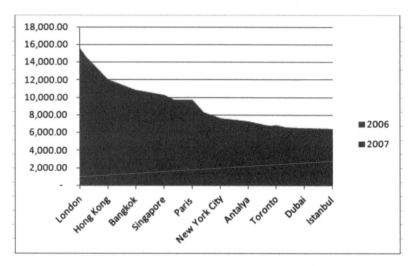

Figure 5–26. Tourist areas: tourist data in a Area chart

You see the initial problem. Because the Area chart fills in that space all the way down to the Horizontal axis, the data series in the "front" can obscure the data series behind it. There are ways to reformat the chart and work around the issue (you can make the areas transparent, for example), but again, you'll need to ask yourself who's going to be viewing this chart, and how effectively it will capture your data. Think about using an Area chart to portray data series that have substantial differences in their values—say changes in salaries across different occupational groups, where one group's salaries may tower above the others, avoiding the Area chart overlap problem you see with the tourist data.

The Scatter Chart

Scatter charts compare sets of values, and are better understood with the visual evidence. Here's a Scatter chart of the same tourist data (Figure 5-27):

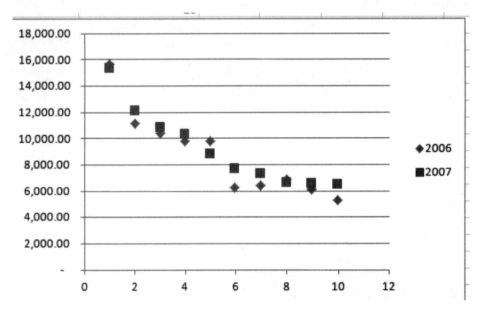

Figure 5–27. The data pared into pairs: The Scatter chart

Here the Scatter chart takes the tourist data for each city, pairing each with its 2006 and 2007 tourist totals. However, the Horizontal axis doesn't use the city names—it simply *numbers* each element in the sequence in which it appears in the source data. Thus, London is 1, Hong Kong 2, etc.

Bear in mind that Excel offers a collection of additional chart types, all of which are available in the Chart button group (you'll have to click **Other Types** to see them), at least some of which you may well find worth exploring. We've devoted our discussion to what are by far the most utilized types.

The Design Tab—A Closer Look

Excel's charting tools are stored in three different button groups—Design, Layout, and Format. True—if you woke Bill Gates in the middle of the night, he might not be able to tell you what *really* distinguishes the three. Still, those are the three tabs Chart Tools gives us, and it's time to review some of their respective options a bit more closely.

Change Chart Type

We've already explored the first Design Tab option—Change Chart Type, in the Type Group. To review—whenever you want to change your current chart, Change Chart Type will unroll Excel's charting alternatives. Just click the one you want.

Save As Template

The *Save As Template* button enables you to save a customized chart (say, a chart you've reformatted with different colors—stay tuned), so that you can retrieve it whenever you wish:

1. Click on the chart.

2. Click the Save As Template button.

3. Type a name for your customized chart and click Save.

If you're starting a new chart, you can then retrieve the template:

1. Select the data that you want to appear in the chart

2. Click the Insert tab.

3. In the Charts group, click the Dialog Box Launcher (Figure 5-28):

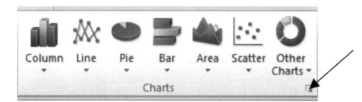

Figure 5–28. Where to start accessing your templates

You'll then click the *Templates* option in the left column of the Insert Chart dialog box, which will list existing templates (Figure 5-29):

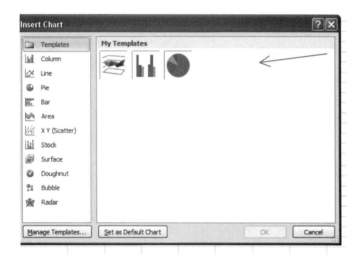

Figure 5–29. Your templates

4. Click on the template you want, and click OK.

Your data will now populate the chart. Make sure you've selected a chart that will work with your data.

If you want an *existing* chart to utilize the template, click on the chart and click ***Change Chart Type*** (remember—we're in the Design tab) (Figure 5-30):

Figure 5–30. *Where to start applying a template to an existing chart*

which will bring you to the same Insert Chart Dialog box—only here it's titled ***Change Chart Type***. Click Templates, and choose the one you like (Figure 5-31):

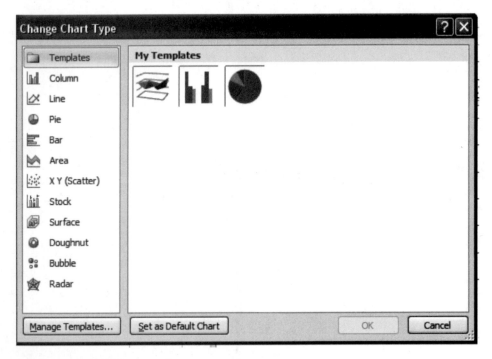

Figure 5–31. *Changing your chart to a template*

Switch Row/Column

We've already discussed the first button in the Data group—the Switch Row/Column button—back in the "Flipping the Data Series" section. You may recall that this button allows you to change the appearance of your chart by exchanging data series.

Select Data

The **Select Data** button does a few things, most importantly giving you the chance to *change the range* of the data in your chart. First click your chart, then click the Select Data button, and you'll see the **Select Data Source** dialog box onscreen (Figure 5-32):

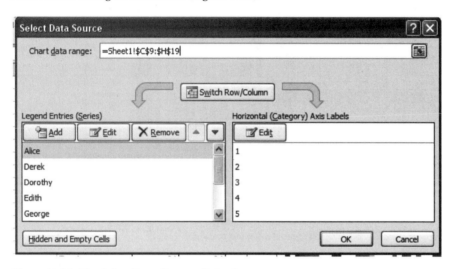

Figure 5–32. The Select Data Source dialog box

If you click in the **Chart data range** field, you can enter different range coordinates, if you've decided you want the chart to use different data. This command may be particularly relevant if you've selected a chart range and accidently left out a row you wanted to include in the chart. You could thus replace:

=Sheet1!$C$9:$H$19

with:

=Sheet1!$C$9:$H$20

(Sheet1 refers to the name of the sheet on which the chart data is contained, implying that a chart can be posted to one sheet even as its data appear on another one. More on multiple sheets in Chapter 7). As you see, Select Data also lets you execute the Switch Row/Column command, as well as *delete* a data series from the chart. If I click on Alice in the above screen shot and click the Remove button, all the columns representing Alice's test scores will disappear from the chart (but not from the source data).

The up and down arrows in the **Legend Entries (Series)** area can *reposition* a data series (Figure 5-33):

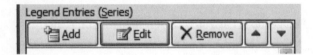

Figure 5–33. Ups and downs: where to reposition a chart data series

If I click on Edith, followed by the Legend Entries up arrow, her series will appear as the *third* in the chart, even though in the source data she appears *fourth* (Figure 5-34):

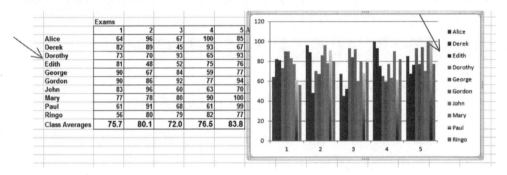

Figure 5–34. Edith: fourth in the table, third in the chart

Chart Layouts

The next group of buttons in the Design tab, ***Chart Layouts***, is pretty self-evident (Figure 5-35):

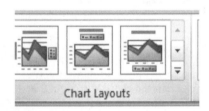

Figure 5-35. The Chart Layouts button group

Clicking its arrows reveals a selection of layouts tied to the chart you're working with. (The lowest of the three arrow buttons reveals all the options at one time) As you'll see, the options sometimes enable you to enter a chart title and other elements, such as a ***data table***, which brings your source data to the table (Figure 5 -36):

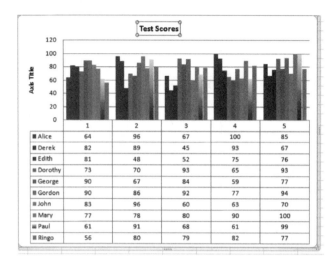

	1	2	3	4	5
■ Alice	64	96	67	100	85
■ Derek	82	89	45	93	67
■ Edith	81	48	52	75	76
■ Dorothy	73	70	93	65	93
■ George	90	67	84	59	77
■ Gordon	90	86	92	77	94
■ John	83	96	60	63	70
■ Mary	77	78	80	90	100
■ Paul	61	91	68	61	99
■ Ringo	56	80	79	82	77

Figure 5–36. Back to the source: a column chart with its data table

(Note: some tweaking required here; more on this soon. Note as well that not every chart type can accommodate every kind of feature. For example—you can't apply a data table to a scatter chart.)

Chart Styles

The next Design group, **Chart Styles**, is no less obvious. Click its up/down arrows and a bounty of coordinated styles commands your screen (Figure 5-37):

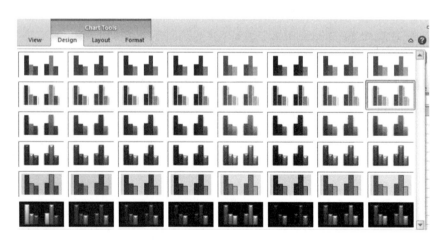

Figure 5–37. Stylish options: Chart Styles

Click any one. Don't like it? Click another one.

177

Move Chart

The next button group, *Location*, comprises exactly one button—*Move Chart*. Clicking it brings an old, pre-2007 dialog box in view (Figure 5-38):

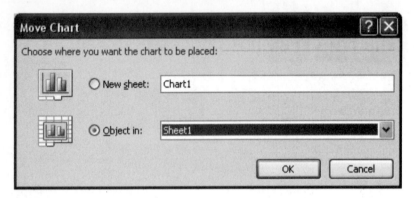

Figure 5–38. Changing your sheets: the Move Chart dialog box

Clicking the default Object In drop-down arrow enables you to resituate the chart to one of the other worksheets in the workbook—and remember: you get three worksheets for starters. The chart's location on the destination sheet corresponds to its original position on the original sheet. Clicking the New sheet option puts the chart on a new sheet, manufactured for the purpose of receiving the chart. That sheet is called Chart1 (sheet names can be changed, as we'll see) and when the chart moves there, it appears significantly larger than in its original version. (*Note*: If you move the chart to a new worksheet, it will *still* reflect any data entry changes you make in the source data. You can also *copy* a chart to a different sheet via standard copy-and-paste procedures. The copy will also remain "live.")

The final option, new to Excel 2010, is *Draft Mode*, on the far right end of the Design Button groupribbon. This option withholds fancy formatting elements that may slow your computer processing speed. When you're ready to display the chart as it really appears, click Normal. In reality, Draft mode won't appreciably change the onscreen appearance of the chart in many cases.

Changing the Chart Default—and the *2*-Second Chart

You may wonder what "chart default" means, because when we begin the charting process we *choose* the chart we want—no chart is imposed upon us by default, is it? Well, no, not exactly, unless you do the following:

1. Select a chart range of data cells.

2. Click the F11 key.

What happens? What happens is that a *column* chart will automatically appear, assigned to its own, new worksheet—and there's your default. You've just engineered a veritable, one-click, 2-second chart—and Excel has decided it's going to be a column chart. But what if you want a 2-second *line* chart instead?

1. Just click the chart you've realized onscreen,

2. Click Change Chart Type on the Design Tab,

3. Click a different chart, and click Set as Default, at the bottom of the Change Chart dialog box.

4. Click OK, and the chart *you've* selected will spring to the screen whenever you select a chart range and tap F11—in any workbook, not just the one in which you changed the default.

Done deal.

The Layout Tab

Among other things, the *Layout* tab helps you introduce and reposition new and existing chart objects, such as a chart title, the chart legend, and axis titles (not there by default). It also contains a basic *formatting* command option, which you'll also find on the Formatting tab (Figure 5-39):

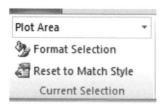

Figure 5–39. The Format Selection option

Format Selection is an important option, and appears elsewhere in charting activity in different guises. Any chart object—say, a data series—can be reformatted by clicking that object and choosing Format Selection. *Note:* If you want to reformat just one data series—say, the color of the column bar for exam 5, just click *any one* of the bars in that series, and all the others will follow suit (Figure 5-40):

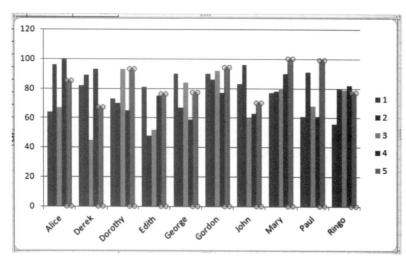

Figure 5–40. Select group: selecting one data series

Note the selection handles atop all the scores for exam 5. Again, I achieved this result by clicking any one of these columns. Click it a second time, and only that particular data *point* will be selected. Click away from it to start over.

Once the object is selected, its name will appear in the Format Selection window. You can also click the drop-down arrow and *then* select the object to be formatted there (Figure 5-41):

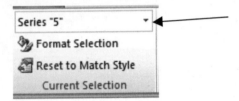

Figure 5–41. The selected data series

Then click Format Selection, and the ***Format Data Series*** dialog box containing formatting options peculiar to that object appears (Figure 5-42):

Figure 5–42. Formatting options for the selected data series

On the other hand, it's important to realize that you can access formatting options in several additional ways:

- You can also call up the Format Data Series dialog box by *double-clicking* the object you want to format.

- You can also *right-click* the object, and select the Format Data Series option (Figure 5-43):

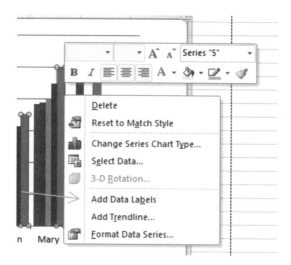

Figure 5–43. *Right-clicking: another route to formatting a selected chart object*

- Moreover, that same right click also sparks a **mini-toolbar**, whose available formatting options depend on the object which you've clicked:

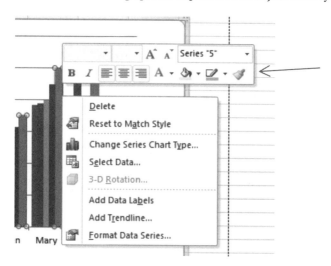

Figure 5–44. *More object-specific formatting options*

Note here that because we've clicked on a Series 5 bar, options enabling you to change the bar's fill and border colors appear on the context menu (the latter option is called **Shape Outline**); right-click on a title and text formatting options also become available. Thus if you're bothered by the slanted student names crowded into the Horizontal Axis, you could right-click any name, trigger the context menu, select or type a smaller font size, and press Enter (Figure 5-45):

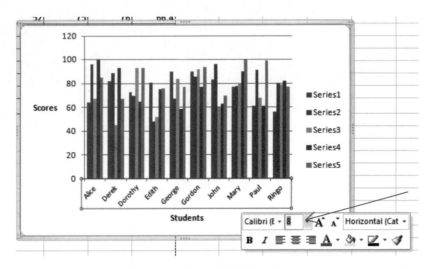

Figure 5–45. Con-text: Changing data labels' font size

If that little repair doesn't straighten your names—and it might not—you can resize the chart horizontally, until you've made room (Figure 5-46):

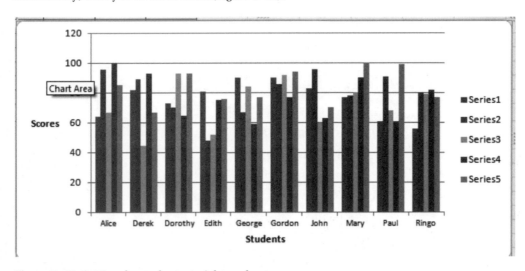

Figure 5–46. Getting the students straightened out

That looks better, though you've paid a small price for the improvement: you've changed the chart's aspect ratio a bit.

Again, these options are peculiar to the object and chart type selected. Options for exploding pie chart slices naturally won't appear in our data series dialog box above, and so on. One common option, however, is for recoloring the object. A column bar can be *filled* with a different color (you'd click Fill on the dialog box in Figure 5-47, whereas it's the *line* that would be recolored in a line chart, etc. Clicking Fill in the Series 5 object, for example, will take you to the Format Data Point dialog box (Figure 5-47):

Figure 5–47. The Format Data Point Dialog dialog box

enabling you to select the appropriate coloring option, including gradient fills, in which a blend of colors can be selected and customized (Figure 5-48):

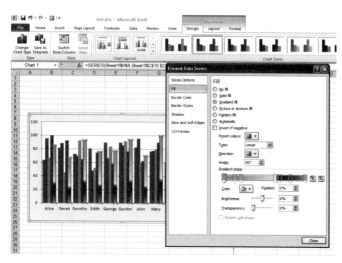

Figure 5–48. Good point: gradient fills can embellish data points

Note the gradient effect is previewed in the Series 5 bars even *before* you click to approve that option.

Working with Chart Labels

The *Labels* button group contains some important and slightly quirky options, and you need to know a bit about the quirks. The first two labeling options, *Chart Title* and *Axis Titles*, place text boxes on the chart at suggested locations, for example (Figure 5-49):

Figure 5–49. Chart label options

If you choose the Title Option, you can enter title text by selecting the title and typing. Note the text appears in the Formula bar, where it can be edited. When you complete the title, just press Enter. True, nothing quirky about that; but look at the Chart title in Figure 5-50 below, because it describes a common consequence of chart labels: when they're placed on a sheet, they often grab space from the chart itself and compress it (Figure 5-50):

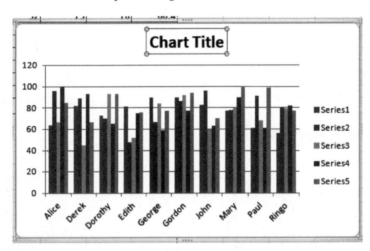

Figure 5–50. Pressed for space: A chart label moves in

The distortion can be quite pronounced, particularly if you insert a data table, as we'll see. As a result, you may need to resize the chart.

Note also that, while Excel's drop-down menus offer a series of locations at which you can place these various labels, you can also reposition them wherever you want on the chart by clicking on the object to select it (if you haven't already selected it), clicking anywhere on its border until you see a four-sided arrow, and dragging it to the desired location. And if you want to remove the object instead, just select it and press Delete. (Note: the ***More…..Options*** selection on all the Labels drop-down menus always takes you to the Format… dialog box for that object).

Axis titles let you apply identifying labels to either the Vertical and/or the Horizontal Axis (Figure 5-51_):

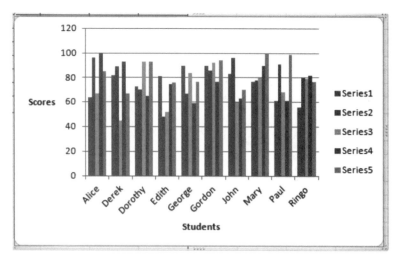

Figure 5–51. *Knowing the score(s): An axis label enters the chart*

Note that the Scores label has barged into the chart's territory, shrinking it a bit.

The ***Legend*** option works similarly; it deposits the legend to one of the locations suggested by the drop-down menu.

The ***Data Labels*** option does more than position the label—it supplies information about the chart's data, by posting the actual number associated with each data point. For example (Figure 5-52):

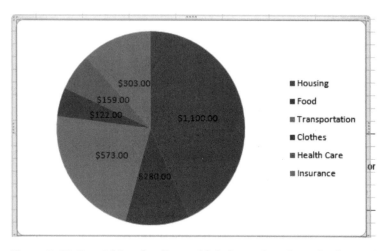

Figure 5–52. *Garnishing the slices, with information about the data points*

Data Labels supplement the chart with the source data used to generate it, adding an instructive touch to the graphical picture. (*Note*: you can initiate the *Data Labels* command by clicking *anywhere* on the chart, on any object. As a matter of fact, clicking a data point will turn the data labels on *only* for the series of which on which you've clicked, so you're actually better off *not* clicking directly on the data themselves.) However, data labels can congest the chart if the data points are numerous (Figure 5-53):

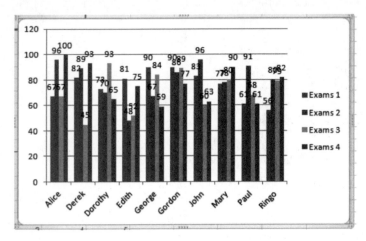

Figure 5–53. Information overload: An excess of data labels

You'll think twice about handing *that* one to your boss. Remember, though, that you can improve the scenario by recoloring and/or changing the size of the numbers. Take any of the prescribed routes to the chart formatting options, and make the appropriate changes. Be advised, though, that you'll have to click on *each* data series and make the changes to each series individually.

The **Data Table** option, already portrayed in Figure 5-36, presents all the data giving rise to the chart. It's a greedy object, however, and by implementing this option you may find yourself looking at something like this (Figure 5-54):

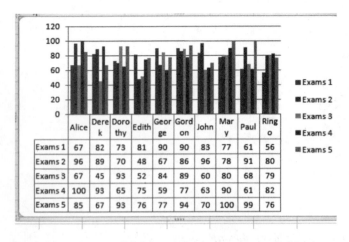

	Alice	Dere k	Doro thy	Edith	Geor ge	Gord on	John	Mar y	Paul	Ring o
Exams 1	67	82	73	81	90	90	83	77	61	56
Exams 2	96	89	70	48	67	86	96	78	91	80
Exams 3	67	45	93	52	84	89	60	80	68	79
Exams 4	100	93	65	75	59	77	63	90	61	82
Exams 5	85	67	93	76	77	94	70	100	99	76

Figure 5–54. Bet you didn't know George was two syllables

Needs work, as they say. Widening the chart would do wonders.

Axes to Grind

The *Axes* button group allows you to redraw certain aspects of the Horizontal and Vertical Axis (Figure 5-55):

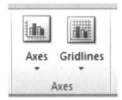

Figure 5–55. The Axes button group

The Vertical Axis options are particularly important. What's called the ***Primary Horizontal Axis*** allows you to flip the order of your Horizontal Axis labels, and also throw the Vertical Axis to the right edge of the chart (Figure 5-56):

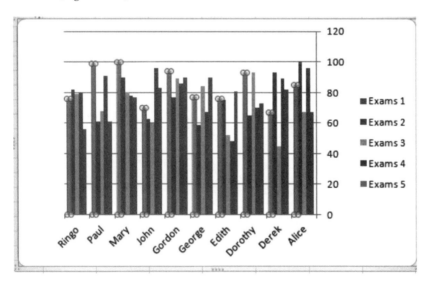

Figure 5–56. Right-handed Vertical Axis

But when your axis works with numerical data, as is the case with the ***Primary Vertical Axis***, the options look like this (Figure 5-57):

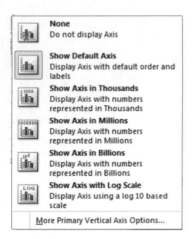

None
Do not display Axis

Show Default Axis
Display Axis with default order and labels

Show Axis in Thousands
Display Axis with numbers represented in Thousands

Show Axis in Millions
Display Axis with numbers represented in Millions

Show Axis in Billions
Display Axis with numbers represented in Billions

Show Axis with Log Scale
Display Axis using a log 10 based scale

More Primary Vertical Axis Options...

Figure 5–57. The Primary Vertical Axis option

The **Show Axis in...** selections enable you to show the axis data in different orders of magnitudes, something you may find useful when you're working with large numbers. Thus a simple salary chart such as this would read originally (Figure 5-58):

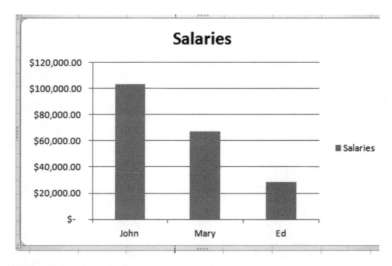

Figure 5–58. Bet John has an expense account, too

But if I select **Show Axis in Thousands**, it would look like this (Figure 5-59):

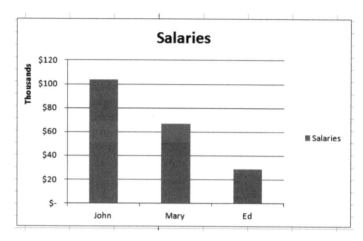

Figure 5–59. The Vertical Axis—same values, different look. Note the axis label.

The numbers are trimmed, even though they continue to represent the data in thousands. That is, the 120 on the axis stands for 120 thousand.

But clicking ***More Primary Vertical Axis Options...*** calls up a particularly important dialog box, and we'll review some of its options (Figure 5-60):

Figure 5–60. The Format Axis dialog box.

Suppose I wanted to line-chart the hypothetical closing values of the Dow Jones index for one week (Figure 5-61):

	DJ Close
Mon	10456.89
Tue	10781.05
Wed	10589.34
Thu	10427.49
Fri	10700.76

Figure 5–61. *A week's worth of stock averages*

Excel will yield, for starters, Figure 5-62:

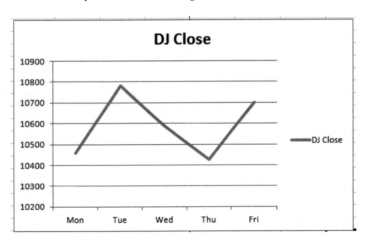

Figure 5–62. *Note the values in the Vertical Axis*

That minimum value—10200—was chosen by *Excel*, based on its reading of the chart data. But let *me* enter 0 as the lowest chart value, and the chart looks like this (Figure 5-63):

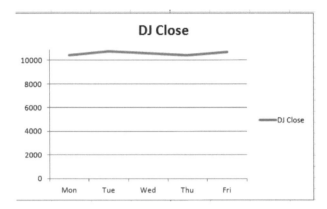

Figure 5–63. Same data, different Vertical Axis starting point

And that makes the fluctuation in the closing prices look a lot less dramatic. It's a classic charting issue.

Major Unit enables you to change the numeric *interval* Excel has selected for the Vertical Axis. In our test-grade chart, the Excel-chosen interval for the grades is 20—0, 20, 40, 60, etc. Enter a Major Unit of 10 to our grade data, and you get (Figure 5-64):

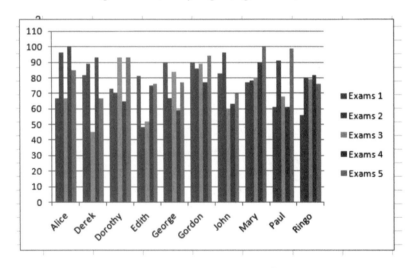

Figure 5–64. The grades represented in intervals of 10

Note that the Horizontal Gridlines in the plot area are drawn to this interval. **Minor Unit** lets the user choose an additional, smaller axis interval that can supplement the major unit. But gridlines associated with the minor unit don't appear on the chart by default, a point that takes us to….

The **Gridlines** option, which enables you to turn on the **minor** unit gridlines as well. Note in Figure 5-60 the minor unit on our Dow Jones chart is set by default at 4000. If we work with that interval and select **Gridlines: Major and Minor Gridlines**, we'll see (Figure 5-65):

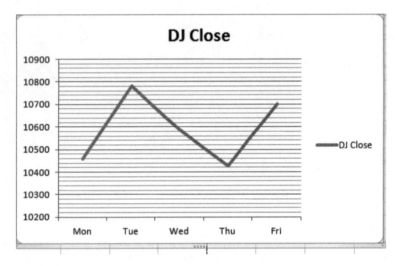

Figure 5–65. Major and minor scales: Turning on the minor unit gridlines

(*Note*: the Gridlines command here is not to be confused with the Gridlines command on the Page Layout tab, coming in Chapter 9).

And just by way of brief introduction, take note of the *Analysis* button group. Clicking these options will, among other things, let you supplement a chart with a trendline drawn atop the chart data, which tries to portray the trajectory of the data you're charting (Figure 5-66):

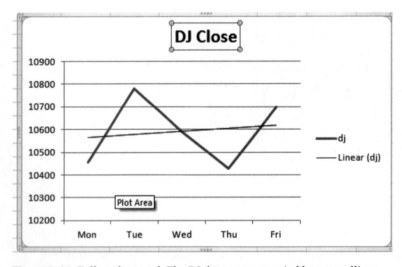

Figure 5-66. Follow the trend: The DJ data accompanied by a trendline

The Analysis group also lets you depict the likely degree of error in a series of values drawn from a sample, and the like.

The Format Tab—Getting Your Objects in Shape

This is probably the easiest Chart tab to figure out, the one whose options can be learned easily through click-this-button experimentation. The Tab offers a medley of ways to color and slightly reshape any chart object on which you click, with its options keyed to that object. Thus if you click on a chart plot area, the *Shape Styles* drop-down menu (when completely revealed) offers this (Figure 5-67):

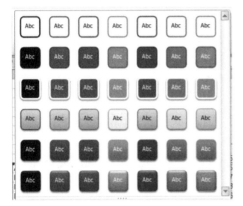

Figure 5–67. The Shape of styles to come

Click an option and the plot area takes on the selected color and border effect. The *Shape Fill* and *Shape Outline* buttons are really extensions of *Shape Styles*, serving up more fill color and border shaping options. The *Shape Effects* button makes additional shape embellishments available. Thus click on a chart plot area, and this Shape Effects potpourri appears (Figure 5-68):

Figure 5–6. Special effects: Shape effects options

Clicking any arrow above reveals still more options.

The *WordArt Styles* group and its associated *Text Fill, Text Outline*, and *Text Effects* options can reformat any selected text—be it in titles, axes, or legends (Figure 5-69):

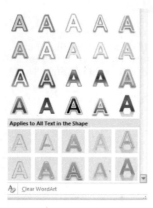

Figure 5–69. Word Art: Shape effects for text

Note that as indicated earlier, the Format tab has the same Format Selection button on the far left of its ribbon that you'll find on the Layout tab.

Sparklines: Mini-Charts with Big Impact

It's possible that no new feature of Excel 2010 has, uh,—sparked—more advance publicity than Sparklines, the brainchild of renowned graphics guru Edward Tufte. Sparklines aren't exactly new, having been marketed for several years by an array of providers; but once Excel decided to absorb the product into its interface, it was time to raise an eyebrow or two in the spreadsheet community.

Sparklines are charts of a special sort. Unlike the charts we've described to date—objects which occupy a layer *atop* the worksheet, as if they were laminated over it—Sparklines *are positioned in worksheet cells*, just as any other data are. They have addresses; and thus it's perfectly reasonable to refer to the Sparkline in cell I14—something you can't say about a conventional Excel chart.

And the fact is we've already encountered Sparklines—way, way, back in Chapter One, when we first trotted out that grading worksheet (Figure 5-70):

	Exams						
Student	1	2	3	4	5	Average	
Alice	67	96	67	100	85	83.0	∿
Derek	82	89	45	93	67	75.2	∿
Dorothy	73	70	93	65	93	78.8	∿
Edith	81	48	52	75	76	66.4	∿
George	90	67	84	59	77	75.4	∿
Gordon	90	86	89	77	94	87.2	∿
John	83	96	60	63	70	74.4	∿
Mary	77	78	80	90	100	85.0	∕
Paul	61	91	68	61	99	76.0	∿
Ringo	56	80	79	82	77	74.8	╱
Class Averages	76.0	80.1	71.7	76.5	83.8		

Figure 5–70. Sparklines—mini line charts

Eyes misting with nostalgia? Sentiment aside, those yellow cells contain Sparklines.

Apart from their placement in specific cells, Sparklines differ from conventional Excel charts in some other important ways:

- They contain *no* textual information—no titles, axis data, or legends.

- They can only characterize *one* data series at a time.

- They permit far fewer formatting options.

Thus in view of these limitations, you're likely ready to ask what's the up side—that is, why turn to a Sparkline when a typical Excel chart seems to offer so much more? The answer is that Sparklines can easily fill a *range* of cells with their data-capturing magic, allowing for numerous, concise charts keyed individually to a large span of columns or rows—like our gradebook. As such, they give a quick, illustrative, graphic read on your data.

So let's see how Sparklines work. We can return to our set of grades, entered in cells C8:I20. Note this range *includes* the class averages as well as the Student name in C9 I warned you about earlier this chapter (Figure 5-71):

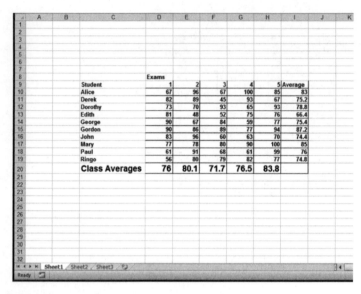

Figure 5–71. The grade data, pre-sparkline

To start the Sparkline:

1. Select cells J10:J19. The Sparkline for each student will go here.

2. Click the Insert tab, and then, in the *Sparklines* button group, click *Line*. You'll see (Figure 5-72):

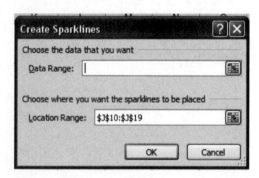

Figure 5–72. The Create Sparkines dialog box

3. In the Data Range field, click D10:H19—the range containing all the student grades. Here, we're not worried about that row containing the name Student or that "Class Average" row—rows 9 and 20, respectively—because we've *excluded* them from the data range.

4. Click OK. The Sparklines in line-chart form should appear in the cells of the location range—J10:J19, each Sparkline tied to each row of student data.

It's all pretty easy. One subtle virtue of Sparklines is that you can select a large range of data— say, daily stock closing prices for an entire year entered across one row, or down one column—and pack it into one Sparkline, delivering a long-term, global picture of financial activity. Sparklines are also dynamic—they will continue to register changes in the original source and change accordingly.

And note that because the Sparklines are lodged in cells just like other data, you can select a Sparkline range, click the Home tab, and click the Fill Color button on the Font button group and color the cells in which the Sparklines appear. You can then click the **Sparkline Tools** tab that has magically appeared above the Design tab (Figure 5-73):

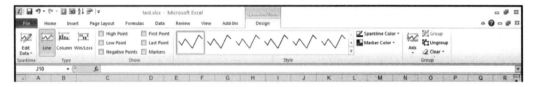

Figure 5–73. The Sparklines Tools tab

and then click the Sparkline Color button on the far right to recolor the Sparklines (Figure 5-74):

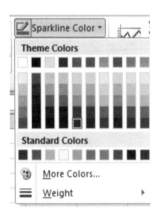

Figure 5–74. Where to color Sparklines

You can also modify the lines' thickness with the **Weight** option on the same menu.
To emphasize data points in the Sparklines, move left to the **Show** group (Figure 5-75):

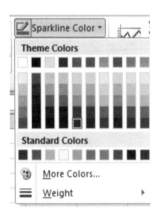

Figure 5–75. The Show group's buttons, for emphasizing Sparkline data points

The *Markers* button allows you to attach markers to each data point in a line-chart Sparkline (Figure 5-76):

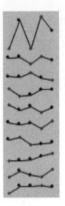

Figure 5–76. Data points on Sparkline line charts

And the other options in that group—***High Point, Low Point, Negative Points, First Point***, and ***Last Point***—attach differently-colored markers to each of those points—the highest value in the chart, any negative values, the very first point in the Sparkline, etc. The Style drop-down menu allows you to select an overall Spakline motif, coordinating colors for the line and any data markers.

And if you decide you'd rather see your data in columns, you can select the range containing the Sparklines and click ***Column*** on the ***Sparklines Tools/ Type*** button group (Figure 5-77):

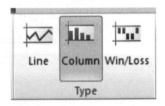

Figure 5–77. Sparkline chart type options

And boom—there's your data in columns.

You Win Some, You Lose Some

As the above screen shot attests, you only have three Sparkline chart types to choose from, but in spite of that modest lineup, the third—Win/Loss—is one that *isn't* directly available in the larger conventional Excel chart roster. The Win/Loss chart is oddly binary—it places a bar above its Horizontal Axis for *any* positive number in a cell, and installs a bar below the axis for *any* negative one. To demonstrate: Say you begin with this range of numbers (Figure 5-78):

| 3 | 7 | -6 | 9 | -12 | 1 | 9 | 5 | -3 |

Figure 5–78. All or nothing: Positive numbers win, negative numbers lose

Select this range, select the Sparklines **Win/Loss** chart, and select a one-cell location range to the right of the range when prompted (though it can really be placed anywhere), and you'll produce this (Figure 5-79):

Figure 5–79. In the black: a win-loss chart

Notice there is no magnitude here. All the positive and negative values are recorded equally—they're in the same place, either above or below the axis. So why would you use Win/Loss? You could use it to track the *incidence* of profits and losses in a business for example, though again, not their exact values. Win/Loss is often applied to chart wins and losses of sports teams (hence its name); you could enter a 1 for every team win along a selected range, and a -1 on that same range for every loss. Do this across a 162-cell range and you could compile a trajectory of the fortunes of a major league baseball team, by placing a Sparkline in the 163rd cell—again, giving the big picture of an entire season. (*Note*: Widening a column, or heightening a row, in a Sparkline cell brings about the same kind of aspect ratio distortion we discussed earlier).

To remove a Sparkline, just right-click it and select **Sparklines → Clear Selected Sparklines**—it's expressed in the plural because you can drag across a range of Sparklines and delete the whole group.

There's one other important Sparkline set of options, and you'll find them when you click the **Axis** down arrow, in the **Sparkline** button group (Figure 5-80):

Figure 5–80. Sparkline Axis options

199

You'll want to know about the *Vertical Axis Maximum* and *Minimum Value Options.* The default Automatic for each Sparkline option means that Excel will decide which numeric intervals will appear on each Sparkline's Vertical Axis, after looking at the data. Thus two Sparkline line charts—to return to two previous examples, one charting a player's batting averages across his career, the other a series of weight measurements—will use different intervals on their axes, because the magnitudes are very different. If you select the same for both Sparklines here, the batting averages and weights will use the *same* interval scale—bringing about highly distorted outcomes (Figure 5-81):

Batting Averages	.273	.312	.302	.288	.301	_ _ _ _ _
Weights	145	152	147	150	142	■■■■■

Figure 5–81. Heavy hitters: Batting averages charted next to player weights

When they say a player can't hit his weight, they mean it. The way to make these data readable in their own terms is to remain with the default *Automatic for Each Sparkline*, and to set the *Custom Value...* option to 0. If you don't carry out that latter step, the lowest value in each data series is treated as a de factto zero value, with the other values keyed to it.

As implied above, Custom Value enables you to *enter* the lowest and highest values of any number that you'll allow to appear in a Sparkline. If I enter a lowest allowable value of 1 for the batting average Sparkline, I'll see nothing in it—because all the batting averages are fractions, and thus all less than 1.

In Conclusion…

Charting Excel data calls for a two-front approach to the data—understanding how to portray the data in a lucid and appealing format, and understanding at the same time what you need to do in order to bring that end about. As we've seen, charting options are numerous and variable, depending on the chart you've selected. As always, a bit of practice with real-world charting questions is key. Next up is a closer look at the data contributing to charts and other Excel capabilities—the world of Excel databases.

Now go out there and cell those charts.

CHAPTER 6

■■■

Setting the Table: Database Features of Excel 2010

By now you've established a close relationship with the concept of a range—that collection of adjacent cells occupying a rectangular area on the worksheet (we'll leave aside any additional nuances I may have bothered you with earlier). Now, a range can be blank, of course—a collection of adjacent, rectangular-shaped *empty* cells is no less a range because of its dearth of data. But when a range is filled with records—that is, a series of consecutive rows and columns containing related information topped by headings of the First Name-Last Name-Address variety—you and I might call that assemblage of data a ***database***. If you were compiling a seating list for a formal event—even if you wrote it out on paper—you could enter Name and Table Number headings at the top of the page, and pencil in the data accordingly. Two headings, beneath which you write in the appropriate information; sounds like a database. In Excel, it could start looking like this (Figure 6–1):

Name	Table
Ted	3
Mary	4
John	3
Emily	6
Jack	1
Bill	6
Barbara	4

Figure 6–1. A basic Excel database

That all sounds and looks good to me; but as a terminological matter Excel isn't always so sure. Microsoft has had some difficulty making up its mind about exactly what it means by the term *database*, though you're not likely to lose any sleep over the matter, and you shouldn't. How Microsoft Access defines "database" doesn't quite dovetail with the ways it's been used in Excel, for example—but that won't stop us from plunging ahead in any case. I know you like a challenge.

For our purposes, we can go ahead and define a database as a collection of data that occupies adjacent rows and columns. Each row comprises a ***record***, and each column is a termed a ***field***. Note I've omitted the ***headings*** requirement from the definition. Headings are surely a very good thing to find at the top of a database, but you can still do productive work in a database if they're not there. What *is* required, however, is that the records in a database be *consecutive*—because a completely empty row ropes off the database from any data that may appear on the other side of the blank row. Note, however—and this is important—that a record need *not* be complete. As long each record contains at least *one* populated field, the database remains in force. Now let's turn to one classic database option.

Sorting—Sort Of Easy

Think of your little black book—if you still have one—and ask yourself how its contents are arranged. The probable answer: in alphabetical order, more or less. That's an equivocal reply, because your book's little lettered tabs naturally present themselves in that order, but the names on each page are likely to be slightly *dis*ordered, aren't they? You'll post Jones, Jepson, and Jackson to the J's, but if you've entered them in that sequence, now what? The three aren't exactly alphabetized, or *sorted*—and you obviously won't erase and rewrite the names each time you make a new entry, in order to ensure a precise listing. I'd pay big bucks to see you do *that*.

But spreadsheets (and even word processors) make the sorting process easy, and they can do far more with the data than anything your black book—or maybe even your Blackberry—can. When I taught sorting in Excel for a training firm in New York, the manual with which I worked described sorting as an advanced subject. It isn't.

The basics—or at least the basic basics—of sorting are most elementary. If you want to sort our old favorite, the gradebook database:

1. Click anywhere in the column (field) by which you want to sort. Do *NOT* select all the cells in that column; just click one cell, as shown in Figure 6–2. (Selecting the column in its entirety may result in you sorting *only* that column, and not the ones on either side of it.)

Student	Exams 1	2	3	4	5	Average
Alice	67	96	67	100	85	83.0
Derek	82	89	45	93	67	75.2
Dorothy	73	70	93	65	93	78.8
Edith	81	48	52	75	76	66.4
George	90	67	84	59	77	75.4
Gordon	90	86	89	77	94	87.2
John	83	96	60	63	70	74.4
Mary	77	78	80	90	100	85.0
Paul	61	91	68	61	99	76.0
Ringo	56	80	79	82	77	74.8

Figure 6–2. The gradebook with one cell in the test 3 column (field) selected—and ready to sort

2. Click one of the *Sort* buttons...There's one—the *Sort & Filter* button—in the *Editing* group in the Home tab (Figure 6–3):

Figure 6–3. One place to start sorting…

And there are three sorting buttons in the *Sort & Filter* group on the Data tab (Figure 6–4):

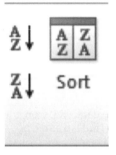

Figure 6–4. …and here's the other

3. Select the A-Z or Z-A options, representing lowest to highest, or highest to lowest, respectively. Note the Sort & Filter option in the Editing group requires you to click a drop-down arrow in order to reach those commands.

That's it. And to anticipate a common question, the data—*all* the *other* adjacent data—are sorted, too. That means that if you're sorting these grades by test 3, in Z-A (highest to lowest) order, you'll get this (Figure 6–5):

Student	1	2	3	4	5	Average
Dorothy	73	70	93	65	93	78.8
Gordon	90	86	89	77	94	87.2
George	90	67	84	59	77	75.4
Mary	77	78	80	90	100	85.0
Ringo	56	80	79	82	77	74.8
Paul	61	91	68	61	99	76.0
Alice	67	96	67	100	85	83.0
John	83	96	60	63	70	74.4
Edith	81	48	52	75	76	66.4
Derek	82	89	45	93	67	75.2

Figure 6–5. The grades, post-sort

Meaning all the data in all the other adjacent columns remain lined up; nothing is out of whack. We see Dorothy is still the owner of that 93. Gordon is still jealous. Pretty easy, no? Just click in the desired column (field), and click A-Z or Z-A.

Using Header Rows

Now there *is*, however, another big question we need to address. If we sort the above data, why won't the very first row be sorted? That is, why isn't the 3—the number of the test being sorted—treated as just another test score (a rather low one, too), and thrown to the bottom of the sorted list?

The answer is that sometimes that's exactly what *will* happen. But Excel really wants your data to have a header row—so if it sees a discrepancy between the *kind* of data in the first row of any field and the other data in that field, it *assumes* the first row is a header. And because the last field—Average—is topped by a text entry, even as the data beneath it are numbers, Excel interprets that data disconnect as an indicator of a header row; and as a result, it leaves the header row alone. That's how it works; and it means in turn that if the Average field had originally been called 6, the first row *would* have been sorted, had you clicked in that or any other column.

And the Sort capability also allows you to sort the data by more than one field. Why would you want to do such a thing? Consider this case: you have a long database of university students, and you want to sort the records by the Last Name field. Because it's highly likely that some students will share the same last name, you would probably want to sort the names further by the First Name field, so that Wilson Henry is sorted before Wilson Nancy. (If you don't sort by two fields in cases such as this, the last names will obviously be sorted together—but the first names will simply remain in their current order). On the other hand, there's *no* reason to sort by a second field if *no* duplicate data exists in the first. And it also then follows that if two or more students share the same first *and* last name, you could sort by a third field–say, middle initial, or major.

To demonstrate, enter this small database in cells J11:L17 (it should go without saying allthis works with much larger databases, too) (Figure 6–6):

Last Name	First Name	Major
Jones	Ed	Poli. Sci.
Walston	Tanya	Physics
Jones	Bill	Ed.
Quincy	Sally	Phil.
Edwards	Ralph	Zoology
Jones	Ed	Soc.

Figure 6–6. Note the two Ed Jones entries.

The duplicate data are clear—but I hear some murmuring in the back rows. The eagle-eyed among you are whispering about the fact that, since all the data—including the headings—are *text* in nature, when we go ahead and sort *even the header row should be sorted.* Very good—it's all true. So in order to obviate that problem, let's move to the next section.

Sorting by More than One Field

To sort by more than one field, click anywhere in the database, and click either the Sort button in the Data tab, *or, in the Home tab,* the Sort & Filter button's down arrow, followed by ***Custom Sort...*** (rather inconsistent, isn't it). Either way, you'll be brought to this dialog box (Figure 6–7):

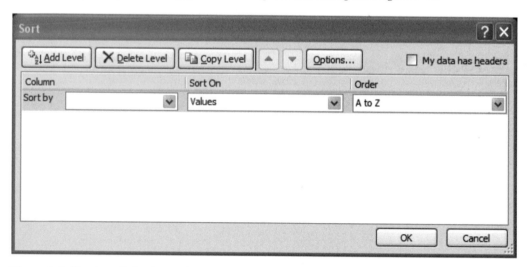

Figure 6–7. The Sort dialog box: Where to sort by multiple columns

Note the check box in the upper right of the dialog box: ***My data has headers***. By checking that box, you'll be instructing Excel *not* to sort the first, or header, row. Then, because we want to sort initially by Last Name, click the ***Sort By*** drop-down arrow and select ***Last Name*** (Figure 6–8):

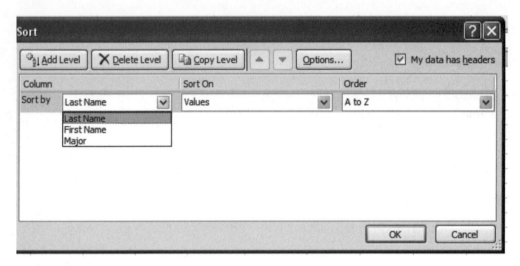

Figure 6–8. Choosing the fields by which to sort

The **Sort On** drop-down menu provides you four choices by which to sort—**Values, Cell Color, Font Color,** and **Cell Icon.** Values denotes any data in the cell—and Values here also means *text,* not just numbers. The next three options enable you to sort by cells whose *appearances* may have been changed by a *Conditional Format or even by standard formatting.* Thus if you have a range of numerical data, and you've Conditionally Formatted all the numbers in the range greater than 100 red, and all those less than 50 green, you can sort the green cells before the red (Figure 6–9):

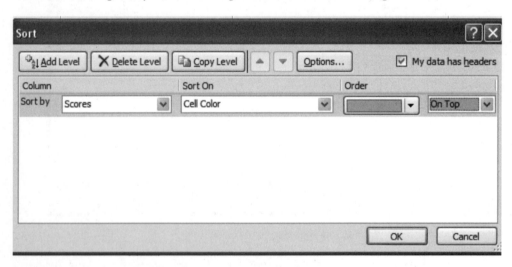

Figure 6–9. Sorting by color. It's done on more than just socks.

The ***On top/bottom*** options are the color-ordering equivalents of A-Z and Z-A. There's no inherent ascending or descending color order, after all.

The same idea applies to Cell Icon—if you've conditionally formatted certain values to exhibit this or that *icon,* they can be sorted first. In our case, though, we're sorting on values.

Order refers to the direction of the sort—A-Z or Z-A. But there's another option there, too—***Custom List...***. If you have a field whose data consists of days of the week, for example, clicking Custom List and then clicking the built-in days of the week Custom List (remember that?) lets you work with a sort order in which Monday can be sorted before Friday, even though the latter comes first alphabetically (and remember: you can compose your own custom lists, and sort by any of these, too, Figure 6–10).

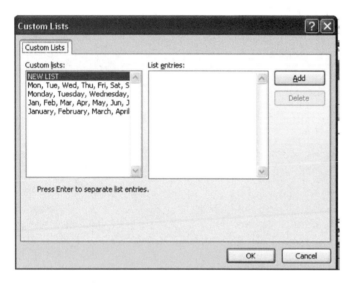

Figure 6–10. Where to initiate a custom sort

So now we're ready to sort the database by Last Name—but because we have *duplicates* in that field, we want to sort by First Name, too. As a result, we need to click the ***Add Level*** button, and select ***First Name*** on the new drop-down arrow alongside that field (Figure 6–11):

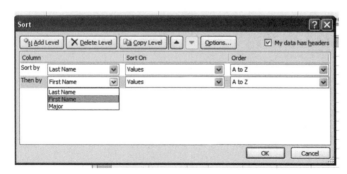

Figure 6–11. Sorting by two fields...

But remember that the database contains *two* students named Ed Jones, and so we want to sort by still a *third* field (and that's all we have here), in this case, by Major (Figure 6–12):

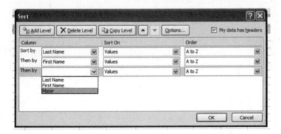

Figure 6–12. …and now by three

Now that we've selected our sort fields, click OK. Here's what happens (Figure 6–13):

Last Name	First Name	Major
Edwards	Ralph	Zoology
Jones	Bill	Ed.
Jones	Ed	Poli. Sci.
Jones	Ed	Soc.
Quincy	Sally	Phil.
Walston	Tanya	Physics

Figure 6–13. Keeping up with Joneses: Note the sort order

Note the two Ed Joneses—sorted together, but with the Poli. Sci. major positioned above Soc.—P sorted before S. Well done.

There are a few additional Sort dialog box buttons that need to be explained. **Delete Level** simply allows you to remove a sort field if you have second thoughts about needing it. Just click the field, select Delete Level, and it's gone. **Copy Level**? Click on a field you've already selected to be sorted, click Copy Level, and that same field appears a second time in the dialog box (Figure 6–14):

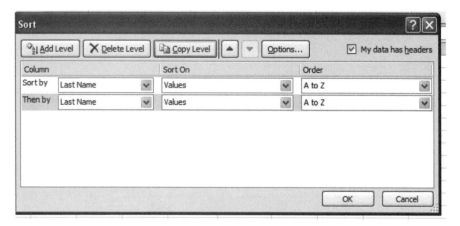

Figure 6–14. Double vision: sorting by the same field twice?

Ok, ok—the question is obvious: Why would you possibly want to copy the same field? And how do you sort it *twice*? The answer takes us back to a previous illustration. If you Conditionally Format a range of values—e.g., cells above 100 red, below 50 green—copying the same field to the Sort dialog box lets you tell Excel which color in that field gets sorted first, second, etc. Note that some values in the field might be *neither* above 100 *nor* below 50, and thus may have *no* color. They could be sorted in between two color priorities, and so you may *indeed* need to establish a sort order within the same field (there is a *No Color* sort option).

The up/down arrows allow you to adjust the order by which fields are sorted. Thus, if you decide you want the First Name field sorted first, click on First Name and then the up arrow.

Options... delivers a fairly exotic set of choices. First, if you have duplicate names in a field to be sorted, some of which are lowercase and others capitalized (jones, Jones), sorts the lowercase names first. *Sort left to right* allows you to sort by *column* instead of row. Thus I can sort the columns in the student database, such that *they* appear in A-Z sequence: First Name, Last Name, Major.

The AutoFilter: Picking and Choosing Your Data

Sorting data is one of those database have-to-knows, equipped with its variety of options for reorganizing your information. But sometimes you need to look at only *part* of the data, based on some criterion that you've established. If you track the sales activity of a team of salespersons, for example, you may want to see all of Jack and Jill's transactions, and *only* their transactions. Or you may want to generate a list of all the major league players who hit more than 20 home runs last year, or only those students with test scores under 65. Excel's *AutoFilter* does just this kind thing, and it's even easier than sorting. It lets you identify which data you want to see with a couple of clicks, and in a couple of seconds.

Let's try out AutoFilter on our student gradebook. Just click anywhere among the data, click the Data tab, and click Filter (Figure 6–15):

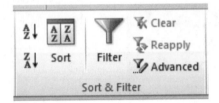

Figure 6–15. The Sort & Filter button group

The data look like this (Figure 6–16):

Student	Exams					Average
Alice	67	96	67	100	85	83.0
Derek	82	89	45	93	67	75.2
Dorothy	73	70	93	65	93	78.8
Edith	81	48	52	75	76	66.4
George	90	67	84	59	77	75.4
Gordon	90	86	89	77	94	87.2
John	83	96	60	63	70	74.4
Mary	77	78	80	90	100	85.0
Paul	61	91	68	61	99	76.0
Ringo	56	80	79	82	77	74.8
Class Averages	76.0	80.1	71.7	76.5	83.8	

Figure 6–16. Filters in place

You'll note the handles attaching to the field names (and note AutoFilter assumes the first row is a header). Now let's say I want to pull Dorothy's test results from the data; and while you could object that Dorothy's results are *already* perfectly visible as is, consider that

1. Your list may be hundreds of students long, and Dorothy's name may not be quite so evident.

2. Depending on the kind of records you're keeping, Dorothy's name could appear more than once, and in various places down the column, and

3. You may want to print *only* Dorothy's data, and hence, need to see only her information onscreen (Figure 6–16).

Student	Exams					Average
Dorothy	73	70	93	65	93	78.8

Figure 6–16. Filtered data—you may need to see Dorothy's data alone

Keeping all that in mind, click the down arrow alongside Student. You'll see (Figure 6–17):

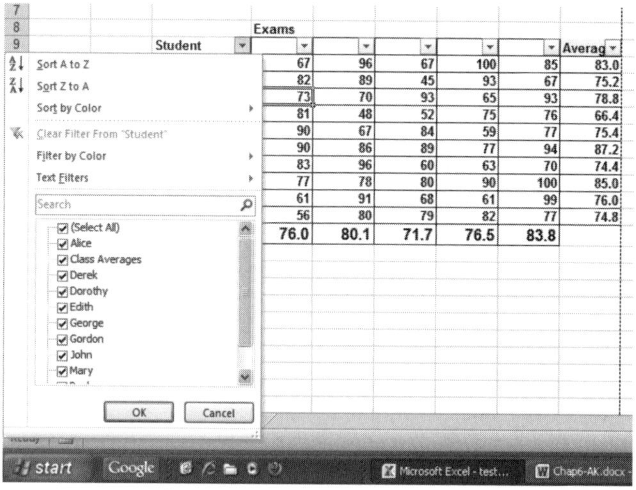

Figure 6–17. The filter drop-down menu

Among other things, you're presented with a list of all the student names, listed *uniquely*, that is, once each. Even if the same student name should appear in the field many times, the AutoFilter drop-down list will record it once. Note all the names are selected, and we want to see Dorothy's alone, so:

1. Click the Select All button. The check marks disappear from all the names.

2. Click Dorothy.

3. Click OK. You should see (Figure 6–18):

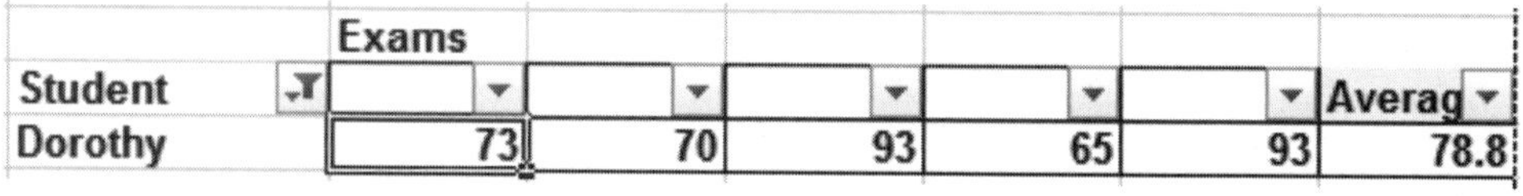

Figure 6–18. There's Dorothy, again—now that we know how it's done

There she is. Had her name appeared multiple times in the Student field, each "Dorothy" row would appear in your filtered result. (You could also type Dorothy in the Search field appearing right above the list of student names, and then click OK. (You can also use wild cards here, too—meaning if I type Dor* in the Search field, the records of all student names beginning with Dor will be filtered, including Doris, too.)

Now at some point you'll naturally want to restore all the other rows to the screen. To do this, just click the **Clear** button in the Sort & Filter group, and you're back where you started. You can now apply the filter to any other name, or names—meaning you can click on *several* names in the drop-down list above. If you need to see the grades for both Dorothy and George at the same time, just click those two names (Figure 6–19):.

Student						Average
Dorothy	73	70	93	65	93	78.8
George	90	67	84	59	77	75.4

Figure 6–19. Group shot: Filtering for two students

Or for an alternative but related example, if we had a database of students and their majors, for instance (Figure 6–20):

Student	Major
Alice	Soc
Derek	Poli Sci
Dorothy	Soc
Edith	Eng
George	Phil
Gordon	Poli Sci
John	Eng
Mary	Geog
Paul	Eng
Ringo	Lit

Figure 6–20. Ringo a Lit major? What a concept.

We could filter by major, and say, click on Soc. We'd get (Figure 6–21):

Student	Major
Alice	Soc
Dorothy	Soc

Figure 6–21. Singling out Soc

And just as we could filter for both Dorothy and George, we could filter for both Soc and Poli Sci. Again, transpose all this to a university of 10,000, and you get a pretty swift and effective way to learn about large numbers of students.

Playing—or Plying—the Numbers

Numerical data, on the other hand, can be subjected to a range of filtering criteria, all of which are pretty easy to figure out. If I click the down arrow by exam number 2 (if you don't actually see the exam number names, by the way, it's because the filter handles are obscuring the single digits. Just center the exam names, and they'll return to view), I'll see (Figure 6–22):

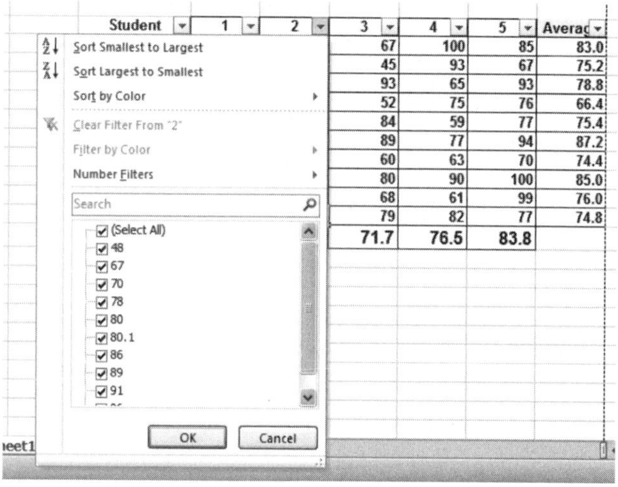

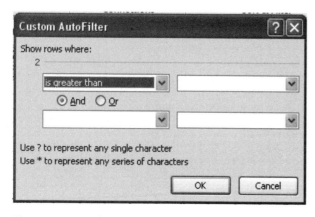

Figure 6–22. Filtering numeric data

Note that the numbers in the drop-down result are sorted in ascending order, making it easier for you to select a particular test score. (The names in the previous example were also sorted in that drop-down, but because the names were already sorted in the original database, you may not have noticed.) If, however, I want to see all the exam results for that exam 2 that exceed 75, I can:

1. Click Number Filters ➤**is greater than** (Figure 6–23):

Figure 6–23. Looking for all scores above 75

2. Then just type 75 in the field alongside "is greater than" and click OK.

The records should be filtered as per your instruction (Figure 6–24):

Student	1	2	3	4	5	Average
Alice	67	96	67	100	85	83.0
Derek	82	89	45	93	67	75.2
Gordon	90	86	89	77	94	87.2
John	83	96	60	63	70	74.4
Mary	77	78	80	90	100	85.0
Paul	61	91	68	61	99	76.0
Ringo	56	80	79	82	77	74.8
Class Averages	76.0	80.1	71.7	76.5	83.8	

Figure 6–24. Test scores above 75—for exam 2

Note that the Greater Than dialog box we summoned in Figure 6–23 is really the same for *all* the Number Filters options, even Custom Filter. As you see, the dialog box allows you enter up to *two* filtering conditions of the And or the Or variety, if you wish, and the drop down arrows enable you to select which kind of mathematical operations you wish to apply. You could have indicated that you wanted to see all scores for exam 2 which are greater than 75 *or* less than 60, for example.

And note that you can apply AutoFilters in sequence. Leaving the above results in place (that is, *not* restoring all the records), you can then filter *another* field. Let's say I now want to apply precisely the same criterion to test 1—that is, all tests over 75. I can carry out exactly the same Numbers Filters sequence, yielding (Figure 6–25):

Student	1	2	3	4	5	Average
Derek	82	89	45	93	67	75.2
Gordon	90	86	89	77	94	87.2
John	83	96	60	63	70	74.4
Mary	77	78	80	90	100	85.0
Class Averages	76.0	80.1	71.7	76.5	83.8	

Figure 6–25. Filtering scores above 75 on both exams 2 and 1

We've now AutoFiltered *both* exams 1 and 2, and have learned that Derek, Gordon, John, and Mary are the only students to have bettered 75 on both. Note in addition the AutoFilter symbol posted in the AutoFilter handle of fields 1 and 2, indicating that they are the ones that have been filtered. Click *Clear* in the Sort & Filter button group, and all the records return.

Note you can also do sorting via the drop-down menu, and also sort and filter by *color*, as per our sort discussion. Just keep in mind that if you sort one exam field in Z-A order, for example, the Class Averages row will *also* be sorted, even if you'd prefer otherwise. As a result, you may want to go ahead and delete that row, or insert a blank row between the last actual test score and Class Averages. But we're getting back to this issue soon.

And finally, if you want to turn the AutoFilter off altogether, just click the Filter button on the Sort & Filter button group—and the handles disappear (but *note*: AutoFilter handles *won't* print, even if you leave them on screen).

The Advanced Filter—Setting Your Data Aside

The AutoFilter is a great and speedy way for sifting your data, but it suffers from a few shortcomings that could impair your analysis of the information, depending on what you need to do. For one thing, the AutoFilter is temporary; that is, because it works by hiding any rows that *don't* meet the criterion you've specified, you're going to want to restore those rows to view sooner or later—and then you're back where you started; the filtered results are gone. In addition, those hidden rows may contain information *elsewhere* in other columns, far from the data with which you're working—but they'll be hidden too. Finally, the AutoFilter presents the results for *all* the database fields, even if you don't need all of that information. For example: I need to know the names of those students whose test averages equal or exceed 85, and *don't* need to see the data in their individual exam fields. That is, I may want the filter result to display data for the Student and Average fields *only*. But AutoFilter isn't selective—it shows results for *all* the database fields, whether I want to see them or not. And here's where the *Advanced Filter* comes in: it lets you *copy* your filtered results to a *separate* area of the worksheet, giving you a new set of results to work with, while leaving your original table data untouched and unhidden.

So let's say you want to carry out the above task—you want to see which students have compiled a test average of 85 or better, and you want to see those results displayed compactly, in the Student and Average fields alone. Now we need to do a bit of preparation in order to get the Advanced Filter going.

First, we need to designate a small area on the worksheet (it could be anywhere, except inside the database) in which we'll enter the *criterion*, or criteria, we need to define which data we want to filter. We'll select cells N9:N10, and enter (Figure 6–26):

Student	1	2	3	4	5	Average		Average	
Alice	67	96	67	100	85	83.00		>=85	
Derek	82	89	45	93	67	75.20			
Dorothy	73	70	93	65	56	71.40			
Edith	81	48	52	75	76	66.40			
George	90	67	84	59	77	75.40			
Gordon	90	86	89	77	94	87.20			
John	83	96	60	63	70	74.40			
Mary	77	78	80	90	100	85.00			
Paul	61	91	68	61	99	76.00			
Ringo	56	80	79	82	76	74.60			
Class Averages	76	80.1	71.7	76.5	80	76.86			

Figure 6–26. A criterion range for an advanced filter. "Average" in N9, >=85 in N10.

What is this pair of cells trying to do? It's identifying

1. The name of the field bearing the criterion we need—Average-—in N9, and

2. The criterion itself—the 85-or-greater grade threshold—in N10.

Remember—we want to filter all students who've achieved a test average of 85 or better. The averages are recorded in the Class Averages field, and so we've entered that name in N9. The >=85 in

N10 is the standard way in which to express equal to, or greater than, a specified value—in this case, 85.

If, by way of a different example, we had wanted to filter all the students who had scored less than 65 in *exam 4*, we could have entered this in N9:N10 instead (Figure 6–27):

Figure 6–27. Not Dean's List Material: A criterion for filtering grades below 65 on exam 4

where 4 represents that exam's *field* name.

Note, without getting too carried away, that you can specify *two criteria* to be met at the same time. If I had supplemented the expression above in Figure 6–27 with these entries in O9:O10 (Figure 6–28):

N	O
4	5
<65	<65

Figure 6–28. Two advanced filter criteria operating at the same time

I'd be searching for all students who scored below 65 in *both* exams 4 *and* 5. But we're sticking with our initial criterion—those students with test averages equal to or greater than 85.

Next, we need to mark out a range on the worksheet to which our filtered results will be *copied*, because we want these results to occupy a place on the worksheet that is *independent* of the original gradebook data in C9:I20; so in cells K9:L9 we'll enter (Figure 6–29):

Figure 6–29. Where our results should appear

because, as per our introduction to this exercise, these are the names of the only two fields for which we want to see the filtered results—and those results will appear directly beneath those two headings when we execute the Advanced Filter. Remember as well that this results area could be designated anywhere on the worksheet.

In the interests off tidying up the worksheet, first either delete the Class Averages row or insert some blank rows between it and Ringo's data (we're doing this because we don't want Class Averages treated as another student). Then click anywhere in the data and click Data➤ Advanced in the Sort & Filter button group. You'll see (Figure 6–30):

Figure 6–30. The database coordinates. Note here Excel uses the word "list"—an inconsistency

- Click the *Copy to another location* option, because that's exactly what we want to do—copy the filter results somewhere away from the original database. Clicking Copy to another location activates the *Copy to:* field, below. Remaining with the Filter the list, in-place option you see in Figure 6–30 would have the effect of executing a standard *AutoFilter*—because that's what AutoFilter *does*—filter data in their *own* place, by hiding rows.

- In criteria range, type or drag this range: N9:N10, the cells in which we entered our greater-than-85 criterion.

- In Copy to: type or drag this range: K9:L9. Even though we're only naming the *headings* in the copy-to location, Excel will still copy all the records that meet our criterion below those headings.

- Click OK. You should see: (Figure 6–31):

Student	Average
Gordon	87.20
Mary	85.00

Figure 6–31. Our results. Note Mary's average: Exactly 85

Thus we see that only Gordon and Mary averaged at least 85 across all 5 tests; and these results can be analyzed on their own, completely independent of the original database. Again, Advanced Filters will work just as well with 10,000 students as it does with 10, and again, the original database in cells C9:I20 is left intact.

Table Talk

There's still another step you can take to add value to your analysis of a database—you can define it as a *table*.[1] A table is really a slightly more souped-up database, which affords you a couple of additional advantages:

- It automatically turns on AutoFilter.

- It supplies you with a large inventory of formats you can easily apply to the database, including some additional customizing options.

- Even after the table is established onscreen you can type *additional* field names to the right of the last field, as well as new records (that is, new rows), and these will be incorporated automatically into the table. The new fields will receive their own AutoFilter handles, and all new fields and records will inherit the same formatting as the rest of the table.

- As you scroll down a table with many records, its headings remain visible onscreen (Figure 6–32):

---

[1] (Note: the term Table here is *not* to be confused with tables as they're understood in Word.)

	Country		Salesperson		OrderID		Order Amount		
729	USA		Davolio		10984		$1,809.75		
730	USA		Davolio		10992		$69.60		
731	USA		Fuller		10983		$720.90		
732	USA		Callahan		10987		$2,772.00		
733	USA		Davolio		10995		$1,196.00		
734	UK		Dodsworth		10951		$458.74		
735	USA		Fuller		10990		$4,288.85		
736	USA		Davolio		10991		$2,296.00		
737	USA		Leverling		10924		$1,835.70		
738	USA		Peacock		10927		$800.00		
739	USA		Leverling		10960		$265.35		
740	USA		Peacock		10966		$1,098.46		
741	USA		Fuller		10982		$1,014.00		
742	USA		Leverling		11003		$326.00		
743	USA		Fuller		10994		$940.50		
744	USA		Callahan		10977		$2,233.00		
745	USA		Leverling		10988		$3,574.80		
746	UK		King		10993		$4,895.44		

Figure 6—32. Heads up: Note the row numbers

- Perhaps most importantly, it enables you to install a *Total* row, which automatically *won't* be sorted.

Creating a Table

Remaking the database into a table is simple: continuing with our gradebook data, click anywhere in the data, click the **Insert** tab, and click the **Table** button in the **Tables** button group (or its keyboard equivalent, Ctrl-T). You'll see something like this (Figure 6–33):

Figure 6–33. *A table range, automatically identified. You can change its coordinates here, though.*

Note that the dialog box assumes your table-to-be has a header row; but the box has also made a more subtle decision. In fact, our gradebook data spans C9:*I20*, but as we see above, Excel has pulled up one row short, bounding the range at row *19*. That's because row 20 contains *formulas* and Excel wants to exclude if from the table as a result, thinking that the row doesn't contain standard data. In this case Excel is correct. (Note: You can also begin the table-making process by clicking the *Format at Table* down arrow in the *Styles* group on the Home tab.)

In any case, when you click OK you get (Figure 6–34):

Student ▾	1 ▾	2 ▾	3 ▾	4 ▾	5 ▾	Average ▾
Alice	67	96	67	100	85	83.0
Derek	82	89	45	93	67	75.2
Dorothy	73	70	93	65	93	78.8
Edith	81	48	52	75	76	66.4
George	90	67	84	59	77	75.4
Gordon	90	86	89	77	94	87.2
John	83	96	60	63	70	74.4
Mary	77	78	80	90	100	85.0
Paul	61	91	68	61	99	76.0
Ringo	56	80	79	82	77	74.8
Class Averages	76.0	80.1	71.7	76.5	83.8	

Figure 6–34. The database—now a table.

Using Table Styles

What is now a table exhibits Filter handles, a new format of Excel's choosing, and a *Table Tools* tab that stakes the top of the worksheet, right above the Design tab (Figure 6–35):

Figure 6–35. The Table Tools tab—rather alliterative, isn't it?

Click the tab and click one of the down arrows by *Table Styles* (Figure 6—36):

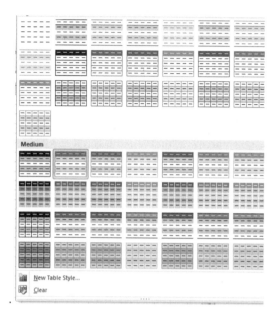

Figure 6–36. Table Styles: No shortage of options

Just click the style you prefer.

Adding a Total Row

If you want to add that Total row to the table, click **Total Row** in the **Table Style Options** button group. You'll see (Figure 6–37):

Student	1	2	3	4	5	Average
Alice	67	96	67	100	85	83.0
Derek	82	89	45	93	67	75.2
Dorothy	73	70	93	65	93	78.8
Edith	81	48	52	75	76	66.4
George	90	67	84	59	77	75.4
Gordon	90	86	89	77	94	87.2
John	83	96	60	63	70	74.4
Mary	77	78	80	90	100	85.0
Paul	61	91	68	61	99	76.0
Ringo	56	80	79	82	77	74.8
Total						776.2
Class Averages	76.0	80.1	71.7	76.5	83.8	

Figure 6–37. This just in: The table Total row

A few things happen here. The Total row has moved in *atop* Class Averages, because that latter row *is no longer part of the table.* If this looks messy and/or puzzling, you could delete the Class Averages data, or insert some rows between Total and Class Averages in order to separate the two, which is what we'll do. In addition, the data in the *last* table field—Averages—has been added, and only that field. But the function the table uses here isn't SUM, but one we've yet to introduce—*SUBTOTAL*, and it looks like this, as it appears in cell I2:

=SUBTOTAL(109,[Average])

Here, SUBTOTAL calculates data for a field—in this case Average, the name of the field on the far right of the table. The 109 refers to the particular *mathematical operation* being conducted on the range—which is the default operation, Sum. But click the down arrow by that cell and you'll see (Figure 6–38):

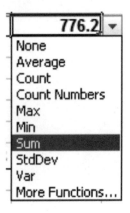

Figure 6–38. Calculation options for the Total row

You can click any of the possibilities above, and it will give SUBTOTAL a new code which carries out that operation instead. These are the SUBTOTAL codes representing each of the above operations, as they appear in the drop-down-menu sequence:

Average - 101
Count All - 102
Count (only cells containing) Numbers – 103
Max - 104
Min – 105
Sum – 109
Standard Deviation – 108
Variance – 110

In fact, the SUBTOTAL codes we see above sport an extra "1" because its codes are really 01, 02, etc. That first digit is still another code, instructing SUBTOTAL to ignore, and so not compute, any data on table rows *you* may have hidden via the Hide Rows command (but more importantly, the data on rows hidden by the AutoFilter *will* still be computed).

And if you click any cell in the Total row for any of the other fields, a similar drop-down arrow appears. Click, and you can select from the same options (in fact, you may want to select None for the Average field in our case—because Sum here is really just *adding* the test averages of the individual students, probably a bit of information you don't need. Note as well that the **More Functions...** option allows you to select *any of the* others in Excel's collection as well).

Examining the other Table Style Options

As for the other Table Style Options:

- When unchecked, *Header Row* actually *deletes* the header row, and doesn't redefine it as just another row of data.

- *Banded Rows* and *Banded Columns* color rows and/or columns with alternating colors, to heighten the clarity of the table data (Figure 6–39):

Student						Avera
Alice	67	96	67	100	85	83.00
Derek	82	89	45	93	67	75.20
Dorothy	73	70	93	65	93	78.80
Edith	81	48	52	75	76	66.40
George	90	67	84	59	77	75.40
Gordon	90	86	89	77	94	87.20
John	83	96	60	63	70	74.40
Mary	77	78	80	90	100	85.00
Paul	61	91	68	61	99	76.00
Ringo	56	80	79	82	77	74.80
Total						776.20

Figure 6–39. Banded rows—alternating row colors

Note that the banding motifs appear by default in many, but not all, Table Styles—and it is only when you select one of *these* that you can turn Banded Rows and Banded Columns on and off. Note as well that you *can't* conduct a Sort By Color with banded colors; that option only works with colors you actively select via a Conditional Format, or fill colors of your choosing.

- The First Column and Last Column options allow you to color those columns differently from the other table columns, should you need to emphasize these (Figure 6–40):

Student	1	2	3	4	5	Average
Alice	67	96	67	100	85	83.0
Derek	82	89	45	93	67	75.2
Dorothy	73	70	93	65	93	78.8
Edith	81	48	52	75	76	66.4
George	90	67	84	59	77	75.4
Gordon	90	86	89	77	94	87.2
John	83	96	60	63	70	74.4
Mary	77	78	80	90	100	85.0
Paul	61	91	68	61	99	76.0
Ringo	56	80	79	82	77	74.8
Total						776.2

Figure 6–40. Recoloring key data columns

Because our gradebook database has special information in those very columns—the student names and averages, respectively—you might then want to apply these options here. But note again that not every Table Style will let you use them.

If you turn left on the Table Tools ribbon, you'll wind up by the ***Resize Table*** command in the ***Properties*** button group (Figure 6–41):

Figure 6–41. Property management: The Table Properties button group

It's a rather curious command, enabling you to exclude rows from the table *without* deleting them. Instead, Resize Table places the unwanted rows on the *other side* of the Total Row, keeping them around even as they're no longer subject to table commands. Let's give it try.

1. ➤ Click anywhere in the gradebook data (the current formatting doesn't matter).

2. ➤ Click Resize Table. You'll see (Figure 6–42):

Figure 6–42. Try this out for size

3. For the sake of the illustration, change the row reference 20 to 17.

4. Click OK. You should see (Figure 6–43):

						Average
Alice	67	96	67	100	85	83.0
Derek	82	89	45	93	67	75.2
Dorothy	73	70	93	65	93	78.8
Edith	81	48	52	75	76	66.4
George	90	67	84	59	77	75.4
Gordon	90	86	89	77	94	87.2
John	83	96	60	63	70	74.4
Mary	77	78	80	90	100	85.0
Total						625.4
Paul	61	91	68	61	99	76.0
Ringo	56	80	79	82	77	74.8

Figure 6–43. Odd men out: Excluding two students via the resize table option

We see that Paul and Ringo have been tabled, so to speak—they're on the outside looking in, having been banished from the table, but not from the worksheet; and any mathematical activity in the Total row is recalculated to reflect the new table range. If however you click Resize Table again and enter the original table range of $C$9:$I$20, Paul and Ringo will return to their original positions and be incorporated back into the table. You may want to use Resize Table if you need to work with a subset of the original data, say, records with dates after January 1, 2010 (you'll have to sort the records by date first, though, so that the older ones appear at the bottom of the table and can be readily excluded by Resize Table).

■ **Note** also the **_Table Name:_** field in the Properties button group. It displays a default name for the table, which you change by typing a different one and then simply clicking elsewhere.

At the Risk of Repeating Yourself: The Remove Duplicates Option

One classic data entry bugaboo is the risk of entering the same name twice. Working with long, multiple lists of names—some of which you may have inherited from other sources—could well result in name duplication, and while you may know that the three John Does in your database are the same person, Excel won't.

Hence the **_Remove Duplicates_** table option in the Tools button group. It's a good one to know, provided you know exactly how it works. Note in addition that this feature also works on a range of data that has _not_ been submitted to the Insert Table command. For non-table ranges you can click:

Data Ribbon ➤ Remove Duplicates, on the Data Tools button.

The command searches for identical values or text in a particular table field or fields and if it finds any, _deletes_ all rows containing that value—_except for the first instance of that value,_ which it leaves in place. Thus if your table has data such as these (Figure 6–44):

Last Name ▼	First Name ▼
Jones	Ed
Walters	Gary
Jones	Grace
Albert	Ida
Troy	Helen

**Figure 6–44.** Not-quite-duplicate names

and you launch a Remove Duplicates search of the Last Name field, the row containing Grace Jones' record will be deleted—and that not may be what you had in mind, because Grace Jones is obviously not a mere duplicate of Ed Jones. She's a different person. What you'd presumably want to do then, is eliminate all duplicates of _Ed Jones_—and if that's your objective, you'd need to search for duplicates in _both_ the Last and First Name fields at the same time. So let's go with this example, and this simple collection of names, which contains an obvious duplicate record. In cells L14:N20, type these data, and execute the Insert Table command (Figure 6–45). The format you choose doesn't matter:

Last Name	First Name	Age
Jones	Ed	34
Walters	Gary	21
Jones	Ed	34
Albert	Ida	26
Troy	Helen	51
Jones	Grace	42

Figure 6–45. Broken record: Two Ed Joneses

You added the Age field, because there could well be two persons in the database named Ed Jones—with different ages. Then click anywhere in the table and click Remove Duplicates on the Tools Button group. You'll see (Figure 6–46):

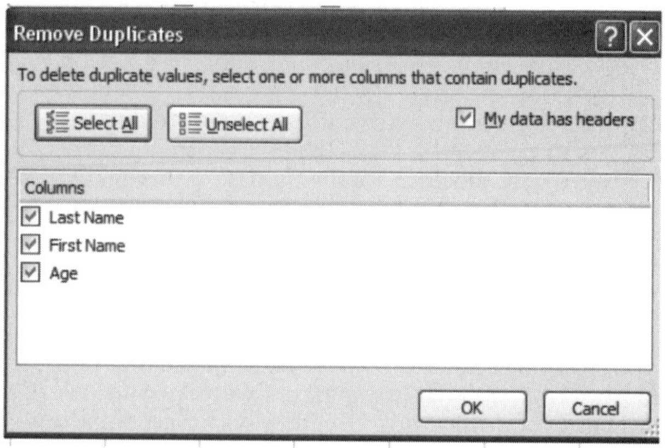

Figure 6–46. Duplication search criteria

Note that by default all three fields are checked, meaning: if we click OK, Excel will remove *only* those records which contain duplicate data in *all three fields*. It's clear in our table that the two records of Ed Jones are indeed identical across all three.

Click OK, and you'll see (Figure 6–47):

Figure 6–47. Results reported

OK—"1 duplicate values" isn't grammatically correct (let's not be too harsh—Bill Gates did drop out of Harvard, after all), but you get the idea. The second Ed Jones has been removed—but had Ed Jones Number 2 been say, 37 years old, he'd have remained in the table, because his *three* fields would no longer completely duplicate those of Ed Jones the First. And Grace Jones has been completely ignored by our duplicate removal, as she should be—because *only* her last name duplicates the other Joneses, and again, we required a match on all *three* fields. Thus if you really wanted the table to display just one record containing Jones, you'd click First Name and Age *off* in the Remove Duplicates dialog box, thus confining your search to duplicates in Last Name *only*—a less restrictive criterion.

Finally, to turn *off* the table's status as a table, should you want to do such a thing, click anywhere in the table and then click Table Tools ➤ *Convert to Range* on the Tools button group. A prompt appears, asking: "Do you want to convert the table to a normal range?" Clicking Yes turns off the AutoFilter, but leaves your current table formatting in place, along with the Total row and any SUBTOTAL calculations you've added (though it does subtly rewrite the SUBTOTAL formulas), by substituting the range being subtotaled (i.e., $I$10:$I$19) for the name of the field (i.e., Average) whose data are subject to the subtotal.

Data Validation: Improving Your Entrée to Data Entry

Whether you're an Excel guru or an Excel tyro, your worksheets are only as good as the quality of the data you post to them. The most elegant formulas and beauteous charts in all of Exceldom won't work if the data they crunch are erroneous, and Excel provides you with a collection of ways for preempting—though not completely preventing—miscues in data entry.

One such collection is warehoused in the *Data Validation* option, which you can access via the *Data* ➤ *Data Tools* ribbon group. Data Validation offers you an assortment of what are, for the most part, pretty simple ways to *restrict* the kinds of data you can enter in any range (no table required), and thus minimize the likelihood of entering the wrong numbers, or even the wrong text.

Using Data Validation

Let's demonstrate how Data Validation works with a simple introductory example. Suppose you need to enter state names as per their post office designations—that is, their two-lettered abbreviations.

1. Select any range and then click the Data Validation button. Its dialog box appears

2. Click the drop-down arrow by *Allow*. You'll see (Figure 6–48):

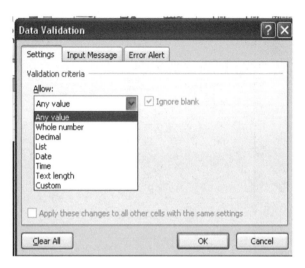

Figure 6–48. The Data Validation drop-down menu

3. Click Text length, and this set of fields appears (Figure 6–49):

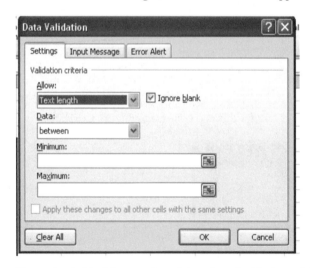

Figure 6–49. Limiting text length in selected cells. Sounds like Twitter.

4. Click the Data down arrow and a series of operators—greater than, less than, equal to, between, etc., appears.

5. Click on *equal to* (Figure 6–50):

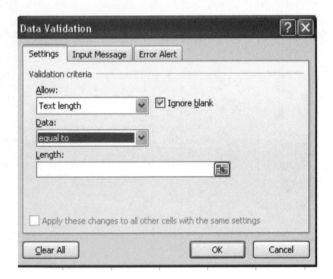

Figure 6–50. Rather taciturn: A two-character data entry limit

6. Enter 2 in the **Length** field.

7. Click OK.

What we've done here is specify a character-entry limit of 2 for any cell in the range we selected. That means you'll only be able to enter exactly 2 characters, no more and no less (and that rule *does* allow exactly two-digit numbers), in those cells—and that's what we want, since we need to insure that we enter the two-character state abbreviations only and be prevented from accidentally entering expressions of any other length. If, then, we inadvertently attempt to enter CAL for California in any cell in the range, we'll trigger this error message (Figure 6–51):

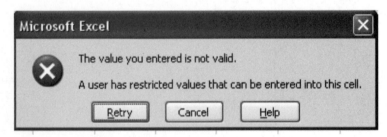

Figure 6–51. Nice try: Can't fool Data Validation!

because CAL is three characters. When we retry and type CA, the entry will be accepted.

That's what Data Validation does: enable the user to establish rules to prevent certain kinds of unwanted data entry. It *can't*, of course, prevent you from entering NY when you wanted to type AZ, because both expressions meet the two-character requirement here, but it will fend off CAL and C, for that matter.

230

Adding Data Entry Rules

The Data Validation Allow field lets you to install a data entry rule, with the same Data drop-down operators (greater than, equal to, etc.) for these data types:

- Any Value—which really institutes no restriction

- Whole number—allows you to restrict data entry via the operators to whole numbers alone, e.g., numbers between 10 and 20. Here you'd be able to enter 12 or 17, but *not* 17.6.

- Decimal—allowing you to restrict data entry via the operators that permit decimal entry. Thus if the rule restricted entry to values between 10 and 20, you'd be able to enter 12 and 17 *as well as* 17.6—but not 34 or 34.1, as both exceed 20.

- Date—allows you to restrict data entry via the operators to dates equaling a particular date, or to a dates falling between two dates, etc.

- Time—allows you to restrict data entry via the operators to times, such as between 10:00 and 12:00, etc.

- Text Length—as discussed.

There are two additional Data Validation Allow options, **List** and **Custom**. List is a rather neat feature, giving you the option to construct a drop-down menu of data entry choices.

To explain: suppose I want to be able to enter the names of any of my five salespersons down a range, say A1:A20, by selecting these from a drop-down menu.

1. First, enter the salesperson names in any range, e.g., P19:P23 (Figure 6–52):

Figure 6–52. These names will appear in your customized drop-down menu, or list.

2. Then select A1:A20.

3. Then click Data Validation ➤ Allow ➤ List. You'll see: (Figure 6–53):

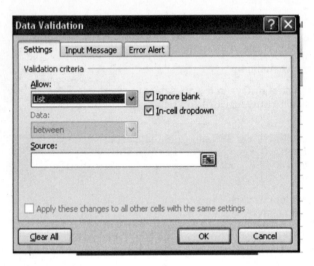

Figure 6–53. Menu venue: Where the drop-down list is constructed

1. In the Source field type or drag this range: P19:P23, the range containing the salesperson names to populate the drop-down menu.
2. Click OK.

Click on cell A1 and a drop-down arrow appears. Click it and you'll see (Figure 6–54):

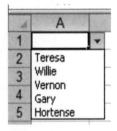

Figure 6–54. There's your list

Just click any name and it'll enter the cell. This, too, is an instance of Data Validation—because it serves as a means for restricting the data entry to the names in the drop-down. Try typing any other name in A1:A20, and you'll encounter the same error message we saw earlier. *Note*: you can *also* enter the salesperson names *directly* in the Source Field, each name separated by a comma. In this way, too, the names will populate the drop-down menu. The ***Ignore Blank*** option, the source of considerable confusion on Internet group posts, here means: if you've entered a Source range by its *range name* (if it has one), and some of the cells in that range are blank, leaving Ignore blank on means you'll still be able to enter data that *isn't* in the Source range list. Turning Ignore blank off here *will* obstruct any data not listed in the Source range. Thus if your list looks like this (Figure 6—55):

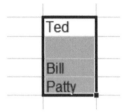

Figure 6–55. Blank look: A list with empty, blank rows

the resulting drop-down list will display that blank space, and you *won't* be able to enter names other than the ones you see in the list. Leave Ignore blank on, and you *will* be able to. It's a rather strange option.

The Custom option allows you to establish a data entry rule based on a *formula*. For example, if you're grading an exam for which you've established a highest possible grade of 50, and you want to prevent yourself from absent-mindedly entering higher scores in student records, you can:

1. Enter the 50 in a cell, say A6.

2. Then, assuming you're entering the grades in cells B5:B20, select that range, making sure the range remains selected.

3. Then click Data Validation ➤ Data Validation ➤ Settings ➤ Custom.

4. Make sure the current cell in the selected range is B5 (by way of review, that's the cell in white).

5. Type =B5=A$6 in the Formula field (Figure 6–56):

Figure 6–56. Customizing a data validation rule

6. Click OK.

What this formula does is restrict the data entry in B5:B20 to a value no greater than the number you've posted in A6, in this case 50. Change that highest-possible-grade value in A6, and your data entry limit for B5:B20 changes accordingly. The formula requires the dollar sign before the 6 in A6, because even though the formula is initially written in cell B5, because you've selected the range B5:B20, Data Validation *copies* this formula to the other cells in the range; and because of relative cell referencing, the A6 would otherwise revert to A7, A8, A9, etc. down the range. But we need to hold to A6 throughout the range—because that's where the grade value is stored.

Adding an Input Message

Data Validation also allows you to fashion a prompt, called an ***Input Message***, which appears over the cell in which you're about to enter data, informing the user what sort of data can be entered in the cell as per your data validation rule. To demonstrate by returning to the two-character state name data validation rule, we can:

1. Select any range, say H3:H40. Leave the range selected.

2. Click Data Validation ➤ Data Validation ➤ Allow ➤ Text Length ➤ Data and select "equal to" on the drop-down menu.

3. Enter 2 in the Length field.

4. Click the Input Message tab.

5. In the Title field enter 2 Characters, Please (or any suitable title.)

6. In the Input Message field, type: You Must Enter a Two-Character State Abbreviation.

7. Click OK.

Rest your mouse over any cell in the H3:H40 range. You should see (Figure 6–57):

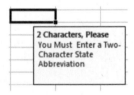

Figure 6–57. An Input Message

Using the Error Alert Option

And there's another option you can implement with Data Validation, which enables you to modify the restrictions on data entry in cells—the ***Error Alert*** option. Error Alert does more than simply alert the user about various validations; it also lets you notify the user about a restriction—and then *allows the restricted data to be entered anyway.*

1. Select cells H3:H40 again, and select Data Validation ➤ Data Validation ➤ Error Alert.

2. You'll see a drop-Down menu entitled *Style* that stores three options. The first is *Stop*, the Data Validation default whose error message is the one we've already seen. The second is called *Warning*. Select it and another Title/Error Message set of fields appears, enabling you to type whatever customized prompts you wish. But when selected, Warning *allows* the user to go ahead and enter data even if it violates the data validation rule. If I choose the Warning option for range H3:H40, and then type CAL in H3, this default message appears (Figure 6–58):

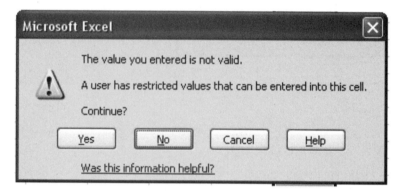

Figure 6–58. Don't say we didn't warn you: Overriding the restriction, if you wish

3. If I click Yes, CAL will be accepted anyway.

4. The third prompt, *Information*, works just slightly differently. It too allows you to proceed with data entry that violates the data validation rule, but its default message simply notifies the user of the violation, *without* asking if he/she wants to continue. Here clicking OK *automatically* accepts the data (Figure 6–59):

Figure 6–59. An information message prompt: Not as informative as the previous warning

Again, all three Error Alert possibilities allow you to customize your own prompts, affording you the opportunity to indulge in some gentle and prudent office humor, such as this (Figure 6–60):

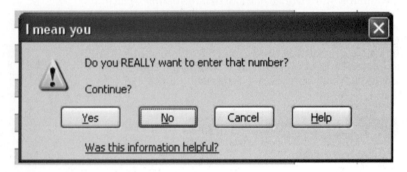

Figure 6–60. Rhetorical question

Use with caution, needless to say.

Adding a Validation Rule to Existing Data

The Data Validation command also lets you institute a validation rule on data you've *already* entered. That sounds like an odd sequence of events, but it has the effect of allowing you to *see* exactly which existing data don't comply with that rule, even if it's issued after the fact. In reality, this option is a way to learn which existing data do and don't meet a specified condition, without rejecting any of the data. To demonstrate, we'll try a simple example.

- Select cells A1:A5.

- Type these numbers in the respective cells: 34, 56, 78, 12, 102.

- Select the range, and click Data Validation ➤ Data Validation ➤ Settings.

- Select Whole Number in the Allow field, and "less than" in Data.

- Enter 60 in the Maximum field.

- Click OK.

- Then click Data Validation ➤ *Circle Invalid Data*. You should see (Figure 6–61):

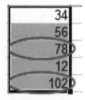

Figurae 6–61. Red pencil: Highlighting invalid data

True, they're not circles, they're ovals—but the point is made. Data Validation pinpoints the values that violate the less-than-60 rule we established, but without expelling or deleting those data (it's also true, by the way, that one could design a Conditional Format that does something very similar—say, color all cells red whose values exceed 60). To turn the error indicators off, select the range in question, and click Data Validation ➤ *Clear Validation Circles*.

Finally, if you want to turn any Data Validation rule off:

- Select the range in question.

- Click Data ➤ Data Validation ➤ Click *any* tab, and click ➤ *Clear All*.

- Click OK. (Figure 6–62)

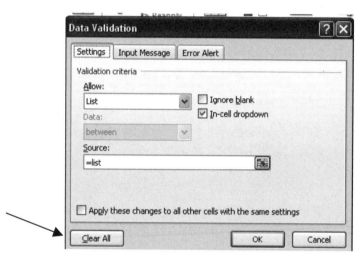

Figure 6–62. *A real turn-off: Clearing Data Validation rules*

All refers to any and all rules you may have introduced to that range, not the entire worksheet.

In Conclusion…

Data is a hopelessly broad term, but working with data organized in adjacent rows and columns is central to the spreadsheet enterprise, if that isn't too high-sounding. Knowing how to sort records and pull out—and even eliminate—records from the data on the basis of this or that criterion are attainments you'll want to be able to list in your Excel skill set, and don't assume these skills are universally shared.

Tables turn your databases into easy-to-sort-and-filter batches of records, and while they're not the last word on the subject (as we'll see), they do very useful work—and speedily.

Data validation options go a long way towards insuring your data's integrity, including nifty data entry drop-down menus and the like.

Good things to know—and there's more to come.

CHAPTER 7

■■■

Working With Multiple Sheets

A worksheet is a spacious place–16 billion or so cells at your disposal, each one accessible in a flash at the tap of a keyboard. The Name Box is your Excel—based satnav; type any address therein and the Box doesn't tell you how to get there—it *takes* you there, in a hot second.

But in spite all of that digital terra firma and ease of navigation, Excel gives you more, three worksheets by default, so you won't have to feel deprived—not with those 48 billion cells at the ready. But if even you don't need 48 billion cells, you might need three—or more—worksheets. Because while it's true that virtually all of the work you need to do in a workbook could be accommodated by *one* worksheet, sometimes it's the way data are *organized* in a workbook that make the multi-sheet approach a good idea, apart from any need for space.

For example, you may want to draw up a chart, or several charts, in a workbook, and keep them at arm's length from the data that gave rise to them (even though by default Excel places a chart on the same sheet as the contributing data, a decision you may want to override. However, Excel *does* assign pivot tables to a new sheet by default, as you'll see in the next chapter). That's a presentational decision, which could be motivated by a wish not to clutter the same sheet with a profusion of numbers and graphic objects. Or you may have a small business in which you want to earmark similarly-structured worksheets for each of your employees, with the same kinds of information about each assigned to the same cells on each sheet. (Remember that each worksheet has the same set of cell address—they all have an A45 or a LR5421, for example. How these addresses can thus be distinguished from one another is coming up soon.) Or you may want to store very different kinds of tables and the like on different sheets, should you need to dramatically redesign one of them and not impact the others. Or put more generally, your workbook may simply look better by placing disparate data in different sheets. More subtly, keeping a large collection of data on the same sheet could entail lots of scrolling up, down, and across the sheet, and as a result it might simply be easier to farm out some data to the upper rows of different sheets.

And even if you do disperse the data across several sheets, you can write formulas that reference cells on different sheets at the same time, a kind of three-dimensional way of working.

And in reality, I've badly undersold Excel's worksheet capabilities. If you wish, you can *add* worksheets to a workbook if events require, though on the other hand you can also delete two of the default three sheets, if you want to downsize your workbook. Finally, if your workbook needs are large, you can change Excel's default worksheet allotment, so that every new workbook starts you off with say, five new sheets.

In fact there's more to all this. Even before you begin to add more worksheets to your workbook, you can in effect enlarge the sheets you *already* have—by adding columns, rows, and even a few cells to existing sheets. Let's start by looking at this subject.

Adding To Sheets—Inserting Rows, Columns and Cells

Having the capability to add rows, columns, and cells raises the obvious question: if you have all those billions of cells to begin with, why would you need to supplement them with even more? The answer—or at least the standard answer—is that after you've constructed a table, for instance, you may decide you need an extra field's worth of data—and that decision means you'll have to introduce a new column into the table. And if you want that column to appear *between* two columns already in place, you'll need to insert another one. If, on the other hand, you've entered data all over the worksheet and you'd like to see them a bit closer to one another, you may want to delete a column or two.

The means for adding and deleting columns or rows are pretty easy (although as usual, there's more than one way. We're demonstrating the most straightforward approach here). But before we demonstrate how it's done, we need to anticipate and answer a big question—namely, what happens to cell references when additions or deletions are carried out?

For example, suppose you've written this formula in cell H3:

=AVERAGE(B17:B32)

If you delete any of columns between C and H, will the cells referred to in that expression change? After all, delete one such column and the formula now appears in cell G3–and as a result, will the formula read

=AVERAGE(A17:A32) ?

The answer is no. When you add or delete rows or columns, Excel *maintains* the existing cell references that might otherwise be impacted by the additions or deletions, so not to worry. *But* keep in mind that if you insert a row or column such that cells *contributing* to a formula are repositioned, the formula *will* rewrite itself correspondingly. If a column is added to the left of the B column in the first example above, the formula will now read

=AVERAGE(C17:C32)

Because the values being added are now in column C.

Inserting a Column

To go ahead and insert a column, just click anywhere in the column to the *right* of where you want the new one to be inserted. Thus if you want to insert a column between H and I, click any cell in I. Then click Home ➤ *Cells* button group ➤ *Insert* ➤ *Insert Sheet Columns* (Figure 7–1):

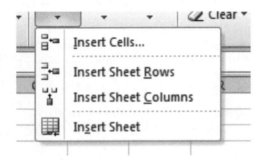

Figure 7–1. Where to insert a column or a row

The new column will slide into place, and will claim the column letter I. The original column I will move to the right, and become J, and so on. If you want to insert multiple columns, just drag across as many consecutive columns as you wish and execute the above commands. You'll insert as many columns as you've selected—and they'll appear to the *right* of the selection. Thus if you select cells R3:S3 and click Insert Sheet Columns, R and S will become T and U—because each will have moved two columns rightward.

Inserting a Row

The procedure for inserting rows is basically identical. Click in the row *beneath which* you want to insert a new one and click the above commands, culminating with **Insert Sheet Rows** instead. Thus if you click in row 17, you'll insert a new row above the original 17— which becomes the "new" row 17, whilst the original row 17 is now bumped to 18. To insert multiple rows select as many rows as you wish to insert.

Deleting Rows and Columns

To delete rows or columns, click anywhere in the column or columns you wish to delete and click Home ➤ Cells button group ➤ *Delete* ➤ **Delete Sheet Rows** or *Columns*. (Yes, you can Undo these commands). Just keep in mind that if you delete the cells whose data contribute to a formula, that formula will suddenly have nothing to work with—and instead of a result, you'll be left with an error message in the cell instead.

Inserting and Deleting Cells

You can also insert and delete selected *cells,* not just entire rows and columns, a possibility which is curiously piecemeal. If you click in cell A12 and carry out the Insert Cells command, you'll push A12 down a row–but you *won't* push down row 12 in its *entirety.* Only the A column will be affected by the command. Any data in cell B12 will remain there, for example.

To insert or delete cells, click in the cell or cells in question and click either the Insert or Delete buttons we described in the previous to command sequences, but click *Insert Cells…* or *Delete Cells…* instead. Click Insert Cells and you'll see (Figure 7–2):

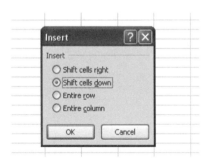

Figure 7–2. Where to insert selected cells

Click OK. If you select **Shift cells right,** all the cells to the right of the cell(s) in which you click will move in that direction—but *not* the cells to their left. The other two options you see—**Entire row** and

Entire column—are nothing but alternatives to the Insert Row and Columns commands we've already described.

To delete selected cells, click in the cells you wish to delete and click Delete Cells... in the Cells button group (Figure7–3).

Figure 7–3. Going in reverse: where to delete selected cells.

Note here that deleted cells move the remaining cells that are to their right to the *left*, and cells beneath them will be shifted *up*.

Hiding Rows and Columns—and Getting them Back

You can also hide rows and columns—not so much in order to maintain the secrecy of your data, but to improve the appearance of a spreadsheet; perhaps columns with complex formulas don't need to be seen—but if you *do* hide them, all the data posted there remain active, and any cell references to them remain in force, too.

To start hiding, click on any cell or cells in a column or row you wish to hide and click Home ➤ Cells button group ➤ *Format* ➤ *Hide & Unhide* ➤ *Hide Rows* or *Hide Columns* (Figure 7–4):

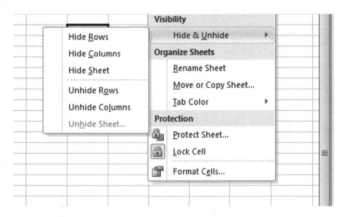

Figure 7–4. Outta sight: where to start hiding rows or columns

Click and the rows or columns will disappear, as will the column letters and/or row numbers of the hidden items. To hide several rows or columns at the same time, just drag across those columns or drag down those rows, leave that selection in place, and click the commands you see in 7–4.

Now sooner or later you may want to reveal these clandestine areas of the workbook—and to do so you need to select rows or columns on *either side* of the hidden ones. For example, if the K column is hidden, just drag across any row in the J and L columns (e.g., J23:L23), leave that selection in place, and click the command sequence as per Figure 7–4—only here you'll click either **Unhide Rows**, or in our case **Unhide Columns**.

Now on to multiple worksheets, because extra space on your single worksheet may not be what you want.

Multiple Worksheet Basics

As you can see, the three start-off worksheets that stock an Excel workbook share the same first name—Sheet1, Sheet2, and Sheet3 (you move between worksheets simply by clicking the tab of the sheet you want to access, or by utilizing these keyboard equivalents: Ctrl+Pg Dn to advance to the next sheet on the right; Ctrl+Pg Up to the next sheet to your left). But as with file names, Sheet1, etc. are default identities which can be changed as your needs require. As a result, you might very well want to rename any or all of these, and it's easy to do so. To rename a worksheet:

- Right-click the tab of the sheet you want to rename. Click Rename on the shortcut menu (Figure 7–5):

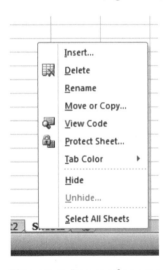

Figure 7–5. By any other name..where to rename a worksheet

- Since the current tab is selected, just type the new name, and press Enter.

You can also rename the sheet by double-clicking the sheet tab in question, which also selects the tab. Type the new name and press Enter. You're allotted 31 characters per name.

Inserting a New Worksheet

Inserting a new worksheet is most easy, too. Just:

- Right-click the sheet to the *right* of which you want to insert the sheet. You'll see again (Figure 7–6):

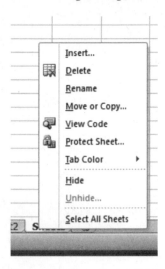

Figure 7–6. One way in which to insert a new worksheet

- Click *Insert...*.In the Insert dialog box. The new worksheet will be selected by default.

Click OK. The new sheet appears, bearing the default name Sheet4, if it's the first new sheet you've inserted. And there's a still easier way to insert a new sheet. Click the *Insert Worksheet* button to the immediate right of the worksheet tabs (Figure 7–7):

Figure 7–7. And here's another

Note the keyboard equivalent, too—Shift-F11. Clicking Insert Worksheet inserts a new sheet to the immediate right of the last sheet. It's the swiftest way to introduce a new sheet, but because it automatically installs the sheet at the end of the worksheet queue, you may decide you want to reposition the new sheet somewhere else.

Deleting an existing sheet entails right-clicking a sheet tab, then clicking Delete, and if it's empty, the sheet simply disappears. If the sheet contains data, this message materializes on screen (Figure 7–8):

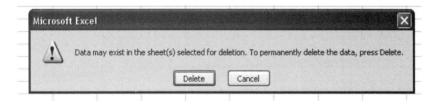

Figure 7–8. In case you need to rethink a worksheet deletion

Note that prompt. The word "permanently" means that if you click Delete, the sheet (and not just its data, in spite of what the prompt states) will not be retrievable via the Undo command. As a result, if you've accidently deleted a sheet you still need, you may have to resort to the classic close-the-file-without-saving-it technique. Don't say you weren't warned.

Busting a (Sheet) Move

To continue our medley of right-click options: If you want to move or copy a sheet, either within the existing workbook or to another open workbook, or sheets (we'll soon see how to select multiple sheets), right-click the relevant sheet tab, and select *Move or Copy...*.You'll see this dialog box (Figure 7–9):

Figure 7–9. Peripatetic worksheet: Where to move or copy a worksheet to another book.

As you see, you'll need to click on the name of the sheet *before* which you want the sheet to be moved. Note here that, by default, the *To book:* field names the workbook in which the sheet is currently positioned. If you want to move or copy the sheet to a different book, click the down arrow by "To book" to view the names of other open workbooks. Alternatively, you can click *(move to end)*, whereupon the sheet will be resituated at the end of the sheet collection, no matter how many sheets you currently have on hand in the workbook. Then click OK.

Note that you can copy the sheet(s) to a different *open* workbook, too. ***Clicking Create a copy*** will do just that, replicating the sheet (including all its data) and placing it in the first position among the sheets (though obviously you can go ahead and move it). Copying a sheet coins a new sheet name based on the copied sheet, e.g., Sheet 2 (2).

■ **Tip** You can also move a sheet by clicking the sheet tab (left button, this time), dragging it to its new position among the tabs, and releasing the mouse when you've reached your destination. A small page icon will accompany you as your drag, letting you know that sheet move is in progress.

And you can also recolor the sheet tab. Right-click the tab, select ***Tab Color,*** and select your hue from the resulting color selection. (Note: Your new color won't actually appear in the tab until you click on a different tab.)

Hiding Worksheets

You can also *hide* entire worksheets, raising the obvious question as to why you'd want to. The principal reason isn't a desire to conceal the sheet from the dark intentions of industrial spies, covetous colleagues, or assorted other bad guys, because hidden worksheets can be revealed easily (there are Visual Basic programming means for securing the sheet with a password, though). Rather, you may want to hide a sheet because it contains complex formulas you'd rather not overwrite, or because all those calculations are unsightly (you can also *protect* all or part of a worksheet for much the same reasons, but protection options leave the sheet in view. More on protection a bit later.) Keep in mind that hidden worksheets remain active; that is, all their data and formulas continue to be available in the workbook, and can still be referenced by formulas in the visible sheets.

To hide a worksheet, right-click the sheet you want to hide and select ***Hide Worksheet***. That's all. You can also execute the Hide command by clicking on the Home tab ➤ Cells in the Format button group ➤ Hide & Unhide ➤ ***Hide Sheet*** (I suspect you'll find the first approach just a bit more efficient). Note as well that you can carry out the Move or Copy, Rename, or Tab Color change commands via the Format button, too. To reveal a hidden sheet or sheets—say we've hidden Sheet 3—right-click anywhere among the still-visible worksheet tabs and click ***Unhide*** (rather an inelegant verb, but Excel seems to be fond of it). You'll see (Figure 7–10):

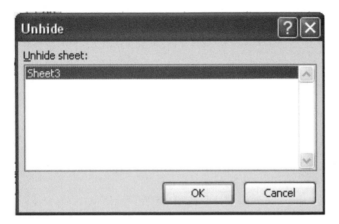

Figure 7–10. Out of hiding: Where to unhide a sheet

Click OK, and the sheet reappears.

Grouping Worksheets

You can also *group* several worksheets, meaning that you can select them simultaneously. Why bother? Because by doing so, any data entry or formatting change you make in a range in one grouped sheet will be reproduced in precisely the same range in all the *other* grouped sheets, affording you a highly efficient way to achieve the same data arrangement and look across sheets. Thus if you enter a series of header rows in one grouped sheet—say, Name, Address, and Age—all those entries will appear in the same addresses on the other sheets.

To group sheets, click on the first one you want to group. You're then handed two group options: If you want to group non-adjacent sheets in a workbook, press Ctrl, leave that key down, and then click on the other sheets you want to group. Then release Ctrl. If you want to group adjacent sheets, click on the first tab you wish to group, then press Shift, leave that key down, and click on the *last* in the series of sheet tabs. To select *all* the sheets in the workbook, you can right-click any sheet tab and click **b**.

To demonstrate, open a new blank workbook and click the tab of Sheet1. Press Shift and at the same time click the Sheet3 tab (yes; you could have also clicked Select All Sheets, as per the instructions in the last paragraph). All three tabs should appear white (or at least whiter than usual, in the event you've colored any tabs), with the tab text "Sheet 1" appearing in boldface, indicating it is the active sheet. Then in cell A1 type Name, then Address and Age in cells B1 and C1, respectively. Then click Sheets 2 and 3—and you'll see the same data in the same cells. To deselect, or ungroup, the sheets, right-click any tab and click ***Ungroup Sheets*** (another dorky verb), or click on any sheet that is not currently grouped.

Far-Flung Formulas: Working with Multi-Sheet Cell References

Now what about those multi-sheet cell references? As stated earlier, you can write formulas in which cells in different worksheets contribute to that formula result. For example, if you allocate a separate worksheet to each of three employees and enter their salary in the same cell on each sheet—say cell

A7—you can write a sum formula, anywhere, on any sheet, which totals the three salaries. (And in fact the salaries don't have to be entered in the same cell address on the respective sheets. They can be situated in any cells.)

Doing a Multi-sheet Calculation

But let's start with a simpler case—you want to add two numbers on different sheets:

1. On Sheet 1 type 56 in cell D12.

2. On Sheet 2 enter 48 in cell B3. (Remember that the formula referencing these two cells can be written on any sheet—even Sheet 3, but we'll enter ther formula on Sheet 1.)

3. Click back on Sheet 1, onto cell A21. Once there, type the usual, and necessary, = sign.

4. Click on cell D12, the cell in Sheet 1 containing 56. You'll see:

=D12

Nothing new so far. Then:

5. Type the + sign, simply because we're about to add the contents of two cells.

6. Click the Sheet 2 tab, and click on cell B3. You'll see (Figure 7–11):

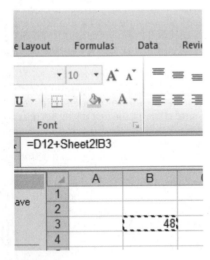

Figure 7–11. *Writing a formula in Sheet1, including a cell in Sheet2*

Note the budding expression in the formula bar: =D12+Sheet2!B3. By clicking on cell B3, the formula supplements that cell reference with the Sheet2! prefix, and why? Because, remember—we're actually writing this formula in cell A21 on *Sheet 1*, and so we need to indicate *which* cell B3 we're now referring to. After all, that cell could be in Sheet 1, Sheet 2, or Sheet 3—or any other sheet we might have inserted into the workbook. As a result, Sheet2! is Excel's way of notifying the formula that we want to call upon the B3 in *Sheet*2. Then press Enter, and we're snapped back to Sheet1, and the answer—104. And as with any Excel formula, its result will automatically recalculate, should either of its two contributing values—the 56 and the 48—be changed.

Now you may want to know why Sheet2! is attached to the second of the two cell references in the formula, but nothing like it accompanies the first. That's because the first cell reference–D12—appears in the *same sheet as the one in which the formula was written*, and Excel assumes, by default, that unless the user indicates something to the contrary, all the cell references in a formula *and* the formula itself emanate from the same sheet—and after all, isn't that usually the case?

Now had we added these two numbers in a formula composed in *Sheet3* instead—the sheet that contains *neither* of the values we wanted to add—we would have clicked in a cell on Sheet3, typed =, and then clicked on the two cells in Sheet1 and Sheet2 respectively. The formula would in this case have looked like this:

$$=Sheet1!D12+Sheet2!B3$$

See why? In this case *neither* cell shares its worksheet location with that of the formula itself, and so Excel needs to specify the worksheets on which *both* cells are positioned.

So that's the general approach to multi-sheet cell references in a formula—enter the = sign and the mathematical operation (or function) you wish to perform, and then click on the sheet and the cell(s) on that sheet you wish to incorporate into the expression. And if you need to reference a range of cells from another worksheet, you can just type = in your current destination cell, click on the first cell in the range on the sheet from which you wish to copy, then drag the appropriate range length, and press Enter. All those cells from the source worksheet are now referenced here, because they'll *all* be accompanied by the Sheet1, Sheet2, etc., identifier.

Now here's a neat variation on that theme. Suppose you want to add a group of cells, all of which have the *same address* in a collection of different worksheets—for example, values in the cell A3 in Sheets 1, 2, and 3. Let's try it:

- In those three cells, enter 86, 72, and 4.

- In cell C19 on Sheet1, enter =SUM(.

- Then click on cell A3 in Sheet1, hold down the Shift key, and click on the Sheet3 tab.

You should see this in the formula bar:

$$=SUM('Sheet1:Sheet3!'A3)$$

Press Enter, and your answer—162—flashes into the cell (note you don't have to type the close parentheses. Pressing Enter automatically supplies it). With this technique, Excel automatically references the same cell in all the selected sheets—and by tapping the Shift key we've really grouped all three sheets (this method works with any Excel function, not just SUM. In fact, once you press Shift and click on the last of the sheets you want to reference, you can go ahead and drag any range you want. That range, with precisely the same coordinates, will be selected on all the sheets, and all will be calculated into the formula. Thus:

$$=AVERAGE('Sheet1:Sheet3!'A6:B14)$$

will calculate the average of all the values in the A6:A14 ranges on the three sheets.

Note in addition that a named range on one worksheet can be directly referenced on any other worksheet, without any concern for relative cell reference complications (note: this assumes the range's scope is the Workbook, which is the default in any case. See the Appendix on range names.) Understand a key point here-that the cell coordinates of a named range don't change—they're treated as absolute references (a point elaborated in the appendix) by default. Thus you can write:

$$=MAX(Scores)$$

on Sheet1, even if the range Scores is on Sheet2.

Extending Your Reach: Referring to Cells in Different Workbooks

But there's still another possibility: you can even reference cells in your formulas that come from other *workbooks,* that is, completely different Excel files. It's possible you'll need to calculate some bottom-line total for sales or budget data assigned to different workbooks, and have it all distilled into just one workbook; and that sort of task is eminently doable once the relevant cells are referenced. True, you'll want to proceed with care here, because if you email someone such a workbook—one containing cell references to data in *another* workbook—and you don't send along the *latter* workbook as well, your data will be missing something.

The way to go about referencing, or linking, data across workbooks is actually pretty easy, and similar to the method we described above for referencing cells across worksheets in the same workbook. Let's try this:

1. Open two new workbooks, and save one as Link, the other as Link2.

2. In cell G13 in Link type 65. In cell I2 in Link2 type 17. Now we're going to try and add the two numbers (needless to say, you can add many more than two, and you can link ranges as well this way).

3. Remaining in Link2, type =I2+ in cell A1.

4. Click on Link, and simply click cell G13. You'll see (Figure 7–12):

=I2+[link.xlsx]Sheet1!$G$13

D	E	F	G
			65

Figure 7–12. Note the more elaborate cell reference, pointing to a different worksheet in a different workbook

5. Then press Enter. The answer appears.

Note the syntax of the formula we've just written. Because we're working with cells in two different workbooks, Excel needs to specify two things: the *workbook* in which the linked cell(s) is located, as well as the *worksheet*, too. The name in brackets—[link.xslx]—obviously points to the workbook. Note as well that it's the cell that *isn't* in the same workbook as the formula that needs all these specifications, and note also that it's written with dollar signs, signifying an absolute reference. That's because if you copy the formula down a column, for example, Excel assumes you want all the copied formulas to reference the same cell in that other workbook.

Keep in mind that if you currently have *only* the workbook open that contains the *linked* cell and you change its data—and then *later* open the workbook containing the formula—the formula *will* recalculate automatically. And by the same token, let's say you change the data in the linked cell, close it and save it, thus leaving neither workbook open. When you open the formula-bearing workbook, it will likewise recalculate. (Note: If you *move* one of the workbooks to a different folder, the current link will be severed and will have to be reinstituted, if that's what you want, requiring a fairly messy repair job. An *Edit Link* dialog box appears, asking you to supply the new location of the moved workbook.) In sum, working with cell references can be a bit dicey, and should be used frugally. Apart from the moving-folder issue, tracking the cell references that contribute to your results can be daunting, particularly if you need to analyze a mistake in a formula.

The Watch Window—Spying On Your Own Data

I've said it before, and I'll say it again: workbooks are vast. You may have formulas scattered all across its worksheets, or even in far flung cells on the same sheet. And what if you've written a formula referencing cells in very different places on the workbook, such that when you changed the data in one such cell you could no longer see the new formula result on screen, because you've scrolled too far away? Well, you can always keep that result in your sights with the *Watch Window* option, located in the *Formula Auditing* button group in the *Formulas* tab. Let's try a very simple illustration, which should prove its point. Just watch.

Type 71 in cell D18 on Sheet1. Then type 21 in cell A2 in Sheet2. Return to Sheet1, and write the following formula in E17:

$$=D18+Sheet2!A2$$

Answer: 92. OK—been there, done that, got the t-shirt. But now click back onto Sheet2, and click Formulas ➤ Watch Window. You'll see (Figure 7–13):

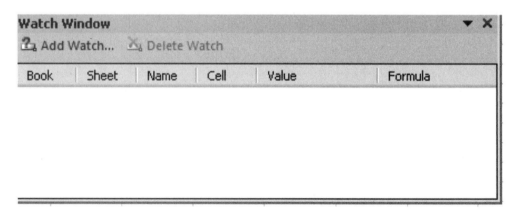

Figure 7–13. Opaque window—watching designated cells

Then click **Add Watch....** You'll see something like this (Figure 7–14):

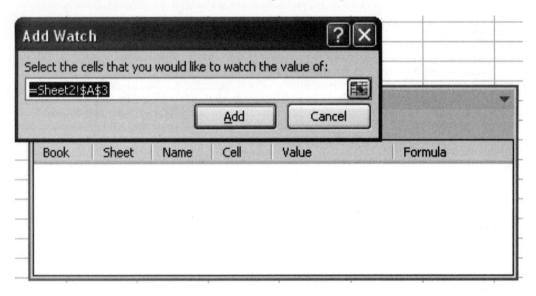

Figure 7–14. *Watch this*

I say "something like this," because the cell reference you actually see right now depends on the last cell you clicked on Sheet2, because that's where we are right now. But we want to track the current value of the formula in E17 on Sheet1, so just click that cell, and that reference should appear in the Add Watch dialog box. (Note: The dialog box asks you to click the cells you wish to watch, suggesting you could select a range. If you do, each cell in the range appears in the Watch Window, along with its value.) Then Click **Add**. You should see (Figure 7–15):

Book	Sheet	Name	Cell	Value	Formula
Book3	Sheet1		E17	92	=D18+Sheet2!A2

Figure 7–15. *The current result for cell E17 in Book3, Sheet1*

Note the dialog box records the workbook name as well as the sheet in which our watched cell is positioned; that tells you that if you have more than one workbook open at the same time, you can watch cells in any and all of them. The **Name** column, currently blank, is reserved for any range name you may have assigned a range you're watching (See Appendix XX). More obviously, the cell address and *current value* in the cell is recorded, along with the formula the cell is housing. Remember that we've clicked on Sheet2; so type 93 in cell A2, the cell on this sheet that is contributing to our formula. The Watch Window experiences a change in its **Value** column to 164—reflecting the new total in the formula in E17 on Sheet1—which we can't actually see right now. That's the point; the Watch Window keeps us posted of changes in the values of cells that, at the moment, aren't visually available to us. To turn off the Watch Window, just click the standard X in the window's upper-right corner. The Watch Window isn't remembered by the saved workbook. It has to be reconstructed if you want to use it again with a reopened workbook.

Protect Your Cells From Unwanted Intruders—Even Yourself

You'll recall that we earlier described how you can hide worksheets from view—an option that surely has its advantages, because the data on that reclusive sheet are gone but not forgotten. You can still refer to the data in formulas and the like, even as the sheet stays out of harm's way. But there's an obvious downside here: the sheet is…hidden, and while you may enjoy the security that worksheet invisibility affords, you may want to have your cake and eat it too—you may want to be able to view your worksheet data even as you fend off the errant mouse clicks that could obliterate your finely-tuned, guru-worthy formulas. Protecting your worksheets—either all or in part, by protecting just some of its cells—is the way to achieve those ends, and the how-tos are pretty simple and reasonably secure, if just a mite quirky.

When you protect a worksheet you can continue to see the sheet and its data, but once the protection is in force you won't be able to enter any additional data in its cells. You *will*, however, be able to view the underlying formulas in cells, and you will be able to *copy* the data you see in protected sheets. At least, that's how the default protection settings work. You can, however, also opt to hide formulas in their cells via protection. And in addition to protecting individual worksheets you can protect workbooks in their entirety (with different consequences, as we'll see), or protect just *selected* cells in a worksheet instead.

Protecting a Sheet

To protect a sheet, click in any cell, then you can either click:
Home tab ➤ Format button (in the Cells button group) ➤ **Protection** ➤ **Protect Sheet…** or
Review tab ➤ **Protect Sheet** in the Changes button group. Either way, you'll see (Figure 7—16):

Figure 7–16. The Protect Sheet dialog box

If you click OK, the sheet will revert to protected status, with the default selections you see checked above put in place. And what do those selections mean? ***Select locked cells*** and ***Select unlocked cells*** mean that you'll be allowed to *click* on any cell in the worksheet—but you won't be able to enter any data in it. (It *does* mean, however, that you'll still be able to see any underlying formulas in any cells.) And what's a *locked* cell? I was afraid you'd ask that question. For starters, what it means is that if you check both of the above default options *off*, you won't even be able to *click* on any worksheet cell. And if you click only Select locked cells *off*, you'll be able to click on unlocked cells *only*.

Locking Cells

But I still haven't defined ***locked*** cells—so here goes. By default, turning on worksheet protection locks *all* of a worksheet's cells. But if you want to able to enter data in just *some* cells and leave the remainder of the sheet protected, you have to inform Excel about this intention *before* you turn protection on (I told you it was quirky). If that's what you want to do—that is, be able to enter data in some cells only—then before turning protection on, *first* select those cells you want to leave available for data entry, and then click either the Home tab ➤ the Dialog Box Launcher in the Font button group, or Home tab ➤ Format in the Cells button group ➤ Format Cells… . You'll be brought to this dialog box (Figure 7–17):

Figure 7–17. Heading toward the Protection tab in the Format Cells dialog box

Déjà vu? We're back to a dialog box we've seen a few million times before in previous chapters, but here you need to click the ***Protection*** tab, something we haven't yet done. Click it and you'll see (Figure 7–18):

Figure 7–18. Protection options—read with care

Then click *Locked* off and OK. Just remember the sequence of events: We want to be able to enter data in only certain cells on a worksheet, and at the same time protect the rest of the sheet. Start the process by selecting those cells that will remain available to data entry, and then call up the dialog box you see above and *uncheck* Locked. Then—and only then—can you go ahead and turn Protection on. That will do the job—and as a result, you'll be able to carry out normal data entry in the unlocked cells. If you attempt to type anything in a protected cell, though, you'll encounter this error message (Figure 7–19):

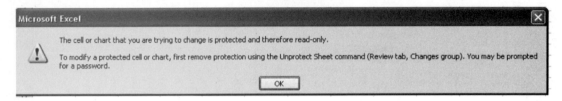

Figure 7–19. Locked out of a cell without a key—the protection error message

Unlocking Cells

The prompt in Figure 7–19 informs you of one—but only one—way of returning the entire worksheet back to normal data entry status, or its unprotected state: Review tab ➤ *Unprotect Sheet*, in the *Changes* button group (another lovely Excel "un" verb). There's an alternative route—namely, Home tab ➤ Format in the Cells button group ➤ *Unprotect Sheet*.

The whole process is curiously backwards, but it's always worked this way: select the cells in which you'll want to able to enter data, uncheck Locked in the Protection tab of the Format Cells dialog box, and then protect the worksheet. And once a cell is unlocked and you go on to protect the sheet, you can't click the *Lock Cell* option (see below in figure 7–15) to lock that cell back along with the rest of the sheet.

There is, however, another command out there—an alternative way to unlock cells before you protect a sheet—that may rank among Excel's most puzzling. If we return to the Cells ➤ Format drop-down menu, you'll see another Lock Cell option (Figure 7–20):

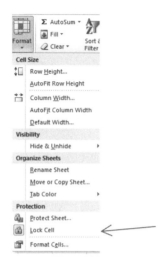

Figure 7–20. Don't be boggled by the toggle: The Lock Cell option

The problem with Lock Cell is that when you click it, it designates any cells you've selected to be *unlocked* if you go ahead and protect the worksheet. Don't ask questions—it's a toggle, an alternately on-off click result.

And what about that ***Hidden*** option offered up in the Format Cells ➤ Protection tab we see in Figure 7–18? Clicking it sees to it that any formulas posted in the selected cells will be *hidden* when you click in those cells. That is, click on one of these formula-bearing cells (once you've turned protection on) and you'll see nothing in the formula bar, and you'll see nothing when you tap the F2 editing key either. The formula *result* remains visible in the cell, however.

You also doubtless noted the password option featured in the Protect Sheet dialog box (Figure 7–21):

Figure 7–21. The password protection option

Entering a password prevents you—or anyone else—from unprotecting the sheet. Once you type a password—which is optional—another dialog box appears (Figure 7–22):

Figure 7–22. The password confirmation prompt. Protect the password, too.

Note the caution. Once you click OK, the password is duly recorded. Try now to unprotect the sheet, and you'll be prompted for the password. Hope you wrote it down.

Protecting a Whole Workbook

You can also protect an entire workbook—but doing so brings about a result you're not likely to expect. Protecting a workbook does *not* seal off every cell in the entire book from data entry. On the contrary; if you protect a workbook, all its cells can continue to receive data. Rather, workbook protection prevents the user from making what Excel calls structural changes in the book—that is, adding, moving, renaming, or deleting worksheets. It will also allow you to protect against changes to current window sizes, meaning if you accept this option and your worksheet currently occupies less than a whole screen's worth of space, you won't be able to restore it to full size via the Maximize button, for example. But that's a less relevant option for most users.

To protect a workbook, click the Review tab ➤ *Protect Workbook* button in the Changes button group. You'll see (Figure 7–23):

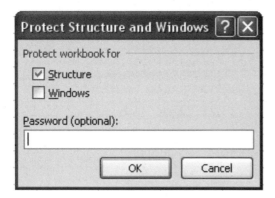

Figure 7–23. Workbook protection: different objects protected here

Note the dialog box isn't titled Protect Workbook, but that is what it's offering to do. And as you see, it's password controllable, and you'll be asked to confirm that password should you choose one. Click OK, and as stated earlier, you won't be able to reposition worksheets, change their names, or delete any of them. To turn Protect Workbook off, just click the Protect Workbook button again. If you've protected the workbook with a password, you'll be asked to supply it.

Consolidating Your Data—Getting It All Together

You may have constructed a workbook—or inherited one—in which similar data are compiled on separate worksheets, say, the sales totals compiled by a set of salespersons across a set of years, each year assigned its own worksheet. If you want to then combine these yearly totals into one summary worksheet, in order to see how much each salesperson has earned overall, you can use Excel's Consolidation tool to do the job.

To demonstrate how Consolidate works, download the Sales By Year workbook from www.apress.com. You'll see a small listing of salesperson data for the years 2008, 2009, and 2010. Note each sheet is identically organized—that is, the ordering of the salespersons is the same in each year, and each sheet's data column is headed Sales (remember that by grouping worksheets you can do this easily—entering labels in one grouped sheet reproduces those same labels in the same cells in the others). On each sheet name the range A4:B8 Sales08, Sales09, and Sales10, respectively (Figure 7 -24):

	Sales
Jane	$ 24,568.00
Ted	$ 36,982.43
Mary	$ 42,602.76
Bill	$ 26,709.42

Figure 7–24. The 2008 sheet data

Note in addition that a fourth sheet, containing the same labels but no data, is supplied as well. If you were consolidating your own sheets you'd need to draw up such a sheet, because this is the one on which the consolidated results will appear. Then to begin consolidating, select cells B5:B8 in the Consolidated Data sheet (Figure 7–25):

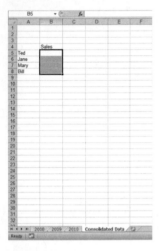

Figure 7–25. The Consolidated data sheet—marking out the range in which the consolidation results will appear

Then click the Data tab ➤ *Consolidate* in the Data Tools button group. You'll see (Figure 7–26):

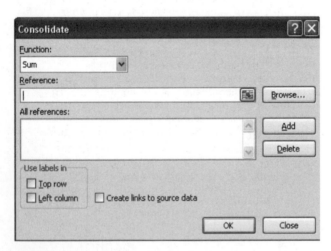

Figure 7–26. The Consolide dialog box

The options presented here require a bit of explanation. You can carry out two kinds of consolidation—consolidation by position and consolidation by category. We're going to start with consolidation by position, which is the approach you'll take when the data labels on the various sheets are all in the same position, as they are in our sheets. Since our three sheets line up their labels in exactly the same way, all we need do in the Consolidate dialog box above is enter the ranges in which the *data* appear in the three yearly sheets. Click in the ***Reference*** field if necessary, and then click the 2008 tab, drag cells B5:B8, and click ***Add***. You'll see (Figure 7–27):

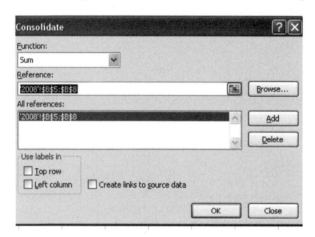

Figure 7–27. *Identifying the first range to be consolidated*

Then click sheet 2009, select cells B5:B8, click Add, and do the same for sheet 2010. (Note that when you click on sheets 2009 and 2010 you should find that B5:B8 is already selected. If not, just drag those cells.) Then click OK in the above dialog box. You should see (Figure 7–28):

	Sales
Ted	$ 129,970.75
Jane	$ 158,375.08
Mary	$ 119,778.51
Bill	$ 73,258.45

Figure 7–28. *The consolidation—you're looking here at the Consolidated Data sheet*

The data are consolidated in the Consolidated Data sheet. Each salesperson's sales totals for the years 2008-2010 are now recorded, or consolidated, in one cell. Again, this is a consequence of the data labels on the three yearly sheets all holding the same relative position. Thus Consolidate knows that because Ted is the first-listed salesperson on all three sheets, the first cells in the three ranges we added to the Consolidate dialog box all represent Ted's sales data, and so on. (*Important note*: Working by position, as we've done here, doesn't require that the salesperson's labels on the respective sheets all share exactly the same addresses. They need to share the same *relative* position, such that Ted would always be listed first, followed by Jane, etc.)

Now for what again is called consolidation by ***category***. Delete the results in the Consolidated Data sheet (but not the data labels) and click on sheet 2008. Switch the positions of the names Ted and Jane, so that Jane is now listed above Ted. Then click back on the Consolidated Data sheet and this time select A4:B8, which includes the data *labels*—something we didn't need to do when we consolidated by position. Then click Data Tools ➤ Consolidate. You should see the three ranges we selected for the previous consolidation listed. Click on each one and click Delete. Then type Sales08 in the reference field, click Add, and repeat the procedure by typing and adding Sales09 and Sales10. Remember that we named these ranges when we opened the Sales By Year sheet, and these ranges include the cells in which the *data labels* appear, in addition to the data.

Then click the ***Top row*** and *Left Column* boxes in the ***Use Labels in*** area of the Consolidate dialog box, and click OK. You should see (Figure 7–29):

	Sales
Ted	$ 142,385.18
Jane	$ 145,960.65
Mary	$ 119,778.51
Bill	$ 73,258.45

Figure 7–29. Consolidating by category

Note the totals here for Ted and Jane differ from our previous results because we've switched the positions of Ted and Jane's names, and hence their sales totals, in sheet 2008. We've just carried out a consolidation by *category*, in which the names of the salespersons *don't* share the same relative position across the three sheets. That's why we needed here to click on Top Row and Left Column to orient us, because Consolidate needs to "find" all the salespersons and their data by looking for their names and the Sales label on each sheet—*wherever* they may be positioned.

That point may call for a bit of review. "Consolidation by category" means that Excel will search for salespersons' names wherever they happened to be positioned on the 2008, 2009, and 2010 sheets. The salespersons *are* the categories here.

There's one other Consolidation option that you may want to explore—***Create links to source data***. Checking this enables you to change the numbers in any of the sheets contributing to the consolidation, such that those changes will be recorded in the consolidation result. To demonstrate, return to the Consolidated Data sheet and make sure range A4:B8 is selected, with the results you've seen above. Then click the Data tab ➤ Data Tools ➤ Consolidate, and click Create links to source data, then click OK. You'll see (Figure 7–30):

4			Sales
+	8	Ted	$ 142,385.18
+	12	Jane	$ 145,960.65
+	16	Mary	$ 119,778.51
+	20	Bill	$ 73,258.45

Figure 7–30. Consolidating by linking to the source data

You'll note the obvious addition to the screen. A collection of plus signs has taken over a new, gray area to the left of the worksheet proper, and you'll note as well that the row numbers exhibit gaps in their sequence, and—less obviously—that a new third column has inserted itself between the salespersons' names and the actual sales data. Click one plus sign and you'll see (Figure 7–31):

	4		Sales
	5	Sales E	$ 36,982.43
	6	Sales E	$ 41,700.10
	7	Sales E	$ 63,702.65
−	8	Ted	$ 142,385.18
+	12	Jane	$ 145,960.65
+	16	Mary	$ 119,778.51
+	20	Bill	$ 73,258.45

Figure 7–31. Expanding Ted's sales data—the three years contributing to his total are revealed

You've viewing an instance of Excel's outlining capability, which in this case breaks out the three years' worth of sales data for Ted. Clicking the plus sign reveals—or *expands*—these data, which had been hidden—thus explaining the row-sequence gaps we noted earlier (you may also want to widen the columns so as to better view the Sales By Year labels). These new data really consist of cell references to the relevant data in the three yearly sheets for each salesperson. Thus by clicking the first such row for Ted, you'll see in the formula bar:

='2008'!$B6

which references the cell in sheet 2008 in which Ted's sales data appears. And because we're working with cell references, changing any data in these linked cells will change the consolidation result here. Then, clicking what is now a minus sign *collapses* these detail rows and hides them again. Click the 2 you'll see in the upper reaches of that gray area housing the plus-minus signs will expand all the hidden row data for all the salespersons, and clicking 1 collapses them (Figure 7–32):

Figure 7–32. Outlining buttons for expanding and collapsing the data

And if you click the Data tab ➤ *Outline* group ➤ the *Ungroup* down arrow ➤ *Clear Outline*, the plus-minuses will disappear, but you'll still be left with the salesperson detail rows, this time all visible.

And that's how to consolidate data across multiple worksheets. On the other hand, the consolidation options aren't terribly flexible, and you may decide that other alternatives to aggregating data, particularly pivot tables, will better suit your data gathering needs. And as it turns out, we're going to take a look at pivot tables in the next chapter.

In Conclusion…

Workbooks consist of worksheets, and those sheets can be treated as stand-alone objects that contain their own, independent data, or they can be connected in various ways to the other sheets. We've reviewed a batch of ways in which those connections can be made—either through cell references, grouping, or consolidation of their data. We've also seen how to protect the data on your sheets, either wholly or partially, on a cell-by-cell basis.

Just remember—you've been entrusted with the care and feeding of 16 billion cells. It's an awesome responsibility—so take good care of them.

CHAPTER 8

■■■

PivotTables and Pivot Charts

There's that word again—Tables. They're back, but this time we're going to look at tables from a different angle—almost literally—by subjecting all those columns and rows to a new and more informative way of presenting their data—the PivotTable.

PivotTables are a most powerful and nimble way to *aggregate* data—but that introduction calls for a bit of...well, introduction. After all, adding a column of numbers is a form of data aggregation, too, but you wouldn't bother to apply a PivotTable to that task (though you could). PivotTables do something else, something more. A lot more.

It's one thing to be able to total a range of numbers—even a very large range—and that can be a most important capability. But to be able to break the numbers out by *categories*—that is when you need to call upon a PivotTable.

It's noteworthy that a decisive definition of PivotTables is hard to come by. Type "PivotTable definition" into Google and scan the results—you'll see what I mean. But what PivotTables do is summarize data by categories, thus allowing you to view patterns in the data that might otherwise escape you.

Let's take a look to see what I mean.

Starting Out with PivotTables

Think back to the very first example with which I inaugurated Chapter 1 (Figure 8–1):

Date	Expense	Sum
01/11/2008	telephone	7.31
15/11/2008	Central Heating	17.00
15/11/2008	Property Tax	232.00
15/11/2008	Life Insurance	29.00
15/11/2008	Medical Insurance	96.00
15/11/2008	Plumbing Insurance	6.24
15/11/2008	Water	65.00
23/11/2008	Cleaner	25.50
23/11/2008	Food	30.00
23/11/2008	Food	7.00
23/11/2008	Food	16.00
23/11/2008	Food	14.00
23/11/2008	Food	4.00
23/11/2008	Newspapers	2.00
23/11/2008	Newspapers	2.00
23/11/2008	Sewing	10.00
28/11/2008	Savings	40.00
30/11/2008	Car Maintenance	58.00
30/11/2008	Cleaner	30.00
30/11/2008	Clothes	21.00
30/11/2008	Contents Insurance	300.00
30/11/2008	Eat out	17.00
30/11/2008	Food	45.00
30/11/2008	Food	11.00
30/11/2008	Food	2.00
30/11/2008	Home Insurance	900.00
30/11/2008	Newspapers	4.00
30/11/2008	gas	38.00
30/11/2008	Sewing	10.00
01/12/2008	telephone	7.00
07/12/2008	Breakdown Insurance	115.00

Figure 8–1. Family budget records, organized by date, category, and amount

—that list of family expenses. Turn this database into a table, as we saw in Chapter 6, and you could, for example, filter Newspaper and/or Telephone expenses and calculate their respective contributions to the budget—and an Advanced Filter would enable you to *save* those data to another location on the worksheet. You could also generate a *count* of the number of Newspaper or Telephone payments, by clicking on Count Number in the Expenses cell in the table's Total row.

But if you need a more comprehensive breakout—say you want to see Newspaper costs by each *month*, in which three variables, or fields, are considered at the same time—Expense, Date, and Sum—then the task becomes more challenging. My professional recommendation: you need a PivotTable.

Indeed, the revised budget portrait we presented in Chapter 1 (Figure 8–2):

Sum of Sum	Date												
Expense	Jan	Feb	Mar	Apr	May	Jun	Jul	Aug	Sep	Oct	Nov	Dec	Grand Total
America trip					264.00								264.00
Annual subscriptions		20.00						45.00					65.00
Breakdown Insurance											115.00		115.00
Car Insurance	281.00												281.00
Car Maintenance								6.00	3.00	58.00			67.00
Central Heating	17.00	17.00	17.00	17.00	17.00	17.00	17.00	17.00	17.00	17.00	17.00	17.00	204.00
Child Tax Credit Repay	12.50	12.50	12.50	12.50	12.50	12.50	12.50	12.50	12.50	12.50	12.50	12.50	150.00
Cleaner	128.00	125.00	95.00	90.00	127.00	76.00	70.00	70.00	94.00	136.00	55.50	30.00	1095.50
Clothes	133.00	24.00	26.00		76.00	48.00	39.00	158.00	115.00	3.00	21.00		643.00
Contents Insurance										347.00	300.00		647.00
Dental Treatment					55.00								55.00
Donation												150.00	150.00
Dry Cleaner						8.00	6.00			18.00			32.00
dry cleaning		7.00		12.00	12.00	8.00							39.00
Eat out	25.00	66.00	10.00		17.00	16.00		62.00	20.00		17.00	14.00	247.00

Figure 8–2. The budget data broken out by category and month

was engineered by a PivotTable. Data from two fields, Expense and Date, form a set of borders around the actual expense data, which are then broken out into individual totals at the intersections of each Expense and each Date, in this case defined in monthly units (of course some of the intersections are blank, simply because that type of expense wasn't incurred that particular month). It's this sort of thing that a PivotTable can do with ease, and the sort of thing that a table can't.

This object used to be called a crosstab—a kind of matrix in which data were organized by one variable displayed horizontally (in the above case, by Date), and another displayed vertically (Expense). PivotTables are latter-day, electronic descendants of the crosstab, and once you acquire a basic understanding of how they work, you can cook one up in about four seconds—at the same speed as an Excel chart.

It's true that PivotTables are viewed by some users as a rather forbidding and daunting object-and I'll allow that when I first set eyes on a PivotTable, in pre-millennium New York, I had no clue what they were about. By the *second* look, however, PivotTables began to make considerably more sense—and if you understand what's going on in the screen shot above, and doubtless you do-you're on your way.

Of course we can't tell you everything about PivotTables in this chapter—whole books have been devoted to just this topic (two by Apress, by the way). But we *are* going to describe the PivotTable essentials-and then some—so you'll be able to do quite a bit of productive work with them.

What's in a Name?

PivotTables are so named because they enable the user to move, or *pivot,* table data to various positions on an area called a pivot grid (you'll see it soon), thus breaking out the data in a wide range of changeable ways. Thus in the above case, the Expense field data occupies what's called the ***Row Labels*** area, the actual budget expenses are assigned to the ***Value*** area, and the Dates here are installed in the ***Column Labels*** area. Now that's a rather abstract description, but consider this illustration, an excerpt from a table of sales data, adapted from one of Microsoft's sample files, one we're going to work with in this chapter (Figure 8–3):

Country	Salesperson	Order Date	OrderID	Order Amount
UK	Suyama	7/10/03	10249	$1,863.40
USA	Peacock	7/11/03	10252	$3,597.90
USA	Peacock	7/12/03	10250	$1,552.60
USA	Leverling	7/15/03	10251	$654.06
UK	Dodsworth	7/15/03	10255	$2,490.50
UK	Buchanan	7/16/03	10248	$440.00
USA	Leverling	7/16/03	10253	$1,444.80
USA	Leverling	7/17/03	10256	$517.80
USA	Peacock	7/22/03	10257	$1,119.90
UK	Buchanan	7/23/03	10254	$556.62
USA	Davolio	7/23/03	10258	$1,614.88
USA	Peacock	7/25/03	10259	$100.80
USA	Callahan	7/25/03	10262	$584.00
USA	Peacock	7/29/03	10260	$1,504.65
USA	Peacock	7/30/03	10261	$448.00
UK	Dodsworth	7/31/03	10263	$1,873.80
USA	Leverling	7/31/03	10266	$346.56
USA	Callahan	8/2/03	10268	$1,101.20
USA	Davolio	8/2/03	10270	$1,376.00
USA	Peacock	8/6/03	10267	$3,536.60
UK	Suyama	8/6/03	10272	$1,456.00
UK	Buchanan	8/9/03	10269	$642.20
USA	Davolio	8/9/03	10275	$291.84
USA	Fuller	8/12/03	10265	$1,176.00
USA	Leverling	8/12/03	10273	$2,037.28
USA	Fuller	8/13/03	10277	$1,200.80
USA	Callahan	8/14/03	10276	$420.00

Figure 8–3. Table data—about to turn into PivotTable data

I say "excerpt" because the table—which for the purposes of this chapter we're going to call the PivotTable's ***source data*-**comprises one header row and 799 records (though again, the number of records with which you work is largely irrelevant-the PivotTable concepts are the same). It's a pretty straightforward collection of information, recording each sale by each salesperson, date, country of sale, order number, and sales amount. Tossing these data into a PivotTable, I could do something like this (Figure 8–4):

Sum of Order Amount	Column Labels		
Row Labels	UK	USA	Grand Total
Buchanan	68792.25		68792.25
Callahan		123032.67	123032.67
Davolio		182500.09	182500.09
Dodsworth	75048.04		75048.04
Fuller		161336.98	161336.98
King	116962.99		116962.99
Leverling		201196.27	201196.27
Peacock		225763.68	225763.68
Suyama	72527.63		72527.63
Grand Total	333330.91	893829.69	1227160.6

Figure 8–4. Sales data compiled by a PivotTable—by country and salesperson

Here the sales data are broken out by Salesperson and Country. Thus Davolio did $182,500.09 worth of business in the USA, and none in the UK (and note the original table data are formatted as currency, but not here; the PivotTable awaits your decision on this). But I could also redesign the table (the PivotTable that is) to take on this appearance instead (Figure 8–5):

Sum of Order Amount	Column Labels									
Row Labels	Buchanan	Callahan	Davolio	Dodsworth	Fuller	King	Leverling	Peacock	Suyama	Grand Total
UK	68792.25			75048.04		116962.99			72527.63	333330.91
USA		123032.67	182500.09		161336.98		201196.27	225763.68		893829.69
Grand Total	68792.25	123032.67	182500.09	75048.04	161336.98	116962.99	201196.27	225763.68	72527.63	1227160.6

Figure 8–5. Same data, different arrangement—the salesperson names are now running across a set of columns

Same exact information—but here I've pivoted the table, so that the Row Labels area shows the Country data, and the Column Labels area displays the Salesperson. I've given the data a different, almost perpendicular look. Which look you prefer is a presentational decision, and PivotTables make these and many other such options available.

Note as well that data from only *three* of the original table's five fields have been invoked in this PivotTable—Country, Salesperson, and Order Amount (see the **Sum of Order Amount** caption in the PivotTable's upper-left corner); that tells us that you can apply the original table fields *selectively* to a PivotTable, and leave out the ones that don't currently interest you. But nothing in PivotTables is forever; you can start over again and introduce whichever fields you like, as your needs warrant.

But all this raises the obvious question: How do you actually start *doing* all this? I thought you'd never ask. So let's go.

Constructing a PivotTable: Let's Go

To give PivotTables a try, download the SampleSalespersonReport workbook from our download page at apress.com.

Let's say you want to construct a first PivotTable, or pivot *report* as it's officially termed, which simply breaks out all sales in dollars by Salesperson. That is, we want to wind up with this report (Figure 8–6):

	Row Labels ▾	Sum of Order Amount
2		
3	**Row Labels** ▾	**Sum of Order Amount**
4	Buchanan	68792.25
5	Callahan	123032.67
6	Davolio	182500.09
7	Dodsworth	75048.04
8	Fuller	162503.78
9	King	116962.99
10	Leverling	201196.27
11	Peacock	225763.68
12	Suyama	72527.63
13	**Grand Total**	**1228327.4**

Figure 8–6. For starters: A basic PivotTable

Inserting the Table

To begin the process, click anywhere in the original table data (on the Source Data worksheet). Then click the Insert tab ➤ *PivotTable* (in the *Tables* button group(➤ *PivotTable* ➤ and OK (we're accepting all the defaults in the dialog box). You'll see (Figure 8–7):

PivotTable 1

To build a report, choose fields
from the PivotTable Field List

Figure 8–7. A PivotTable grid—where to till your fields

Look to the right of your screen, and you'll see (Figure 8–8):

Figure 8–8. The PivotTable Field List: where you decide what goes where

Note as well that when you click anywhere in the PivotTable area, even if it's blank as per the above screen shot, a ***PivotTable Tools*** tab appears onscreen, complete with an array of buttons to help you construct and reconstruct the table on which you're working (Figure 8–9):

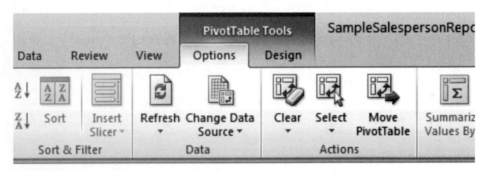

Figure 8–9. The PivotTable ribbon

Needless to say, these screenshots need to be explained. The first shot (Figure 8–8) captures the areas, all currently empty, in which the various data from the data source (that is, the original table) are to be positioned, or dropped. We've already identified most of these: Row Labels, Column Labels, and Values (the fourth, the **Report Filter**, streaming across the upper edge of the screenshot, remains to be discussed). The second screen shot identifies what's called the **PivotTable Field List**, whose upper half simply lists the *names* of the data source *fields*.

Setting Up the PivotTable

Now remember that we want to compile a sales-in-dollars-by-salesperson pivot report. Here goes:

1. To start, click the **Salesperson** check box on the PivotTable Field List. That means we want to see information from that field, which consists simply of the *names* of the salespersons recorded each time they register a sale: You'll see (Figure 8–10):

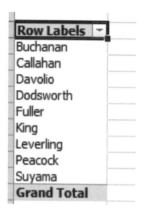

Figure 8–10. The Salespersons. Note that each is listed only once.

This introduces an important point, one of those PivotTables have-to-knows. Note that all the salesperson names are listed in the row area as a result of that click, but each is listed only *once*. Remember our source data contains 799 records, but nevertheless when those data are installed in the Row Label area, each salesperson is *listed once, that is, uniquely*. After all, we want to *aggregate* the sales data by salesperson, so it stands to reason that each name is enumerated once, in order to summarize and report their *total* sales. The general principle here is: *Any field data that is placed in the Row Label area lists its distinct entries once, and only once.* We see that our sales force comprises nine salespersons, and no matter how many sales any one of them records, her name will be listed in the Row Label area *once* (we'll need to qualify this point a bit later, but that's the essential idea).

Note in addition that when we clicked on the Salesperson check box, those data were sent directly to the Row Label area. That was Excel's decision, not ours, because Excel assumes that this kind of data—which is *textual*—is the kind that is typically assigned to the Row area. But as we'll see, *you can place any source data field in any of the PivotTable areas.*

2. Next, click the check box next to the **Order Amount** field. You'll see (Figure 8–11):

Row Labels	Sum of Order Amount
Buchanan	68792.25
Callahan	123032.67
Davolio	182500.09
Dodsworth	75048.04
Fuller	161336.98
King	116962.99
Leverling	201196.27
Peacock	225763.68
Suyama	72527.63
Grand Total	**1227160.6**

Figure 8–11. Finito—your first PivotTable

Don't look now, but we're done. Clicking the Order Amount check box did these things:

- It delivered the data in that field-the sales data in dollars—to the Values area.

- Those data were in turn *aggregated* by each name in the Row Label area, which controls the process by dictating how the data are to be aggregated.

Note also that by default, the salespersons are sorted in A-Z sequence.

So there's your first pivot report, and whether you realize it or not, we've already encountered and worked with three of the most important principles of the report-making process. To summarize these:

- The data from any field placed in the Row Label area are *always listed, and listed once each* (again, we'll need to modify this slightly later). Our nine salespersons are thus each listed once in the Row Label area, irrespective of the number of sales they achieve. Let any salesperson record 1 or 50,000 sales; she or he will be listed only once.

- *Any data placed in the Values Label area is subject to some kind of mathematical operation.* In our case the Order Amount data was *added*, and keyed to or broken out by each salesperson.

- Any source data field can be placed in any PivotTable area. If it's placed in the Row Label area, that field's contents will be *listed uniquely*. If it's placed in the Values area, the field's contents will submit to some kind of mathematical operation.

Keep these principles in mind; they should become clearer as we proceed.

Note in addition that buttons representing the two fields we've selected thus far—Salesperson and Order Amount-are also slotted into their respective places in the lower half of the Field List (Figure 8–12):

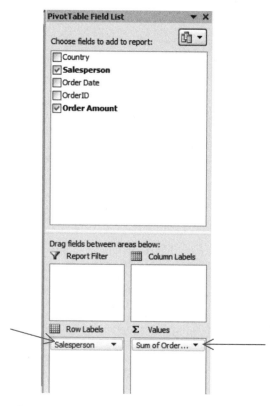

Figure 8–12. Pivoting the Report: Table fields currently in use

Now click the drop-down arrow on the Salesperson button. You'll see (Figure 8–13):

Figure 8–13. Rearranging the PivotTable—we're about to pivot it

Click *Move to Column Labels*. This is what happens (Figure 8–14):

Figure 8–14. The same data, now running horizontally

We've pivoted the report. The Salesperson names now occupy a succession of *columns* stretching horizontally across the report, framing a new way for looking at precisely the same data. (*Note:* You can also move the buttons from one area to another by clicking on a button and dragging it into a different area. You'll also gradually discover, to your delight or befuddlement, that PivotTables offer many ways for doing the same things.) And we're also learning that the Column Labels area is really a horizontal version of Row Labels—as with that latter area, any source data assigned to the Column Label space will be *listed uniquely*.

Updating the Pivot Report

There's something else to keep in mind, this time about the source data that contributes to a pivot report. If you add new records to the source data, or if even if you change any of the data in an *existing* record, you need to *refresh* the pivot report. Unlike standard Excel formulas, PivotTables *won't* automatically recalculate when the data contributing to them is changed. To refresh a PivotTable, click PivotTable Tools ➤ *Refresh* (keyboard equivalent: Alt+F5). To demonstrate, let's add a record to our source data. Return to the source data, and in Row 801 enter these data: UK, Buchanan, 2/5/10, 11111, $567.00. Then click back onto the pivot report and click the Refresh command. You'll see (Figure 8–15):

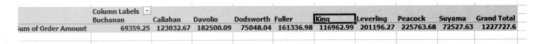

Figure 8–15. The pause that refreshes: updating, or refreshing, the PivotTable with a new record—a new Buchanan sale

Note that Buchanan's sales total has bumped up to 69359.35, reflecting the additional $567.00 sale. Way to go, Buchanan.

The *Refresh All* option, revealed by the drop-down menu by Refresh, also refreshes source data that may be drawn from an external source, such as a Web site or an Access database (You'd click *Use an external data source* in the *Create PivotTable* dialog box to connect to such a source.). Note as well that if you build several different pivot reports, simultaneously drawing on the same source data—and you can—all will be refreshed.

Changing the Calculation

Next point. Suppose instead of having the pivot report calculate the *total* sales for each salesperson—that is the default calculation—you want to determine the *average* sale in dollars each salesperson has executed. To do this (among other ways), first click anywhere in the pivot report data label area, (where the sales numbers appear), then click PivotTable Tools ➤ *Options* ➤ *Summarize Values By* ➤ *Average* (you'll see this command on the resulting drop-down menu) (Figure 8–16):

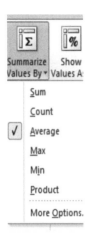

Figure 8–16. *No mean feat: Changing the mathematical operation of a field to Average*

The salesperson data now display average sales by salesperson. Click the Summarize Values By drop-down arrow and you'll see that you can also carry out these operations: ***Count, Max, Min,*** and ***Product*** (which in our case would multiply each salesperson's sales all together, yielding a rather gigantic total). Clicking ***More Options*** gives a few additional possibilities, including ***Standard Deviation.*** (By the way, we'll get to how to format these data in a little while.)

Comparing the Data

And here's another cool way to characterize your data. By clicking anywhere in the pivot report and then clicking PivotTable Tools ➤ Options tab ➤ *Calculations* group ➤ the ***Show Values As*** drop-down arrow, you'll see (Figure 8–17):

Figure 8–17. *The Show Values As drop-down menu: more ways to compare the numbers*

Here you're presented with a wide assortment of options for describing your data comparatively, for example, how each salesperson's sales total ranks. If I click *Rank Largest to Smallest* I'll see (Figure 8–18):

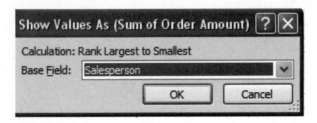

Figure 8–18. Assigning a ranking order to the salespersons by their sales

Click OK (this dialog box asks you which field will be subject to this calculation, should you be working with more than one field). You'll see (Figure 8–19):

	Column Labels									
	Buchanan	Callahan	Davolio	Dodsworth	Fuller	King	Leverling	Peacock	Suyama	Grand Total
Sum of Order Amount	9	5	3	7	4	6	2	1	8	

Figure 8–19. Peacock rules the roost

Thus we see that Peacock tops the sales list. You could then actually sort the data horizontally so that Peacock appears first and Leverling appears second, etc., by right-clicking anywhere in the rankings (and not on the Salesperson names, though) and clicking *Sort* ➤ *Sort Largest to Smallest* (Here "largest" is defined as 1—the higher ranking). Pretty cool, if you ask me; but I do go on. (Note: In order to return to standard calculations such as sum and average, you need to click Show Values As ➤ *No Calculation*.)

Moving and Removing Fields

Now time for a bit of important review. You'll recall that when we launched our pivot report we selected the report fields by clicking those check boxes alongside their names in the PivotTable Field List. Needless to say, you can do the same with any field. But remember that *where* the field will wind up on the report—in the Row or Column Labels areas, or in the Values area—is a decision *Excel* makes, on the basis of where it seems most sensible to place the field. But if you want a field to populate the Column Labels area and you click that field's check box, Excel may decide to refer it to the Row Labels area instead. Ultimately, however, *you* decide where the field goes, and you can always resituate it as we've already seen, by clicking its button arrow and clicking on its new destination, *or* by clicking on the button and dragging it to a different area. Alternatively, you can click on any field name in the PivotTable Field List and drag it *down* into the desired button area, in the lower half of the list pane (Figure 8–20):

Figure 8–20. *Dragging a field into the button area*

On the other hand, if you want to *remove* a field from the report, all you have to is uncheck the box next to that field's name in the PivotTable Field List—*or* click on that field's button, and drag it towards the worksheet proper. As you do, you'll see an X accompanying the field name, and when you do, just release your mouse to remove the field. Either way, the field will disappear from the pivot report. And if you want to start over again and remove *all* the fields from the report, click PivotTable Tools ➤ Options Tab ➤ *Actions group* ➤ *Clear* ➤ *Clear All*. The blank PivotTable grid will remain on screen, however, enabling you to compose a new report right away. And as a matter of fact, let's go ahead and clear the report, because we want to start again and introduce a new report feature.

Adding Data Fields

So far, the pivot reports we've actually designed have called upon two source data fields, Order Amount and Salesperson—and we've pivoted Order Amount to either the Row or Columns areas to demonstrate how the same data can be portrayed differently. But you'll recall that some of the demo reports we've described feature *three* fields, such as the report captured in Figure 8–4, in which the sales data were broken out *both* by Salesperson and Country, or the budget pivot report, broken out by both Date and Expense Type. With that in mind, click the checkbox by **Country** in the PivotTable Field List. Then do the same for Salesperson and Order Amount. You'll see (Figure 8–21):

Row Labels ▼	Sum of Order Amount
⊟ UK	333897.91
Buchanan	69359.25
Dodsworth	75048.04
King	116962.99
Suyama	72527.63
⊟ USA	893829.69
Callahan	123032.67
Davolio	182500.09
Fuller	161336.98
Leverling	201196.27
Peacock	225763.68
Grand Total	1227727.6

Figure 8–21. Adding a third field to the pivot report

(Before you continue, you may want to Autofit the first column (by double-clicking the right boundary of column A), so that the phrase Sum of Order Amount becomes completely visible.) Here we've done something new; we've placed *two fields* in the same area, in this case Row Labels. And what happens as a result should be pretty clear: the Country field serves as a kind of super category within which the Salespersons are housed, to go on and break out the data further. Thus what we've done is learn how much sales activity has been conducted in the respective countries, *by the respective salespersons*; and bear in mind that if any Salesperson had conducted business in both countries (although that isn't the case here), his name would have appeared within *both* the UK and USA super categories.

You've also probably noticed the minus signs flanking the UK and USA items in the Country field. Clicking either or both *collapses* the subcategory data for each country, for example (Figure 8–22):

Row Labels ▼	Sum of Order Amount
⊞ UK	333897.91
⊟ USA	893829.69
Callahan	123032.67
Davolio	182500.09
Fuller	161336.98
Leverling	201196.27
Peacock	225763.68
Grand Total	1227727.6

Figure 8–22. Economic collapse, of sorts—collapsing the UK sales data

Click what is now the plus sign and the Salesperson data reappear. You can also execute this command by clicking in the now-collapsed UK row and then clicking PivotTable Tools ➤ Options tab ➤ *Active Field*, and clicking the accompanying plus and/or minus signs (Figure 8–23):

Figure 8–23. Field work: Another way to collapse and expand a PivotTable field

Now that you've got the Salesperson back, click the arrow on the Salesperson button, summoning this menu (Figure 8–24):

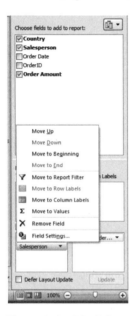

Figure 8–24. Movin' on up—reversing the position of the fields in the row label area

Click ***Move Up***. You'll see (Figure 8–25):

Row Labels	Sum of Order Amount
⊟ **Buchanan**	**69359.25**
UK	69359.25
⊟ **Callahan**	**123032.67**
USA	123032.67
⊟ **Davolio**	**182500.09**
USA	182500.09
⊟ **Dodsworth**	**75048.04**
UK	75048.04
⊟ **Fuller**	**161336.98**
USA	161336.98
⊟ **King**	**116962.99**
UK	116962.99
⊟ **Leverling**	**201196.27**
USA	201196.27
⊟ **Peacock**	**225763.68**
USA	225763.68
⊟ **Suyama**	**72527.63**
UK	72527.63
Grand Total	**1227727.6**

Figure 8–25. Salesperson and Country, having reversed positions

We've literally reversed our fields. The two Row Label fields have changed places; now it's *Salesperson* that has been "promoted" to super category status, while Country now occupies the subordinate, or subcategory, niche. And given this new arrangement, we can see that had the salespersons transacted sales in both countries, UK and USA would have appeared alongside *each* salesperson name in the subordinate area. (Note: Remember that in addition to clicking Move Up, you could have also clicked on the Salesperson button and *dragged* it gently atop Country.)

Changing Field Settings

Now for another point. The screen shot in Figure 8–25 displays *subtotals* for each salesperson (e.g., Buchanan Total, Callahan Total)—those are put in place because had each salesperson done business in both the UK and USA, the *two* country totals would have been reported and added for each salesperson, and those combined totals—UK sales + USA sales—would have told us something new about their sales activity. But because here each salesperson has confined her sales beat to one country each, their subtotals are identical to the individual details of their sales. Thus Buchanan's UK total of 69359.25 is precisely the same as the value in his "Total" row, because there's nothing else to add—there's only one country's worth of data. As a result, the "Total" rows are redundant; and so if you want to remove them, right-click on any entry in the Salesperson Row Label area (but not UK or USA), and click *Field Settings* on the shortcut menu. You'll see (Figure 8–26):

Figure 8–26. The Field Settings dialog box

Click *None* ➤ OK, yielding this view (Figure 8–27):

Row Labels ▼	Sum of Order Amount
⊟**Buchanan**	
UK	69359.25
⊟**Callahan**	
USA	123032.67
⊟**Davolio**	
USA	182500.09
⊟**Dodsworth**	
UK	75048.04
⊟**Fuller**	
USA	161336.98
⊟**King**	
UK	116962.99
⊟**Leverling**	
USA	201196.27
⊟**Peacock**	
USA	225763.68
⊟**Suyama**	
UK	72527.63
Grand Total	**1227727.6**

Figure 8–27. Note the missing Salespeson subtotals

(You can also click PivotTable Tools ➤ *Design* tab ➤ *Subtotals* ➤ *Do Not Show Subtotals*.) There—that's a lot tidier. But remember that there may be many other times when you may want to leave the subtotals in view, particularly if the subcategory displays multiple values. It all depends on what the data tell you, and what you want and need to see.

Pivoting the Table

The Figure 8–27 screen shot tells us still something else about the way data are presented in a pivot report. Earlier, I stated—with some fanfare (in the form of a bullet point, which is about as much fanfare as I can muster here, unless this book can be sound enabled)—that data entered in the Row or Column areas are listed *uniquely*—one time each. Yet in 8–27 we see the words UK and USA any number of times—and they're all deposited in the Row Labels area. Mea culpa—but I *did* say at the time that I'd need to modify my dictum. And here we see why. Data entered in the first, or *super category,* level in the Row and/or Column Labels areas can indeed appear only once each—but data in the *subcategory* tier can appear multiple times—but only *once* for each entry in the super category. Thus USA and UK can only appear once for each salesperson—and, because they occupy the super category in the above shot, each salesperson can only appear once. If that isn't clear, a bit of practice pivot tabling will drive the point home.

Now let's pivot the table.

- Click the arrow on the Country button in the lower half of the PivotTable Field List.

- Click *Move to Column Labels*. You'll see (Figure 8–28):

Sum of Order Amount	Column Labels		
Row Labels	UK	USA	Grand Total
Buchanan	69359.25		69359.25
Callahan		123032.67	123032.67
Davolio		182500.09	182500.09
Dodsworth	75048.04		75048.04
Fuller		161336.98	161336.98
King	116962.99		116962.99
Leverling		201196.27	201196.27
Peacock		225763.68	225763.68
Suyama	72527.63		72527.63
Grand Total	333897.91	893829.69	1227727.6

Figure 8–28. Geography lesson—the countries move into the Columns Labels area

Got that? By moving the Country field to the Column Labels area, we've orchestrated that *crosstab/matrix* look—with the sales data occupying the intersections of Salesperson and Country. And unlike the previous pivot report, in which the Country data appears as a subcategory for each salesperson, here the two Countries are listed only *once*—as a super category. Remember, though—it's all the same exact data.

Counting Totals

Now let's remove both the Country and Order Amount fields from the pivot report, leaving us with Salesperson in the Row Label area (Figure 8–29):

Figure 8–29. Starting over; stay tuned

Then click on Salesperson again in the PivotTable Field, and drag it into the Values area…as murmurs of discontent flit across the hall. First, you're asking rhetorically, haven't we *already* used the Salesperson field, having locked it into in the Row Labels area? And second, didn't I earlier say that fields in the Values area are always subjected to a *mathematical* operation? Well, Salesperson contains *text* data—the names of the salespersons in our pivot report—and how do you subject names to a mathematical operation?

You have a point—or two. To get to the second question first, it's true that you can't add or take an average of text data, but there is one operation to which you *can* subject them: you can *count* them. And when you drag Salesperson into the Values area that's exactly what happens (Figure 8–30):

Row Labels ⏷	Count of Salesperson
Buchanan	43
Callahan	99
Davolio	117
Dodsworth	41
Fuller	92
King	67
Leverling	125
Peacock	151
Suyama	65
Grand Total	**800**

Figure 8–30. Number of sales by salesperson: Using the Salesperson in both the Row Labels and Values areas

The pivot report, then, has no choice but to count the salesperson names once they're assigned to the values area—but why would we want to do such a thing? Here's why: because we've also left the Salesperson names in the Row Labels area, we've engineered a count of the *number* of sales each salesperson has attained. We've told the pivot report to count each instance of each salesperson's name—broken out by the *names themselves,* as displayed in the Row Labels area. That is, we're asking the report to count the number of times Buchanan appears, and then we're tying that count to Buchanan's entry in Row Labels, and so on for all the salespersons. Every time the name Buchanan appears in the source data, after all, it means Buchanan has rolled up one more sale, and so if you need to know how *many* sales Buchanan or any other salesperson has compiled, why not count the number of times his or her *name* shows up in the source data?

Using the Same Field Twice

And as to the first question, that is, how can we deploy the same field twice in a pivot report? The answer, very simply, is: you can. You can situate a field in either the Row or Column Labels areas, *as well as* in the Values area at the same time.

And from all this pivot strategizing we've learned two important new things: you can

- Use the same field twice in a pivot report, and

- You can ship text data to the values area, where it will be *counted.*

And here's a last point in this regard. You can also place the *same* data field in the Values area twice, selecting two different mathematical operations for it. Thus if you've designed this basic pivot report (Figure 8–31):

Row Labels ▾	Sum of Order Amount
Buchanan	69359.25
Callahan	123032.67
Davolio	182500.09
Dodsworth	75048.04
Fuller	161336.98
King	116962.99
Leverling	201196.27
Peacock	225763.68
Suyama	72527.63
Grand Total	**1227727.6**

Figure 8–31. We've seen this report before, but...

where the Order Amount field is summed in the Values area, you can drag that field from the PivotTable Field List into the Values area a *second* time, yielding this, for starters (Figure 8–32):

Row Labels ⌄	Sum of Order Amount	Sum of Order Amount2
Buchanan	69359.25	69359.25
Callahan	123032.67	123032.67
Davolio	182500.09	182500.09
Dodsworth	75048.04	75048.04
Fuller	161336.98	161336.98
King	116962.99	116962.99
Leverling	201196.27	201196.27
Peacock	225763.68	225763.68
Suyama	72527.63	72527.63
Grand Total	**1227727.6**	**1227727.6**

Figure 8–32. Here we've added the same field twice—to the Values area. To be explained—soon!!

That does look rather scary, not to mention redundant; but click any cell containing Sum of Order Amount 2 ➤ PivotTable Tools ➤ Options tab ➤ *Summarize Values By* ➤ *Average*—and you'll see this (Figure 8–33):

Row Labels ⌄	Sum of Order Amount	Average of Order Amount2
Buchanan	69359.25	1613.005814
Callahan	123032.67	1242.754242
Davolio	182500.09	1559.829829
Dodsworth	75048.04	1830.44
Fuller	161336.98	1753.662826
King	116962.99	1745.716269
Leverling	201196.27	1609.57016
Peacock	225763.68	1495.123709
Suyama	72527.63	1115.809692
Grand Total	**1227727.6**	**1534.6595**

Figure 8–33. That same field, but now subject to two different mathmatical operations

A little more intelligible, no? Notice the new *Values* column, because the pivot report needs to differentiate between what are now two set of data values; and Order Amount is now both added and averaged.

And if you think Average of Order Amount2 is a less-than-scintillating title, all you need do is click on that title, and edit it right there in the cell (or in the Formula Bar). Type a different title, and just press Enter.

Filters Again-PivotTable Style

As we've wended our way across the pivot report landscape you've doubtless noticed those drop-down arrow handles sidling the various label headings in the reports. They should look familiar, too, because they bear a not-so-coincidental similarity to the AutoFilter handles we explored in Chapter 6—and basically, that's what they are. And they're just about as easy to use.

Consider our pivot report as it currently stands, as portrayed in Figure 8–30. We're looking at the *number* of sales registered by each salesperson. Now suppose we want to concentrate on King's sales data alone (remember-if our sales force numbered 90 or 900 operatives instead of the nine in our report, our interest in plucking just one salesperson out of the mass of employees might be more illustrative). The method here is pure AutoFilter:

1. Click the handle alongside Salesperson. You'll see (Figure 8–34):

Figure 8–34. You've seen something like this before, too—a filter drop-down menu, here in PivotTables.

2. Click *(Select All)*. All the checks alongside all the Salesperson names disappear.

3. Check King.

4. Click OK. You'll see (Figure 8–35):

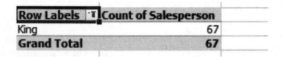

Figure 8–35. Royal total: King's number of sales

You get the idea. To restore all the salesperson names, click the filter handle again and click either *Clear Filter From Salesperson*, or click the now-blackened (Select All) box above all the salesperson names. All the names reappear. If you want to filter several names, just click the check box alongside those salespersons you want to see after clicking Select All off.

And similar to AutoFilters, you can customize what it is you're looking for by selecting either the *Label* or *Value Filters* option on that same drop-down menu (Figure 8–36):

Figure 8–36. *Filter customizing options*

Thus had I clicked **Begins With…** I could have entered the K in the resulting dialog box, and all the salespersons whose name starts with that letter would be filtered. And if you're wondering what **Greater Than** and similar criteria here mean—because we are working with *text*—if I enter the letter K in the Greater Than dialog box, Excel will search for all names with a letter starting *after* K, or K plus additional letters. Thus here I'd get King (because King has letters in addition to K), Peacock, and Suyama.

Note as well that the above menu also offers sort options very similar to those available in the AutoFilter drop-down, with one exception—the **Manual** sort option. Click **More Sort Options ▶ Manual** (Figure 8–37):

Figure 8–37. *Sort options*

Once this option is selected (though this *is* the default selection) you can click on any super category (that is, data in the first Row Labels column) entry, release the mouse, and then rest the mouse again over the lower cell border of that entry. When you see a four-sided arrow, click and drag the entry to any other position in the column. You can do the same with data in the Column Label area; only here, you click on the *right* border of the entry you wish to move, and drag it horizontally to any position in the Column Label area.

Your Very Own Top 10 List

Now here's yet another very useful filtering technique of sorts. For the sake of simplicity, let's scale down our pivot report so that Salesperson occupies the Row Labels area, and Sum of Order Amount holds down the Values area. If you right-click anywhere in the Row Labels area and click the *Filter* ➤ *Top 10…*, you'll see (Figure 8–38):

Figure 8–38. The Top 10 dialog box

Now because we have only nine salespersons, a Top 10 list just won't do. If you either type 5 to replace the number 10 or click the down arrow until you arrive at that number and click OK, you'll see (Figure 8–39):

Sum of Order Amount	
Salesperson	Total
Callahan	123032.67
Davolio	182500.09
Fuller	162503.78
Leverling	201196.27
Peacock	225763.68
Grand Total	894996.49

Figure 8–39. Quite a quintet-the top five salespersons, by dollars generated

Now you're identified the five highest sales achievers. You could also substitute **Bottom** for **Top** in the leftmost field in the dialog box, as well as **Percent** for **Items**. Thus you could determine the either the top ten, or the top ten percent, of test scorers in a class of 500 students, for example. To turn off this feature, right-click again in the Row Table area and click the Filter ➤ *Clear Filter From…* command. All the records return. Bet Letterman can't do any of this.

The Report Filter—Getting on Top of the PivotTable

Now there's still *another* filtering option we've yet to explore, one I've studiously omitted until now—the ***Report Filter*** area. In reality, this area represents a variation on the filtering themes we've already discussed.

As we've seen, when you're working with several different fields at the same, the fields could be arrayed in several different ways. Thus if we want to compose a pivot report in which sales activity is broken out both by the salesperson and the country in which he does business, we could generate this report (Figure 8–40):

Row Labels	Sum of Order Amount
⊟ UK	333897.91
Buchanan	69359.25
Dodsworth	75048.04
King	116962.99
Suyama	72527.63
⊟ USA	893829.69
Callahan	123032.67
Davolio	182500.09
Fuller	161336.98
Leverling	201196.27
Peacock	225763.68
Grand Total	**1227727.6**

Figure 8–40. Country sales, by salespersons

Or, by exchanging the order of Salesperson and Country, this (Figure 8–41):

Row Labels	Sum of Order Amount
⊟ Buchanan	
UK	69359.25
⊟ Callahan	
USA	123032.67
⊟ Davolio	
USA	182500.09
⊟ Dodsworth	
UK	75048.04
⊟ Fuller	
USA	161336.98
⊟ King	
UK	116962.99
⊟ Leverling	
USA	201196.27
⊟ Peacock	
USA	225763.68
⊟ Suyama	
UK	72527.63
Grand Total	**1227727.6**

Figure 8–41. Salespersons, by country

That's not bad, but the recurring UKs and USAs are a touch untidy; and there's a neater approach. Drag Country into the Report Filter area. You'll see (Figure 8–42):

Country	(All)	
Row Labels ·1	**Sum of Order Amount**	
Buchanan	69359.25	
Callahan	123032.67	
Davolio	182500.09	
Dodsworth	75048.04	
Fuller	161336.98	
King	116962.99	
Leverling	201196.27	
Peacock	225763.68	
Suyama	72527.63	
Grand Total	**1227727.6**	

Figure 8–42. Putting the Report Filter in place

Then click the filter handle by Country and click USA. You'll see (Figure 8–43):

Country	USA	
Row Labels ·1	**Sum of Order Amount**	
Callahan	123032.67	
Davolio	182500.09	
Fuller	161336.98	
Leverling	201196.27	
Peacock	225763.68	
Grand Total	**893829.69**	

Figure 8–43. Yankee imperialism: The Report filter applied to USA sales data

Installing a field into the Report Filter area doesn't really introduce any new *information* into the report. What it does is offer a different, sparer look to the data. Here USA appears but once, hovering above the data, and impacting it unobtrusively. And by clicking the filter handle up there you can naturally select UK instead. (You'll also have to remove the check mark by USA).

You can *also* move two or more fields into the Report Filter area. If you drag the ***OrderID*** field there, say below Country (Figure 8–44):

Figure 8–44. *Report Filtering by two fields*

You'll wind up with this (Figure 8–45):

Country	UK	
OrderID	(All)	

Salesperson ▼	Sum of Order Amount
Buchanan	69359.25
Dodsworth	75048.04
King	116962.99
Suyama	72527.63
Grand Total	**333897.91**

Figure 8–45. *This double Report Filter can be tweaked to bring about this result…*

As a result, you'll be able to conduct a double filter, by selecting a particular order ID as well as a country (Figure 8–46):

Country	UK	
OrderID	10255	

Salesperson ▼	Sum of Order Amount
Dodsworth	2490.5
Grand Total	**2490.5**

Figure 8–46. *…where the data are showing all UK sales with the selected OrderID*

It's true that these little tweaks need to be thought through. The primary question you need to ask as you proceed is, of course: What information do I need to see in the pivot report? In the above case, because all the OrderIDs are unique, the Country filter doesn't really do any more filtering, or narrowing down, of the data. There's only one Order ID 10255, irrespective of country. But if for some reason the Order IDs on USA sales were sometimes duplicated by *UK* Order IDs, you *would* be well advised to apply both Country and OrderID filters in order to sift the data more precisely. In this way you'd be able to filter *only* the *UK* Order ID 10255, and exclude Order ID 10255 from the USA.

You also need to keep in mind that the filters don't filter each other. To explain: If you select both Country and OrderID in that order (no pun intended) as filters, and you click UK for Country, *all* the order IDs will still appear when you then click the OrderID drop-down arrow—including the order IDs on USA sales. Thus if you filter for UK along with a USA order ID—which you're able to do-your pivot report will show…nothing.

You can also select two or more items in the same filtered field. If, for example, you move the Salesperson field to the Report Filter area, I can filter data for several salespersons at the same time. To try this:

1. Click the PivotTable Tools ➤ Options tab ➤ Clear ➤ Clear All.

2. Move the *Order Amount* field into the Values area.

3. Move Salesperson into the Report Filter area. Your report should look like this now (Figure 8–47):

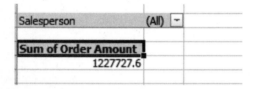

Figure 8–47. Filtering the sales order amounts by salesperson

Note the Total represents the aggregate of *all* sales, because we haven't broken sales out by any other field yet. The *(All)* notation in the Salesperson filter means exactly that-at the moment, the sales of *all the* salespersons are being totaled.

4. Click the filter handle down arrow ➤ Uncheck the All checkbox. ➤ Check *Select Multiple Items* ➤ check Callahan and Dodsworth. ➤ Click OK.

5. The new sum beneath Total is naturally smaller, because now the sales data for only two salespersons has been filtered (Figure 8–48):

Salesperson	(Multiple Items)
Sum of Order Amount	
198080.71	

Figure 8–48. A Report Filter for two salespersons—but which two?

The problem here is that the entry alongside Salesperson—Multiple Items—is not very revealing. You can't tell exactly *which* salespersons have been included by the filter, and you may need to be able to present that information on screen. What to do?

The Slicer—Filter Deluxe

The answer to that question arrived with the release of Excel 2010—with the brand-new *Slicer*. The Slicer is a utility that allows you to filter *any* field in your source data, whether it is—or isn't—currently populating the pivot report. And it lets you *see* the data you've actually selected for the filter.

By way of a first Slicer illustration, here's how Order Amounts as filtered by Salespersons Callahan and Dodsworth would, or could, look (Figure 8–49):

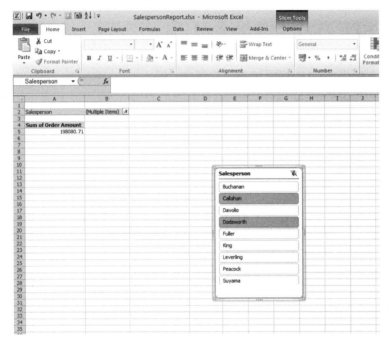

Figure 8–49. Now it can be told: here they are—courtesy of the Slicer

Here the Slicer clearly enumerates the salespersons who've contributed to the current order amount, as detailed in the pivot report. I can click on any salesperson I see listed above, and her sales activity will be added to the existing total. (Note: if you hold down the Ctrl key you can select multiple names as you click. And if you've already selected some, or even one, salesperson name, simply clicking on another name *without* Ctrl turns off the existing selections.)

But note—even if I *remove* the Salesperson field from the Report Filter area, the Slicer *continues* to do its filtering work (Figure 8–50):

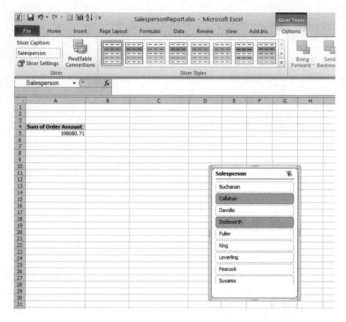

Figure 8–50. Still Slicing, even though the Salesperson field has been removed from the PivotTable

Here the Report Filter is vacant, and yet the Slicer is still slicing. And yes, Slicers can be resized and moved about the worksheet, and they will print along with the pivot report.

Slicers also alleviate a problem we identified a bit earlier. First, you can introduce as many slicers into your worksheet as there are source data fields—and they slice each other. That is, if you call up Slicers for both Country and OrderID, by clicking UK in the *Country Slicer*, you'll restrict the Order IDs that appear in the OrderID Slicer to the *UK* sales only.

With the Slicer, it's now possible to construct a pivot report containing only one field in its grid, with Slicers contributing all the other input. Thus if I place the Order Amount data in the pivot report Values area I can then manufacture a *Salesperson Slicer* and click the names there—right on the Slicer—and still see the sales data change in the Values area. (Clicking the X you see in the Slicer's upper right corner won't turn the Slicer off—it'll turn the *filter* off, meaning it'll click all the items in the Slicer on, for tallying in the pivot report. Thus clicking the X on the Salesperson Slicer means data for all the salespersons will be applied to the pivot report.)

Thus the Slicer is a kind of free-standing, offshore filter which isn't locked into the pivot report grid, rather doing the work of filtering at a distance—sort of a Bluetooth, hands-free extension of the pivot report, meandering around the worksheet wherever you position it, but still impacting the report in important ways.

To add a Slicer—or Slicers—click anywhere in the pivot report and then click PivotTable Tools ➤ Options ➤ *Insert Slicer*....You'll see (Figure 8–51):

Figure 8–51. Choose your Slicers here

Then just click the fields you want sliced, so to speak. Their Slicers appear on screen. Once you've requisitioned them, just click on the names, order numbers, etc., for which you want to see the pivot report results. (You do have to have *some* data in the Values area in order for the Slicers to work. Remember that Slicers are really filters, and they need some data to filter.)

You can move Slicers onscreen by grabbing onto a blank area of the Slicer. Maneuver your mouse across the Slicer until you see a four-sided arrow; then click and drag the Slicer to a new location. You can also resize Slicers by resting your mouse atop one of the dotted sections on any Slicer border, producing a double-sided arrow, and dragging the border in the desired direction.

To remove a Slicer, right-click atop its surface, and click **Remove** [field name].

You can modify the color scheme of any Slicer by clicking the **Slicer Tools** tab (this appears when you click on any Slicer) ➤ **Options** ➤ **Slicer Styles**. You'll see a collection of formats from which to choose (Figure 8–52):

Figure 8–52. A Slicer looks nicer in color

The colors are not mere design touches—they color the field items you've currently selected for filtering differently from the ones you haven't.

Grouping the Data

PivotTables and pivot reports are indeed all about aggregating the data. But data aggregation can assume different forms. Thus far we've described ways in which data vested in the Values area can be aggregated, and that's an essential PivotTable task. But sometimes you also want to aggregate the *categories* by which the values are totaled.

For example—our source data contains an Order Date field, each entry consisting simply of the date on which a sale was executed. But PivotTables allow us to convert, or aggregate, those dates into months, which could make for a more concise, and probably more revealing, report. Let's try it.

1. First, click anywhere in the source data, and click the Insert tab ➤ PivotTable. A new worksheet is manufactured, which asks us to select the pivot report fields we want.

2. Click *Order Date* in the PivotTable. Note these data automatically populate the Row Label area, which is where we want them to go.

3. Then click *Order Amount*, whose data are dispatched to the Value area—again, where we want them. Our report thus looks like this (Figure 8–53):

Row Labels ▾	Sum of Order Amount
7/10/03	1863.4
7/11/03	3597.9
7/12/03	1552.6
7/15/03	3144.56
7/16/03	1884.8
7/17/03	517.8
7/22/03	1119.9
7/23/03	2171.5
7/25/03	684.8
7/29/03	1504.65
7/30/03	448
7/31/03	2220.36
8/2/03	2477.2
8/6/03	4992.6
8/9/03	934.04
8/12/03	3213.28
8/13/03	1200.8
8/14/03	420
8/16/03	2378.4
8/21/03	241.9
8/23/03	2110.42
8/26/03	1743.36

Figure 8–53. A collection of sales transaction dates, to be grouped by their respective months

That's just an excerpt, of course; there are many more records in the report. Thus we see that each sale is broken out by its date—with the proviso that should two or more sales have been conducted on the same date, their data would be aggregated or added *together*—because again, entries in the Row Label area appear uniquely.

4. Now click anywhere in the Order Date data. Then click PivotTable Tools ➤ Options tab ➤ *Group Selection* in the *Group* button group. You'll call up this dialog box (Figure 8–54):

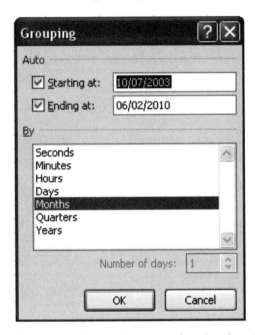

Figure 8–54. Here's where you select time-based grouping interval

5. Note the various grouping options, which obviously apply to date data. We'll leave the default Months selection in place and ➤ click OK. You'll see (Figure 8–55):

4	Order Date	Sum of Order Amount
5	Jan	148398.03
6	Feb	147158.25
7	Mar	125043.89
8	Apr	174498.38
9	May	70907.57
10	Jun	50082.98
11	Jul	58255.21
12	Aug	80345.93
13	Sep	68537.43
14	Oct	117996.88
15	Nov	79904.01
16	Dec	106599.04
17	**Grand Total**	**1227727.6**

Figure 8–55. Aggregating by months discloses important patterns in sales activity

I'd say that's pretty cool—and useful. The pivot report has combined, or aggregated, the dates into a larger category, in this case months, thus enabling us to break out the sales data by that unit. You could also select both *Years* and *Months* in the Grouping dialog box by way of additional example, whereupon the data would be broken out by year, and then by months below each year. And if we want to return the data to their original state, just click in the Row Labels area and repeat the above command sequence, substituting *Ungroup Group*.

The grouping option can also be productively applied to standard numerical data in addition to dates, provided those data are placed in the Row or Column areas. For example-I could place the Order Amount data in the Row Label area—something we've yet to do, because these kinds of data are usually sent to the Values area to be added, averaged, etc. But if I do go ahead and assign Order Amount to the Row Labels area, I'll see, at least in part (Figure 8–56):

Row Labels
$12.50
$18.40
$23.80
$28.00
$30.00
$33.75
$36.00
$40.00
$45.00
$48.00
$48.75
$49.80
$52.35
$55.20
$55.80
$57.50
$57.80

Figure 8–56. Listed numbers: Each transaction sum, arrayed in the row label area

True to Row Label form, the data here are merely *listed* uniquely (and that means if two sales came to say, $50 each, that number would be listed only once). Now, if I click the *Group Selection* command, I'll see (Figure 8–57):

Figure 8–57. Grouping this time by the sales order amounts

The Grouping dialog box here records the highest and lowest values among all the sales—a span—and a suggested grouping interval, which we'll accept. (Note: By typing a larger value, say 100, in *Starting at:*, you can restrict the grouping to begin at the value *you've* designated. The sub-100 values will also be grouped, but in a "<100 category".) By clicking OK, we get (Figure 8–58):

Row Labels ⏷
12.5-1012.5
1012.5-2012.5
2012.5-3012.5
3012.5-4012.5
4012.5-5012.5
5012.5-6012.5
6012.5-7012.5
7012.5-8012.5
8012.5-9012.5
9012.5-10012.5
10012.5-11012.5
11012.5-12012.5
12012.5-13012.5
15012.5-16012.5
16012.5-17012.5
Grand Total

Figure 8–58. Big bucks: The transaction data, grouped in intervals of $1000

See what happens? The pivot report aggregated, or *grouped*, the sales order data by units of $1000 (Note: These aggregated intervals cannot be reformatted). If we then drag the *same* Order Amounts field into the Values area—where it usually goes—but change its mathematical operation to *Count*, we wind up with this (Figure 8–59):

Row Labels	Count of Order Amount
12.5-1012.5	409
1012.5-2012.5	211
2012.5-3012.5	91
3012.5-4012.5	33
4012.5-5012.5	26
5012.5-6012.5	5
6012.5-7012.5	7
7012.5-8012.5	1
8012.5-9012.5	4
9012.5-10012.5	3
10012.5-11012.5	5
11012.5-12012.5	2
12012.5-13012.5	1
15012.5-16012.5	1
16012.5-17012.5	1
Grand Total	800

Figure 8–59. Numbers of sales, grouped by transaction size in dollars

True—you may need to think about this one. What we've done here is break out the *number* of sales *by the size of each sale*, in sales intervals of $1,000. Thus, for example, there were 7 sales carried out that were between $6012.50 and $7012.50, and 211 between £1012.50 and $2012.50. OK, granted-this was a tricky one: take the rest the day off (but before you do, *note* that grouped data may continue to appear grouped on other new pivot reports in the workbook, and so you may need to ungroup these sooner or later in any case).

Formatting the Pivot Report—Values and All

Formatting a pivot report is pretty easy, because most of the options here reiterate the basic options you've already learned. To format numbers, you can do one of two things: either right-click on *any* value in the field you wish to format, select *Value Field Settings* on the resulting shortcut menu, and then click *Number Format*, which is really little more than a tab on the good old Format Cells dialog box that we ran into so often way back in Chapter 4 (Figure 8–60):

Figure 8–60. And we've certainly seen THIS one before; the good old Number tab, here used by PivotTables

Then make your selection as per the formatting instructions in Chapter 4. *Note* that right-clicking on any one value and selecting the appropriate format affects *all* the data in that field. You can also arrive at the Value Field Settings dialog box by clicking PivotTables Tools ➤ Options ➤ Summarize Values By ➤ *More Options*.

You can introduce report-wide format changes by clicking PivotTable Tools ➤ *Design* tab ➤ *PivotTable Styles* (drop-down arrows). These selections emulate the table-wide formats available for standard Excel Tables (Figure 8–61):

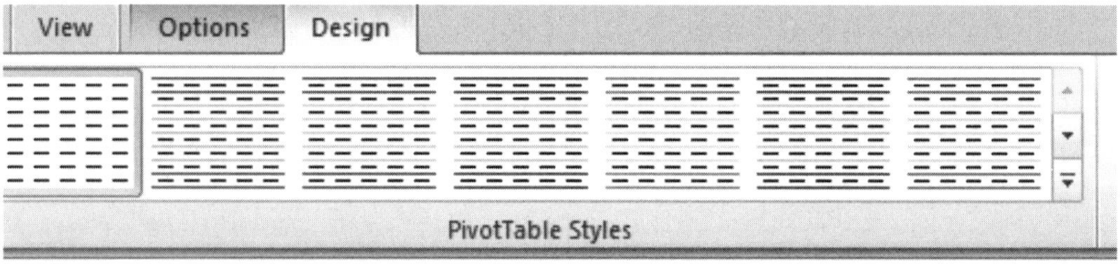

Figure 8–61. Setting the table: PivotTable style options

Just click one. And you have the same Banded Rows/Banded Columns options you're presented with in the standard table styles.

The *Grand Totals* option on the Design tab allows you to remove the pivot report grand totals that appear by default, as well as institute Grand Totals for *rows*, applying to data that reads across columns. You can also select any range of cells and utilize Excel's complement of basic formatting embellishments; including that context menu you've seen before (Figure 8–62):

Figure 8–62. *Just a handy right-click away*

Pivot Charts

It's a pretty short trip from pivot reports to their more showy neighbors, pivot charts, and the trip is a pretty easy one to take. And once your pivot chart beaches up on the worksheet, you can call upon most of the same charting options we described in the charting chapter. As we'll see, however, pivot charts work slightly differently from the conventional chart types.

You can compose a pivot chart in one of two ways, either by grabbing the data from an existing pivot report and routing them to a chart, or by designing a chart from scratch via PivotTable commands (but if you opt for the latter, you should ask yourself whether you need to work with PivotTables at all, rather than Excel's standard charting tools).

Let's give one a try, applying the first method to a simple pivot report.

1. Click anywhere in the source data and click Insert ➤ PivotTable ➤ OK.

2. Then click Salesperson and Order Amount on the PivotTable Field List, and you wind up with this familiar scenario (Figure 8–63):

Row Labels	Sum of Order Amount
Buchanan	69359.25
Callahan	123032.67
Davolio	182500.09
Dodsworth	75048.04
Fuller	162503.78
King	116962.99
Leverling	201196.27
Peacock	225763.68
Suyama	72527.63
Grand Total	**1228894.4**

Figure 8–63. *We'll start charting with these pivot data*

3. Then all you need to do is click PivotTable Tools ➤ Pivot Chart. You'll be taken to this old friend (Figure 8–64):

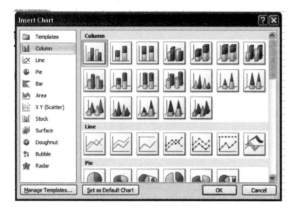

Figure 8–64. The Insert Chart dialog box, brought to PivotTables

4. Click OK to accept the default selections, and view (Figure 8–65):

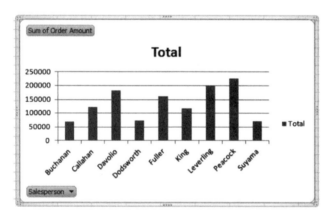

Figure 8–65. From column labels to a column chart

In most respects—save those two buttons nestled in the chart's left area-you've planted a garden-variety Excel chart on the worksheet, subject to the same inventory of charting options as usual. As for those two buttons? Click the lower of the two and you'll behold the standard PivotTable filter menu (Figure 8–66):

Figure 8–66. *Filtering a pivot chart*

Click any salesperson name and his/her column bar will vanish from the chart—***but it will likewise vanish from the pivot report that gave rise to the chart.*** That is, the chart impacts the pivot report, so that, for example, if I check Callahan's name off the chart, Callahan will be missing as well on the pivot report.

As for the other button, in our case entitled ***Sum of Order Amount***, right-clicking it will call up another standard shortcut menu (Figure 8–67):

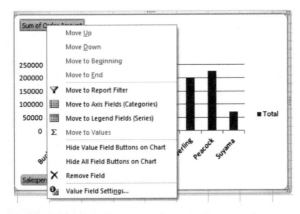

Figure 8–67. *Where to modify the vertical chart axis*

Right-clicking it will, among other options, allow you to change the mathematical operation that gives rise to the chart results—to salesperson average sale, for example. Again, just click Value Field Settings to set that process in motion. But bear in mind again that any such change will *also* change the pivot report results in the same way.

If you find these two buttons obtrusive, you can turn them off by right-clicking either one and selecting ***Hide All Field Buttons On Chart***. To return these to the chart, click the PivotChart Tools tab that appears whenever you click on the chart, and then click the ***Analyze*** tab ➤ ***Field Buttons*** in the ***Show/Hide*** button group ➤ ***Hide All***, which should currently be clicked.

Another note: it's easy to overlook this, but when you click in the pivot chart (and only when you do), the button area in the lower half of the PivotTable Field List changes to this (Figure 8–68):

Figure 8–68. Note the Row and Column Lables areas are temporarily renamed when you work with a pivot chart.

Note the Row Labels area is renamed *Axis Fields* (Categories), and the Columns Labels area is dubbed *Legend Fields* (Series). That may be a bit puzzling, but Axis Fields really denotes the X, or horizontal axis—in our case displaying the salesperson names, which are positioned in the Row Labels area in the pivot report. Legend Fields refers to multiple *data series*. Say we redesigned our pivot report to look like this (Figure 8–69):

Sum of Order Amount	Salesperson									
Country	Buchanan	Callahan	Davolio	Dodsworth	Fuller	King	Leverling	Peacock	Suyama	Grand Total
UK	69359.25			75048.04		116962.99			72527.63	333897.91
USA		123032.67	182500.09		161336.98		201196.27	225763.68		893829.69
Grand Total	69359.25	123032.67	182500.09	75048.04	161336.98	116962.99	201196.27	225763.68	72527.63	1227727.6

Figure 8–69. Redesign the PivotTable and you redesign the chart

where Salesperson has been installed in the Columns Labels area; the pivot chart would look like this (Figure 8–70):

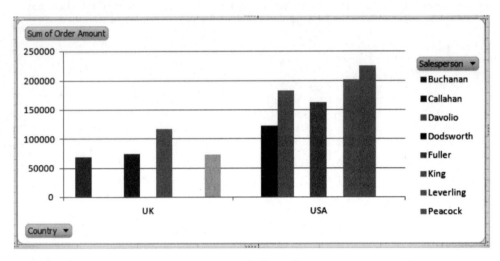

Figure 8–70. Here the Salesepesons appear in the legend

Here the chart legend lists the salespersons, each one now a data series; and as a result the Salesperson button will appear in Legend Fields (Series). (If you can't see all the text in this button area, you can click on and drag the left edge of the PivotTable Field List pane.)

Now for the second pivot chart approach. Here you initiate the process by clicking anywhere in the source data and then Insert tab ➤ the PivotTable down arrow ➤ Pivot Chart ➤ OK (we're accepting the defaults in the dialog box here). You'll see (Figure 8–71):

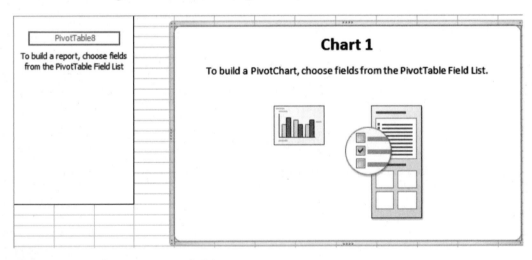

Figure 8–71. Another way to start charting

(Note: the **PivotTable8** legend in the PivotTable grid in the upper left of screen shot merely refers to the number of PivotTables I've constructed on the workbook).

Once this tableau is ushered onto the screen, you can click on or drag the fields in the PivotTable Field List into the appropriate button areas, just as if you were constructing a pivot report. Just remember however that here, Row Labels is called Axis Fields (Categories), and the Columns Labels area reverts to Legend Fields (Series). By simply clicking the checkboxes by Salesperson and Order Amount, I'll produce precisely the same chart you see in Figure 8–70).

And if you want to delete a pivot report, click anywhere in the report and click PivotTable Tools ➤ Options tab ➤ the **Select** down arrow in the Actions button group ➤ **Entire PivotTable**. Then press the Delete key. To delete a pivot chart, just select it (you can select it when you see the four-side arrow over the chart) and press Delete. Interestingly enough, if you delete a pivot report that has been used as the source of a pivot chart, deleting the *report* leaves the chart onscreen, even though it's no longer connected with any data. However, if you click Options ➤ Actions ➤ **Clear** ➤ **Clear All**, you'll delete *both* the PivotTable and its associated chart.

In Conclusion…

Once you get the hang of them, pivot reports and charts equip you with a potent and agile means for aggregating large amounts of data into informative categories. PivotTables grant you the ability to answer these kinds of questions:

- How many sales did each salesperson achieve?

- What's the average grade point average of students, broken out by their major?

- How much money did we spend on transportation in January?

- Who were in the top 5 percent off all home run hitters last year?

The key to understanding PivotTables is to understand which data goes where, and, prior to actually composing the tables, thinking about how to arrange the data that contribute to them. For example, our salesperson workbook could have assigned a different column to each salesperson, but that would greatly complicate the data aggregation tasks at which PivotTables are so adept. Try that approach and you'll see what I mean; you'll have more aggravation than aggregation.

Remember that the data you want counted, summed, or averaged go in the Values area. The *categories* by which the data are broken out go into the Row and/or Column Labels, or Report Filter areas. It's tempting to say that by merely clicking and dragging various source data fields around the pivot report you can experiment and simply see what happens. But it really helps to appreciate *how* the areas interact with one other—the what-goes-where question-and that appreciation will speed the table construction process.

It's true—nail these concepts down and you can assemble a PivotTable in about four seconds. Ok—maybe five.

But now that you've mastered all these sophisticated number-crunching techniques, you still need to know how to bring these results to good old hard copy pages—at least once in a while. Next up: Printing in Excel.

CHAPTER 9

■ ■ ■

Getting It On Paper— Printing in Excel 2010

Stop me if you've heard this one before: An efficiency expert intercepts a 911 call from a desperate boss, begging her to drop everything, don her flak jacket and sensible shoes, and zoom over *now* to do something about his workplace, overrun to the breaking point with unstoppable, rectangular blobs of paper. Throwing caution to the winds, our fearless expert pokes through the debris, and after skidding on a couple of 8½ x 11s and running her paper cuts under the water cooler, finally doffs her helmet and announces hopefully: "It's really very simple: All you need to do is just scan all these hard copies, and burn them onto a couple of CDs; in a few hours you'll be able to see your floor again."

"Great idea!" exults the grateful boss. "But just one thing: before I start scanning, let me make some Xeroxes for backup…"

Paperless office? Probably not *your* office, and probably not your home, either. They still make Excel with the Print command, and sooner or later you're going to have to beam that digital doc to your local neighborhood output device and turn it into something you can actually hold in your hand and spill coffee on. It's retro, but true; you need to know how to print, and when you do, Excel makes it pretty easy to navigate the transition from software to hard copy.

The first thing to understand about Excel printing is to know exactly how much of the workbook you want to print. By default—that is, if you work with the initial print settings supplied by Excel— carrying out the print command will print the entire worksheet (but not the entire workbook). And by the entire worksheet, Excel means *all the cells in the sheet containing data*. And that means in turn that, if you want to print the cells spanning A3:B20 and you've also squirreled a clandestine value in cell X4578, Excel will print 258 pages or thereabouts. That's because when it goes ahead with those default print settings Excel prints all the empty space *between* the data-bearing cells in addition to those cells you really want to print; it preserves the relation in space between all the cells from A3:B20 through X4578. As a result, I'll print 256 empty sheets in addition to the two that contain my values.

Of course, that's an extreme—but not unprecedented—scenario. Worksheets can be teeming with data, and even if those data are confined to one particular area of the worksheet—say, to a 20,000-row table, of which you want to print just 500—going with the default print settings will get you 20,000 rows worth of paper.

Hard Copy? Pretty Easy

Needless to say, Excel is happy to let you overrule its defaults, but it's time we tried this all out. Let's call up the Sales by Year spreadsheet, and click on the 2010 tab, containing that small range of sales data for that year. Let's say we want to print the entire sheet, at least for starters. To start printing (after you'd made sure you're duly connected to a printer, and that it's turned on), you can click the *File* tab ➤ *Print*, or click the primeval keyboard equivalent, Ctrl-P. You'll see (Figure 9-1):

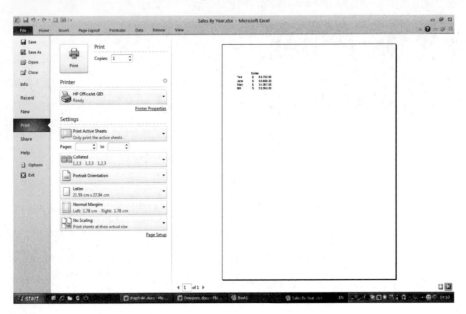

Figure 9–1. *The Excel 2010 Print Preview—part of what's called the Backstage View in 2010*

Note first of all the Print Preview occupying the right half of the screen. The desired print range is captured, and all the default settings remain in place at the outset. To review the settings:

- The *Copies* option is pretty self-evident. If you need to print multiple copies, just type the copy total or click up the spin control arrow.

- *Printer* designates the printer that will output the copies. Because you may have access to more than one printer, you may have to click this option's drop-down arrow and select the appropriate device. Among the "devices" you may see a *Print to PDF* option—not really a bit of hardware but the widely-used document *format*, through which an Excel workbook can be read by users who don't have Excel. By selecting this option you'll "print" a PDF file to your computer. And if you need to identify your printer for the first time, the Printer command's *Add Printer...* options lets you start that process.)

- The *Settings* area features a number of important fields, its options presented in drop-down menus. *Print Active Sheets* serves as the default in the first of these, and when selected prints all the data in the active sheets. But why the *plural*— why *sheets*? That possibility refers to sheets which may have been grouped, and if you *have* grouped multiple sheets, the data on all of them will be printed, and on separate pages—at least by default. Continuing with the field's other options: *Print Entire Workbook* will print all the data on all the sheets of the workbook, each worksheet assigned its own print page. Of course, if the data on any one worksheet is extensive, that sheet may require a multi-page printout in its own right. *Print Selection*, sub-captioned Only print the current selection, lets you select a range on the sheet and designate *just* that range for print output. Thus if you select 500 of the 20,000 rows in the table we cited earlier, only the 500 will print—and you'll see evidence to that effect in the Print Preview (note that a multi-page Print Preview lets you click to each page via the arrows at the bottom of the screen). However, if you click in a table, a new option presents itself in the drop-down menu—*Print Selected Table*. Click it, and just the table prints.

The Print Area Option

The final option in this field—*Ignore Print Area*—requires a bit of a digression. We've already seen how the Print Selection command works, but you can also select a range of cells before you click the Print command and then click the *Page Layout* tab ➤ *Print Area* in the *Page Setup* button group ➤ *Set Print Area*. Doing so draws a dotted border around the range you want to print, and lets you carry on other spreadsheet activity before you decide to print. When you're ready, execute the Print command sequence. You can leave the default Print Active Sheets option in place because you've already established, or saved, your specific print area—and that's what will print. Setting a Print Area also means you can print that area several times, separating each print with other spreadsheet activity and returning to printing when you wish. All the printouts will remember that print area, until you change it. In any case, selecting Ignore Print Area means you can leave the Set Print Area range in place but select a *different* range, or even the whole sheet, to print in its stead on an ad-hoc basis. If you then select the Print Selection option, you can print this improvised range, and then click Ignore Print Area back off, and the range you've identified via Set Print Area reverts to the operative print range.

To illustrate this option, open the SampleSalesPerson report on which we tried out our pivot tables. Click if necessary on the Source Data tab at the bottom, and select cells A1:E50. Then click Page Layout ➤ Print Area ➤ Set Print Area. A dotted border bounds the range. Then click File ➤ Print. You'll see (Figure 9-2):

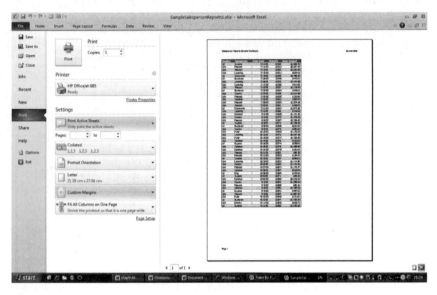

Figure 9–2. The current print range, as displayed in the Backstage

Note the selected print area we've established—A1:E50—appears in the preview. Then click Ignore Print Area, and you'll see (Figure 9-3):

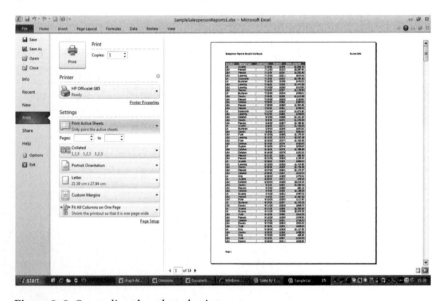

Figure 9–3. Overruling the selected print area

Note the page count at the bottom of the page: 14. That means if we launched a printout right now Excel would print the *entire* table, because we've temporarily overridden the A1:E50 print range and returned to the Print Active Sheets default, as it's shown in the Backstage. Then by clicking Ignore Print Area *off*, we'll return to the A1:E50 selection. And you can turn your Print Area off *permanently* by clicking Page Layout ➤ Print Area ➤ *Clear Print Area*.

- The *Pages* option enables you to indicate which pages you want printed, in the event your selected print range—or the entire active sheet - spans more than one page. Note by default the page number fields are blank. By clicking the horizontal arrows at the bottom of the page you can view how your data appear before selecting your pages. What this means is that if you select some, but not all, of the pages to print you're really carrying out a kind of alternative Print Selection command. Note as well that, unlike Word, you can't print non-consecutive pages in Excel.

- The *Collated* options really only apply to multi-page, multi-copy printouts and work very similarly to the way in which they work in Word. By default, Excel collates by printing copies separately in their page sequence. Thus if we were to print three copies of the entire Source Data sheet in the SampleSalesPerson workbook, we'd roll out all 14 pages, 1-14, three times. The *Uncollated* (another Un word—even Word redlines it) option, however, prints *all* the page ones, twos, threes, etc. together in that sequence. Printing the Source Data sheet in Uncollated fashion would yield three page ones, three page twos, etc. And why would one want to print this way? Perhaps because a lecturer who needed to enter some handwritten corrections on all the page ones, for example, could more easily grab every copy of that particular page via an Uncollated printout.

- *Portrait Orientation* is Excel's default print orientation. That is, leave this option as is and your printout will appear in a vertical, upright position. Your print needs may often require a landscape, or sideways orientation, though, and if that's the case simply click the *Landscape* orientation. Either way, the Print Preview will display the pages in the selected orientation. (Note: You can also access the Orientation option by clicking the *Printer Properties* link beneath the Printer drop-down menu, as well as by clicking the Page Layout tab ➤ Page Setup ➤ Orientation.)

- The *Letter* drop-down menu provides a series of paper sizes you can select for your print. Naturally, the standard 8½ x 11 size appears by default (or A4 if you're on the other side of the pond), but the associated drop-down menu stocks a long list of additional options. And if those aren't enough, clicking the *More Paper Sizes...* selection calls up the ageless *Page Setup* dialog box (Figure 9-4):

Figure 9–4. The Page Setup dialog box

Click its **Paper Size** down arrow and still more possibilities materialize. You can even print to an index card, or a Japanese postcard. We'll have more to say about Page Setup later.

Margin-al Utility

The **Margins** option lets you adjust this print dimension. We generally don't think of spreadsheet margins in the same terms we ascribe to word processing, where they play an essential role. As a rule we don't trouble ourselves with Excel margins, because working electronically on formulas and tables doesn't require a uniform layout, at least not usually. But a printout is a printout, and you have no choice but to consider its margins once you put toner to paper. By default, Excel starts you off with margins of .7 inches left/right, and .75 inches top/bottom—what it calls **Normal Margins** (the Headers options will be discussed soon), but you can obviously change these as you wish. Click the drop-down arrow by the Margins option and you'll be brought to two additional built-in recommendations, **Wide** and **Narrow**. The former suggests measures of 1 inch in both directions, while Narrow offers a top/bottom of .75 inches, and .25 inches left/right. Not happy with any of these? Click the **Custom Margins...** option, and you'll be returned to the Page Setup dialog box, this time its Margins tab (Figure 9-5):

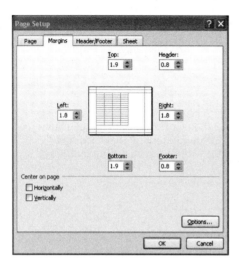

Figure 9–5. The Margins tab in Page Setup

Page Setup allows you to type or click margins of your own choosing, and also introduces a different and useful option as well—***Center on Page***, which enables you to center a print range horizontally across a page, and/or vertically over the length of the page. Select both possibilities and your printout winds up smack-dab in the middle of a page. Note the change in position of the sample image when I click both centering options (Figure 9-6):

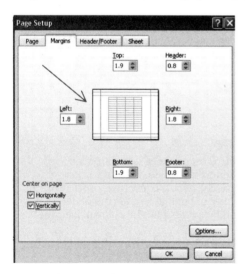

Figure 9–6. Centering the page horizontally and vertically

(Note: The Page Setup dialog can also be accessed by clicking the ***Page Setup*** link at the bottom of the Print dialog box, as well as by clicking the dialog box launcher in the Page Setup button group on the Page Layout tab.)

Printing As You See Fit

The final option in the Settings group in the Print menu controls *Scaling* (sounds like a hair shampoo). By default, Excel prints sheets "at their actual size," a rather ambiguous instruction that means that the printout will emerge as it initially looks in the Print Preview. But you can modify that hard copy outcome, and there may be good reasons to want to do so. Note these drop-down scaling options (Figure 9-7):

***Figure 9–7.** Print scaling options*

Moving past the No Scaling default we're brought to the ***Fit Sheet on One Page*** option, an important one that addresses a classic spreadsheet print challenge: how to deal with a worksheet whose contents when printed will spill onto a second page—barely, by just a few rows or so. Printing here with No Scaling will yield an unsightly Page Two, consisting of but that smattering of data. Click Fit Sheet on One Page however, and all the worksheet data will be ever-so-slightly-downsized, all amicably sharing one, smartly presented page.

Of course, Fit Sheet on One Page needs to be used with care. I once accidently printed a lengthy worksheet under that option, and the one-page result looked like raw seismographic data, or someone's EKG readout. Ah, well...we learn from our mistakes.

The other two drop-down options—***Fit All Columns on One Page*** and ***Fit All Rows on One Page***—address related print issues. If your printout as engineered by the No Scaling mode results in one lonely column being elbowed onto a second page, that's not going to look very nice—but we need to figure out what's really going on here. The printout in question could in fact be dozens of pages long—

because, for example, you may have to print a couple of thousand rows of data—and so we're *not* dealing with the one-versus-two page spillover problem we described earlier in the Fit Sheet on One Page discussion. Here the issue is one of print width versus print length. We're prepared to roll out dozens of pages worth of table rows—but we still want the table fields, or *columns*, to *all* appear on every page of the printout, and it's this print objective that Fit All Columns on One Page carries off. Thus if you have 50 pages worth of table rows streaming down the pages vertically, so be it—but if one table column *also* spills over onto a second page *horizontally*, you'll wind up with a 100-page printout, because every row needs to display its data beneath that excess column, too. And that's downright gauche—but it doesn't have to happen, unless you have dozens of table fields to work with, and fitting them all horizontally on one page crunches the data into text best viewed under an electron microscope.

The companion option—Fit all Rows on One Page—resolves the same sort of print issue, but in a perpendicular direction. If you want to print a table say, three columns wide by 50 rows high, it's possible that a row or two will creep onto a second page, depending on your current margins, row heights, and the like. Use Fit all Rows to reel those truant rows back onto one, all-encompassing page.

But note that the Scaling drop-down menu also sneaks in the **Custom Scaling Options...** selection, which when clicked opens the stalwart Page Setup dialog box, treating you to a couple of additional scaling possibilities (Figure 9-8):

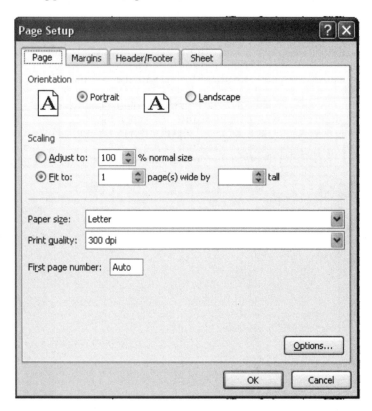

Figure 9–8. Adjusting the print size

Adjust to lets you modulate the size of the printout by a percent of the original, "actual" print size. It thus affords you a way to enlarge a small print range so that it occupies more of the page if you type a percentage greater than 100. On the other hand, entering a percentage less than 100 can act as a variation on the Fit Sheet on Sheet One Page option. Type say, 92 in the Adjust to field and you may be able to make room on page 1 for those few excess rows that have tip-toed onto page 2.

Fit to represents a variation on the Fit All Columns or Rows On One Page options. It lets you resize the printout either horizontally or vertically, and again may come into play if your printout experiences a small surplus of columns or rows. If, say, the last five of the 200 rows you want to print get bumped onto a new page—say page 4—you can click 3 in the *tall* Fit to field, and Excel will shrink the row sizes just a bit in order to achieve a three-page-tall output, which now encompasses all 200 rows. These options are also available via the Page Layout tab ➤ *Scale to Fit* button group (note that modifying Fit to automatically changes the percentage you'll see in the Adjust to box. After all, scaling a four-page tall printout down to three pages brings about a change in the way the worksheet is proportioned).

Headers and Footers—Getting to the Bottom (and the Top) of Your Printout

It may not be something that immediately comes to mind to Excel users, but you can add header and footer information to your prints, so that a recurring bit of information—such as today's date, the current page number, or your workbook title—will appear at the top and/or bottom of your pages. There are two rather different routes to headers and footers, and we'll start with the original, classic approach.

The basic tools for adding headers and tooters are stored in the Page Setup dialog box, which, as stated earlier, can be accessed in several different ways. To demonstrate, let's open the SampleSalespesonReport workbook, if you haven't already done so. Select cells A1:E100, and set the print area via the Page Layout tab ➤ Print Area (in the Page Setup button group) ➤ Set Print Area. Then access the Page Setup dialog box, and click the Header/Footer tab. You'll see (Figure 9-9):

Figure 9–9. The Header and Footer tab

This dialog box, little changed from previous Excel versions, offers you a pretty extensive array of pre-packaged header/footer options. Click the down arrow by Header, for example, and you'll get (Figure 9-10):

Figure 9–10. Customizing a header

Click on the first drop-down option and your printout will display the page number at the top of each page. The next selection, ***Page 1 of ?***, indicates the current page number relative to the total number of pages in the printout, e.g., Page 1 of 3, Page 2 of 3, etc. Source Data refers to the name of the particular ***worksheet*** on which you're working in the header, and so on; and these options are likewise available on the Footer drop-down menu.

You've also doubtless noted the ***Custom Header…*** and ***Custom Footer…*** buttons posted in the dialog box, too. These enable you to do two things that aren't available in those initial drop-down menus: They allow you to align a header or footer on the left, center, or right of a page, and they allow you to enter your own, customized text, e.g., your name, or Acme Widgets, Inc., as well. To see what I mean, click Custom Header…. You'll see (Figure 9-11):

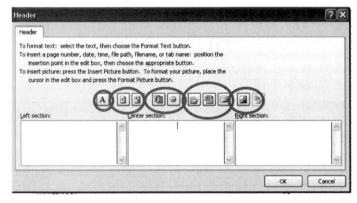

Figure 9–11. Header options, and where to place them

Note the instructions contained in the dialog box as well. The buttons are more-or-less organized in groups, as you see here, surrounded by the ovals. If you want to enter your own text header, just click in the appropriate section above and start typing. To format the text, just select what you've written, click the *A* button, and select the font and its size. The next two buttons when clicked post *page* references in the form of codes—page number and number of pages in the printout, respectively. You can enter both in one section, and insert the word "of" between the codes, thus yielding 1 of 2, 2 of 2, etc. The next two buttons insert date and time codes. Time inserts an updatable current-time code, such that whenever you print the document the correct time will appear on the printout and/or Print Preview. The next three buttons will insert the file path (e.g., c:\My Documents\SampleSalespersonReport.xlsx—often used in offices, so that other employees will be able to locate the workbook), the file name, and the *sheet* (tab) name. The last buttons will, when clicked, let you insert a picture in the header or footer, and allow you to edit it with assorted picture tools (enabled by the very last button).

For example, if I type my company name in the left header section, enter today's date in the center (whenever that is), and the page number in the right, these selections will look like this, as Excel codes them (Figure 9-12):

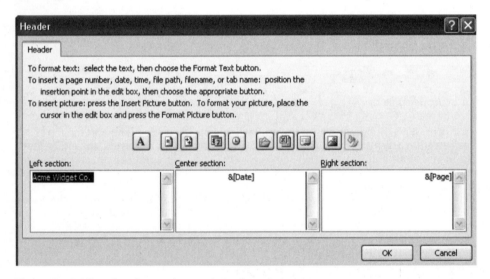

Figure 9–12. Three header entries, one in each section

Click OK and these elements will appear in your header. Needless to say, all these options can be applied to footers as well. You can easily see how it all looks by clicking the Print Preview button in the Page Setup dialog box, or even by just viewing the small preview screens in the Page Setup Header/Footer tab.

You'll also note four check box options on the Header/Footer tab. **Different odd and even pages** lets you supply different headers and/or footers for odd and even pages. By checking that box and then clicking Custom Header or Footer, you're brought to a slightly changed dialog box (Figure 9-13):

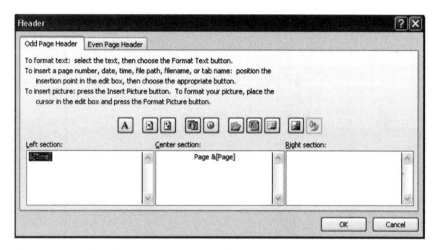

Figure 9–13. The odd and even page header option

Note the tab names, easy to overlook, but now changed; and what they do is pretty self-evident: click **Odd Page Header** and any header elements placed here will only appear on the odd pages of the printout - and you can guess what **Even Page Header** does.

Different first page likewise pulls no surprises, enabling you to treat the first page header/footer differently from the remainder of the printout - an option that includes imparting *no* header/footer to page one, even as the other pages show them. Check that box and then click Custom Header, and you'll see at the top of the dialog box (Figure 9-14):

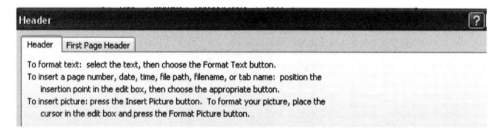

Figure 9–14. The different First Page Header option

By now you know how this works. While this is the kind of option you'd expect to see in Word, and you do, **First Page Header** may have a place in Excel printouts too. You may want to see a date on page one alone, for example.

The next two check-box options are turned on by default. **Scale with document** changes the size of header/footer text in line with the rest of the worksheet if you resize the sheet. Clearing the option preserves that text size even if you do make a print-size change. **Align with page margins** moves the header/footer along the page *horizontally (but not vertically,* even if you change the top/bottom margins) if you change the left and/or right margins. Turning off the default keeps the header/footer in place, even if the margins do change. Thus if I post a page number header in the left section of SampleSalespersonReport as per the default, Normal margins, I'll see (Figure 9-15):

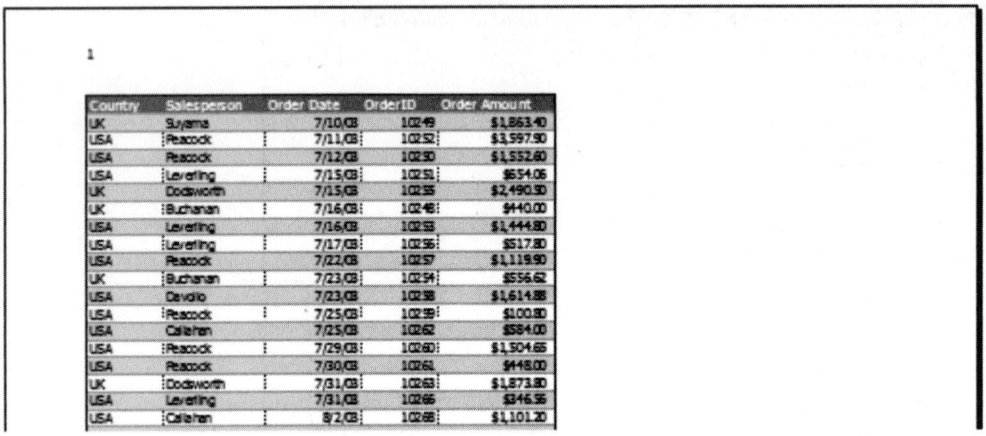

Figure 9–15. A Print Preview, before changing the default margin

But if I change the left margin to 3 inches and leave Align with page margins selected, I'll see (Figure 9-16):

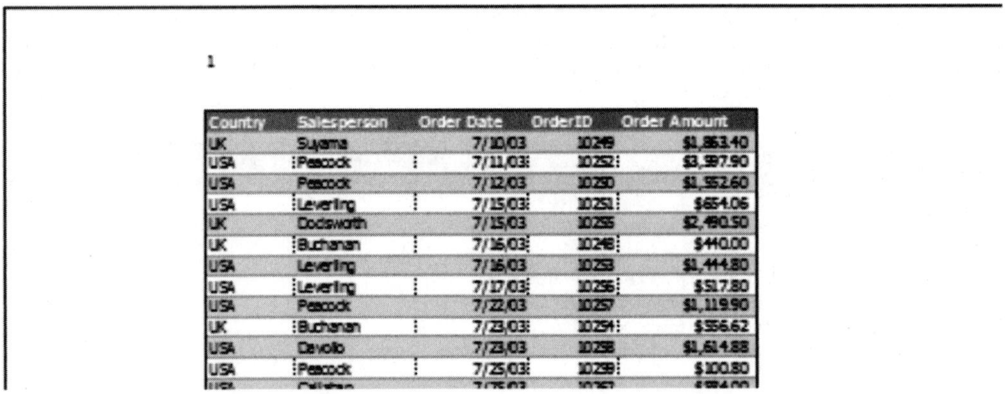

Figure 9–16. After a margin change

The entire printout, including the header, has moved to the right.

Note as well that the Margins tab allows you to select the position of headers and footers relative to the physical top and bottom of the printed page (Figure 9-17):

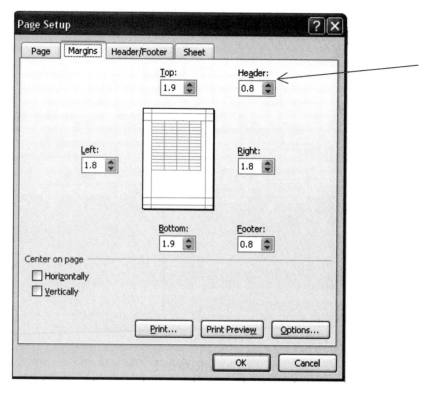

Figure 9–17. Where to relocate the header and footer inside the existing margins

Remember that the values you choose here enable you to reposition the header and/or footer relative to the *physical edges* of the page, and is independent of any Top/Bottom *margin* changes. Thus ratcheting the Top margin up to 3 *won't* automatically push the Header distance down along with it.

Title Search

Time for another classic, and related, print problem: you want to print a lengthy table, which is as usual topped by a header row (not the headers we've just discussed, but rather, the first row of the table). Once the printout reaches page two, the header row is nowhere to be seen. Because it's the very first row in the table, the header row is naturally going to make its appearance on page one—and *only* page one. But you want *all* the pages to show the header row on top, so that a viewer of the printout can always clearly tell which data belong beneath which field. The way to carry this off is with the *Sheet* tab in the all-purpose Page Setup dialog box. Note that our SampleSalespersonReport illustrates this problem: Click anywhere in that report and turn to the Print Preview (all you need do is click Ctrl-P), then click the horizontal page-scroll arrow at the bottom of the screen to page 2. You'll see (Figure 9-18):

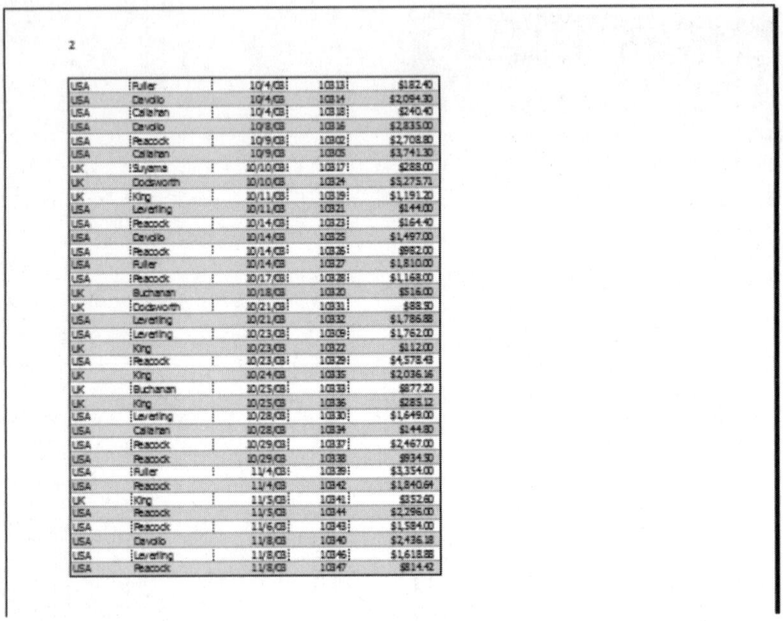

USA	Fuller	10/4/03	10313	$182.40
USA	Davolio	10/4/03	10314	$2,094.30
USA	Callahan	10/4/03	10315	$240.40
USA	Davolio	10/8/03	10316	$2,835.00
USA	Peacock	10/9/03	10302	$2,708.80
USA	Callahan	10/9/03	10305	$1,741.00
UK	Suyama	10/10/03	10317	$288.00
UK	Dodsworth	10/10/03	10324	$5,275.71
UK	King	10/11/03	10319	$1,191.20
USA	Leverling	10/11/03	10321	$144.00
USA	Peacock	10/14/03	10323	$164.40
USA	Davolio	10/14/03	10325	$1,497.00
USA	Peacock	10/14/03	10326	$982.00
USA	Fuller	10/14/03	10327	$1,810.00
USA	Peacock	10/17/03	10328	$1,168.00
UK	Buchanan	10/18/03	10320	$516.00
UK	Dodsworth	10/21/03	10331	$88.50
USA	Leverling	10/21/03	10332	$1,786.88
USA	Leverling	10/23/03	10309	$1,762.00
UK	King	10/23/03	10322	$112.00
USA	Peacock	10/23/03	10329	$4,578.43
USA	King	10/24/03	10335	$2,036.16
UK	Buchanan	10/25/03	10333	$877.20
UK	King	10/25/03	10336	$285.12
USA	Leverling	10/28/03	10330	$1,649.00
USA	Callahan	10/28/03	10334	$314.80
USA	Peacock	10/29/03	10337	$2,467.00
USA	Peacock	10/29/03	10338	$934.50
USA	Fuller	11/4/03	10339	$3,354.00
USA	Peacock	11/4/03	10342	$1,840.64
UK	King	11/5/03	10341	$352.60
USA	Peacock	11/5/03	10344	$2,296.00
USA	Peacock	11/6/03	10343	$1,584.00
USA	Davolio	11/8/03	10340	$2,436.18
USA	Leverling	11/8/03	10346	$1,618.88
USA	Peacock	11/8/03	10347	$814.42

Figure 9–18. Where's the header row?

You see the problem. The reader can't easily determine how the respective data are labeled on page two, because the header row just isn't there. By clicking the Page Layout tab ➤ Page Setup ➤ Sheet tab, you'll see Figure 9-19:

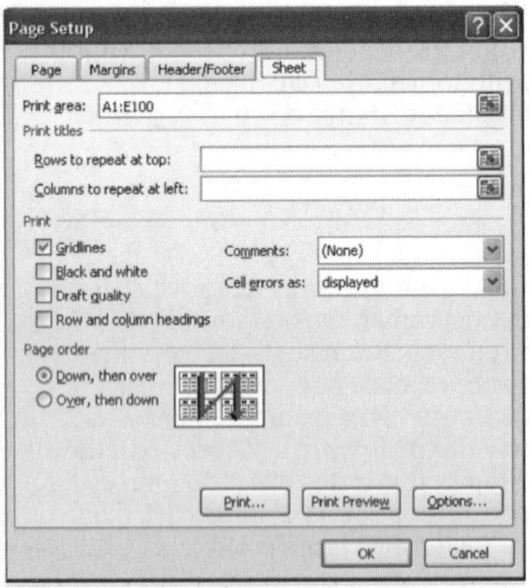

Figure 9–19. Where to print titles on the top of every page

Click in the **Rows to Repeat at Top** field, and then click anywhere on row one in the worksheet. You'll see Figure 9-20:

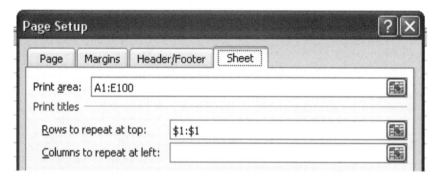

Figure 9–20. Row 1 will now repeat on the top of all the printed pages

That selection guarantees that the contents of row one—which contains the table header row—will appear at the top of every printed page, even if the print is 100 pages long. Now page two of our salesperson report looks like this (Figure 9-21):

Country	Salesperson	Order Date	OrderID	Order Amount
USA	Fuller	10/4/03	10313	$182.40
USA	Davolio	10/4/03	10314	$2,094.30
USA	Callahan	10/4/03	10318	$240.40
USA	Davolio	10/8/03	10316	$2,835.00
USA	Peacock	10/9/03	10302	$2,708.80
USA	Callahan	10/9/03	10305	$3,741.30
UK	Suyama	10/10/03	10317	$288.00
UK	Dodsworth	10/10/03	10324	$5,275.71
UK	King	10/11/03	10319	$1,191.20
USA	Leverling	10/11/03	10321	$144.00
USA	Peacock	10/14/03	10323	$164.40
USA	Davolio	10/14/03	10325	$1,497.00
USA	Peacock	10/14/03	10326	$982.00
USA	Fuller	10/14/03	10327	$1,810.00
USA	Peacock	10/17/03	10328	$1,168.00
UK	Buchanan	10/18/03	10320	$516.00
UK	Dodsworth	10/21/03	10311	$88.50
USA	Leverling	10/21/03	10332	$1,786.88
USA	Leverling	10/23/03	10309	$1,762.00
UK	King	10/23/03	10322	$112.00
USA	Peacock	10/23/03	10329	$4,578.43
UK	King	10/24/03	10335	$2,036.16
UK	Buchanan	10/25/03	10333	$877.20
UK	King	10/25/03	10336	$285.12
USA	Leverling	10/28/03	10330	$1,649.00
USA	Callahan	10/28/03	10334	$144.80
USA	Peacock	10/29/03	10337	$2,467.00
USA	Peacock	10/29/03	10338	$934.50

Figure 9-21. The evidence!

The header row has been instated here as well, insuring a much more readable report. You can also select the **Columns to repeat at left** option, which will allow a column or columns to likewise appear on every print page on the left of the page. Thus if you have a column of months in the leftmost column of a wide, multi-columned worksheet and you need to see those months on every print page, click anywhere in the month column and it will appear on every sheet. (***Note***: This option is *only* available via the Page Layout tab ➤ Page Setup ➤ Sheet sequence. You can't access it in the Print Preview – you'll find Rows to Repeat on Top grayed out there if you do.) And there's something else to keep in mind here, too: by selecting the A1:E100 print range *as well as* choosing row 1 to repeat on top, you might think that row 1 will print *twice* on the first printed page as a result. But it won't: Excel is smart enough to understand what you had in mind, and you'll see row 1 but once on page one.

The Sheet tab also contains a few other options you may want to know about. The ***Print*** section there lists a quartet of check box items, starting with ***Gridlines***. Checking this will enable you to print the gridlines that you see traced around every cell (at least by default) on the worksheet. This is an all-or-nothing command, however, meaning that any empty cell you've included in a print range will *also* sport gridlines in the printout. (As a result, you may want to use one of the ***Border*** options in the ***Font*** button group on the Home tab instead, in order to draw lines around only the cells you want.) ***Black and White*** will output your worksheet in those famously binary colors, even if you're working with a color printer, the better to save color toner. ***Draft quality*** is another economical print option, instructing your printer to roll out your worksheet at a lower print resolution—assuming your device is capable of varying its print quality in this way.

Row and column headings is a selection you see utilized now and then, enabling you to actually print the alphabetical and numeric column and row borders of the worksheet. Avail yourself of this option and your print will look something like this (Figure 9-22):

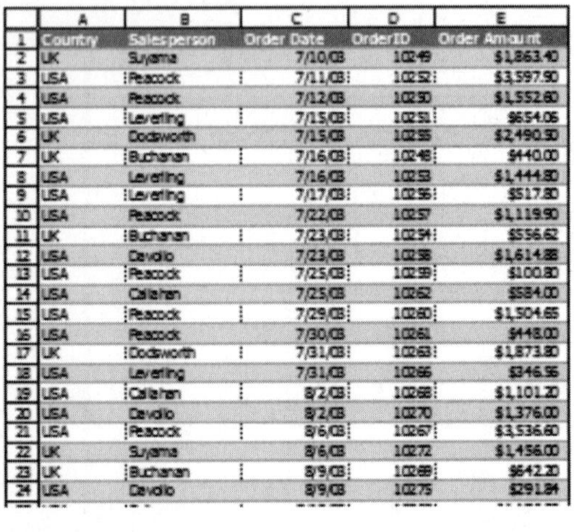

	A	B	C	D	E
1	Country	Salesperson	Order Date	OrderID	Order Amount
2	UK	Suyama	7/10/03	10249	$1,863.40
3	USA	Peacock	7/11/03	10252	$3,597.90
4	USA	Peacock	7/12/03	10250	$1,552.60
5	USA	Leverling	7/15/03	10251	$654.06
6	UK	Dodsworth	7/15/03	10255	$2,490.50
7	UK	Buchanan	7/16/03	10248	$440.00
8	USA	Leverling	7/16/03	10253	$1,444.80
9	USA	Leverling	7/17/03	10256	$517.80
10	USA	Peacock	7/22/03	10257	$1,119.90
11	UK	Buchanan	7/23/03	10254	$556.62
12	USA	Davolio	7/23/03	10258	$1,614.88
13	USA	Peacock	7/25/03	10259	$100.80
14	USA	Callahan	7/25/03	10262	$584.00
15	USA	Peacock	7/29/03	10260	$1,504.65
16	USA	Peacock	7/30/03	10261	$448.00
17	UK	Dodsworth	7/31/03	10263	$1,873.80
18	USA	Leverling	7/31/03	10266	$346.56
19	USA	Callahan	8/2/03	10268	$1,101.20
20	USA	Davolio	8/2/03	10270	$1,376.00
21	USA	Peacock	8/6/03	10267	$3,536.60
22	UK	Suyama	8/6/03	10272	$1,456.00
23	UK	Buchanan	8/9/03	10269	$642.20
24	USA	Davolio	8/9/03	10275	$291.84

Figure 9–22. *Print preview, with row and column headings set to print*

This option might prove instructive to readers who want to visually line up the data in their cell addresses.

And moving down a bit on the Sheet tab you'll see ***Page Order***, an option that comes into play for unusually long and wide printouts. If you need to print a large number of columns and rows you may wind up printing pages in both directions—that is, pages that print the rows downward across the width of the page, but also another set of pages that print the "excess" columns spilling across horizontally, containing the row data sitting beneath those columns. By default, Excel will print data ***Down, then over,*** meaning that if your print area is say, 20 columns wide by 500 rows high, the printout will first print "downwards", until all 500 rows are printed with as many columns as can be accommodated on those pages, and *then* will print the remaining columns streaming across the extra pages—those columns and row data that couldn't fit on the first set of pages. Select *Over, then down*, and the printout will print everything "across"—that is, all 20 columns across the first two pages, with as many rows beneath them as can be fit, and then another 20 columns across, with the *next* batch of rows, etc.

There's More Than One Way to View A Worksheet

Open a worksheet and by default its contents flash onscreen in what's called the Normal view. But Excel makes alternative views of the worksheet available, too, and there are reasons for wanting to switch to them, at least on occasion. In fact, we've already worked with one such alternative—the Print Preview—throughout this chapter. But other viewing options are out there, too, among these the Page Layout view, available in a button bearing that name in the *View* Tab ➤ *Workbook Views* button group. The tool tip caption accompanying the *Page Layout* button states that clicking the button allows you to "View the document as it appears on the printed page," and it goes on to recommend that you should click here "…to see where pages begin and end, and to see any headers and footers on the page." All this sounds good, but that summary could apply just as accurately to the Print Preview, too. There must be something different about Page Layout, then, and there is. Click it on our Salesperson report print area and you'll see (Figure 9-23):

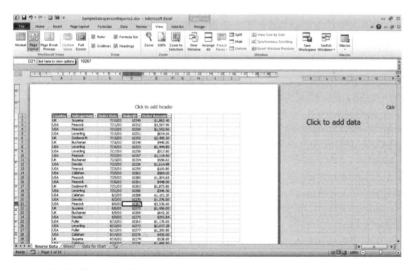

Figure 9–23. The Page Layout view

This view really *is* different in some important ways. The worksheet column and row headings remain visible in this view, but they're separated from the page, to indicate that they won't be printing by default (but if you *do* elect to print the row and column headings, they'll appear *twice* in this view—on the margins, as you see in our screen shot, but also on the worksheet proper). Note in addition the ruler, which allows you to determine how much space on the printed sheet each row and column will occupy. Moreover, you can see that Page Layout delineates the contours of the paper page, showing where the edge of a sheet gives way to the next sheet.

It's also important to understand that the Page Layout view is live—that is, you can actually enter data while working in it. You'll note the *Click to Add Data* prompt on the far right of the screen shot above, a slightly misleading instruction because it implies you can only enter data there. Not true; you can work as usual in any cell on the worksheet here, including those cells that already contain data. Just remember that by entering information in the Click to Add Data area you're including those data in your default print range. Note as well that if you guide your mouse into the narrow gray corridor between pages in the Page Layout view, you'll encounter a ***Hide White Space*** caption (Figure 9-24):

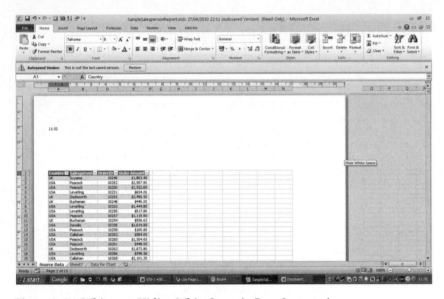

Figure 9–24. White out: Hiding White Space in Page Layout view

Click there and the header/footer areas on the worksheet—that extensive white space—will be banished from the screen, leaving you with more of the worksheet proper on which to work. Slide back into that sliver again between the pages and you'll see a ***Show White Space*** prompt; click there to expose the header/footer areas.

Any print range you've set will continue to be bordered by a dotted line in the Page Layout view. Recall that we've established A1:E100 as that range, an area of cells that should yield a two-page print. But—and this is easy to miss—check out the left edge of the status bar in our screen shot (Figure 9-25):

Figure 9–25. Print page count in the Page Layout view.

This looks like the sort of message you'd see in Word, but in any case it raises a question: Why 14 pages? It's because Page Layout tallies the number of pages you'd get were you to print *all* the data in the worksheet—even though we want to print just 100 rows. And along these lines, note that Page Layout continues to display the filter buttons on the table's header row—but these *won't* print.

You've also probably caught the Click to add header area (of course there's a parallel Click to add footer section here, too); but before you actually click, roll your mouse over there and note that the header area turns blue over whichever of the three header sections you're rolling—that is, the left, center, and right sections that emulate the sections we saw in the Custom Header/Footer option in Page Setup (Figure 9-26):

	A	B	C	D	E	F	G	H	I	J
1	Country	Salesperson	Order Date	OrderID	Order Amount					
2	UK	Suyama	7/10/03	10249	$1,863.40					
3	USA	Peacock	7/11/03	10252	$3,597.90					
4	USA	Peacock	7/12/03	10250	$1,552.60					
5	USA	Leverling	7/15/03	10251	$654.06					
6	UK	Dodsworth	7/15/03	10255	$2,490.50					
7	UK	Buchanan	7/16/03	10248	$440.00					
8	USA	Leverling	7/16/03	10253	$1,444.80					
9	USA	Leverling	7/17/03	10256	$517.80					
10	USA	Peacock	7/22/03	10257	$1,119.90					

Figure 9–26. Kind of blue: Designating a header section in the Page Layout view

Once you've clicked here a ***Header & Footer Tools*** tab tops the screen (Figure 9-27):

Figure 9–27. More of the same: Buttons in the Header & Footer tab, duplicating the options in the Page Setup dialog box

This tab contains what are really the same custom header/footer options we viewed in the Page Setup dialog box. Click any Header & Footer Element button (no, I can't explain Excel's fondness for the ampersand here instead of the word "and") and you can add a page number, date, file path, etc., just as you can via Page Setup. And if you want to add your own text-based header, just type it after you've clicked in a section (Figure 9-28):

Header

This is a header in the left section				
Country	Salesperson	Order Date	OrderID	Order Amount
UK	Suyama	7/10/03	10249	$1,863.40
USA	Peacock	7/11/03	10252	$3,597.90
USA	Peacock	7/12/03	10250	$1,552.60
USA	Leverling	7/15/03	10251	$654.06

Figure 9–28. A user-devised text header

Gimme a (Page) Break—Another View

When you set a print area for a multi-page printout of the worksheet, Excel will naturally occupy the entire first page with data and then move on to page two when it runs out of space, and so on across all the printed pages. But sometimes you want a next page to start with a particular row on top, for the sake of appearances—but Excel can't know that, at least not by default (Note: We're *not* referring to the rows-to-repeat-on-top issue here. Here we want the row to appear just once, but at the top of a specific printed page.) You can, however, instruct Excel to relocate the point at which a page breaks—at least within limits, with the ***Page Break Preview*** option. By clicking the View tab ➤ Page Break Preview in the Workbook Views button group, you'll see (Figure 9-29):

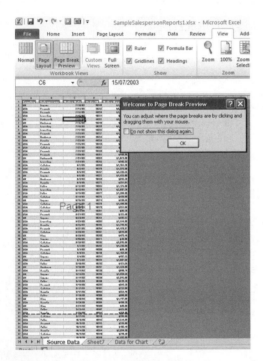

Figure 9–29. *The Page Break Preview*

This is an old Excel option, with a curiously shrunken image of the worksheet (to enable you to get a bird's eye view of the print breaks) and a quaint dialog box to boot (I mean, how many of them start with "Welcome to…"?). Click OK, and you can then begin to adjust your page break settings.

The dotted line you see above at row 61 represents the current point at which Page 1 breaks (note the watermark reference to the page number), and if you click on that line and drag it either *upwards or downwards*, you'll be able to move the page break point to a different row. (If you drag downwards, you'll naturally be adding rows to the page—requiring Excel to rescale the page downwards in order to accommodate those rows in view of the existing print margins. There's only so much physical space on the page!) Drag, say to row 56, release the mouse, and you'll see (Figure 9-30):

Figure 9–30. *I draw the line: Moving the page break to row 56*

The dotted line page boundary has been replaced by an unbroken line, indicating that the break has been introduced by the *user,* not by Excel. And because we've lifted the page break on Page 1 by five rows, establishing the break five rows "earlier" on the page, Page 2 will now break five rows earlier, and so on.

And while it's easy to miss, you can click and drag on the *vertical* boundary of a print range and *widen* the range by adding columns to it, or narrow the print by excluding columns you had originally earmarked (Figure 9-31):

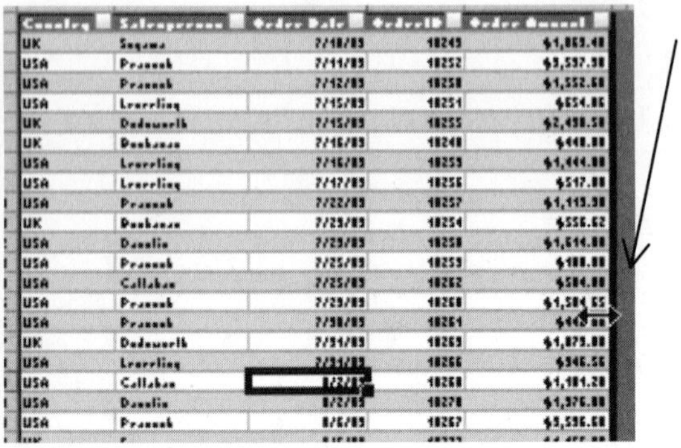

Figure 9–31. Where to click to expand or narrow the printpage horizontally

Note again that, as with the Page Layout view, the Page Break Preview is live, allowing you to enter data in this viewing mode, too—though the text appears so small that typing may pose a challenge (Note: By clicking the View tab ➤ *100%* button in the *Zoom* button group, or the Zoom buttons stashed in the lower right of the status bar, or by holding the Ctrl button down as you roll the mouse wheel, if you have one of those, you can achieve the normal 100% magnification while remaining in the Page Break Preview. The downside of course is that you'll see less of the page onscreen.) To exit the Page Break Preview just click the Normal button in the Worksheet Views button group. (Note: The Normal, Print Layout, and Page Break views can also be activated via a trio of buttons in the lower right of the status bar, to the immediate left of the Zoom buttons.)

Now there's another, closely related option to the Page Break Preview stored in the Page Layout tab ➤ Page Setup button group—*Breaks*. As a matter of fact, it seems so similar you may think the two are identical, but they aren't. Whereas Page Break Preview allows you to reposition an *existing* break by dragging it, Breaks allows you add a *new* page break to the printout. And note the legend that appears when you rest your mouse atop the Breaks button: "Page breaks are inserted above and to the left of the selection." What does that mean? It means that if you click in cell D77 and select Breaks ➤ *Insert Page Break*, you'll get this, whether you wanted it or not (Figure 9-32):

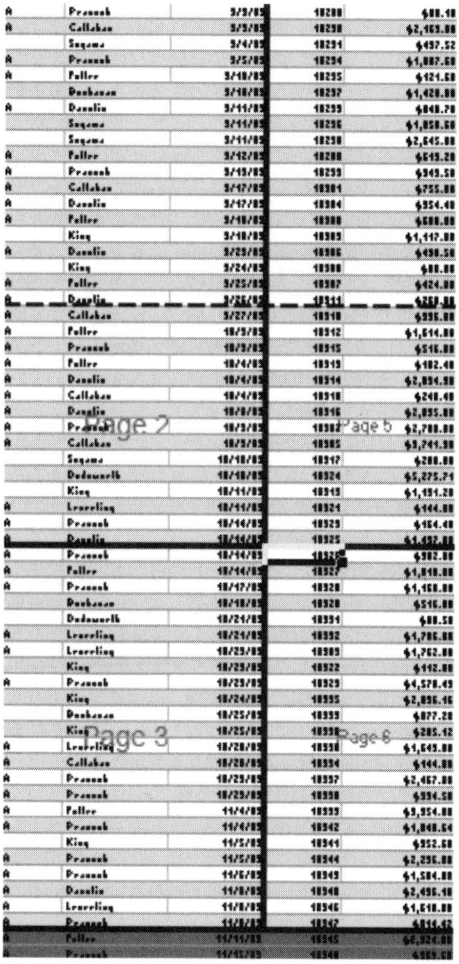

Figure 9–32. The breaking point? Clicking Breaks in Cell D77

Is that what you had in mind? Maybe—but maybe not. Clicking in cell D77 and clicking Breaks does what it told you it would do—it institutes a page break above D77, but also *another* one to the *left* of that cell, resulting in more pages in all directions. If all you really wanted was one more page running down the printout, you'd have clicked in *A77, or the 77 row header* instead, and then clicked Breaks, yielding this Print Preview (Figure 9-33):

Figure 9–33. That's more like it; Page breaking in cell A77

But not to worry. If you've introduced page breaks in all the wrong places, you can click Page Layout ➤ Breaks ➤ *Reset All Page Breaks*, and start over. If you want to merely remove one page break, say at the 77 row juncture, click back on A77 or its row header and click Page Layout ➤ Breaks ➤ *Remove Break*.

Customize Your View, Too

You can also prepare a print setting complete with a set range, hidden rows and columns, and filter settings in effect (i.e., all sales over $5,000), and save all this as a *Custom View*, so that you can change that filter setting, etc., and go on to do other things on the worksheet. You can then trot out the View when you're ready to print, and all those saved settings return to the screen.

Note that you can't save a Custom View to a worksheet that has a defined table on it, so in order to demonstrate how this works, click in the Salesperson Report table and click the **Table Tools** context tab ➤ **Design** ➤ **Convert to Range** in the **Tools** button group. Answer yes to the prompt. Click the Data tab ➤ Filter in the Sort & Filter button group. Filter the Country field to show sales from the USA only. Then hide column C. You should see (Figure 9-34):

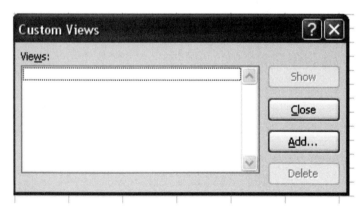

Figure 9–34. Have it your way: the range, filtered for USA records only, while hiding column C

(Remember that we've already set the print range.) Then click the Views tab ➤ **Custom Views** in the Worksheet Views tab. You'll see (Figure 9-35):

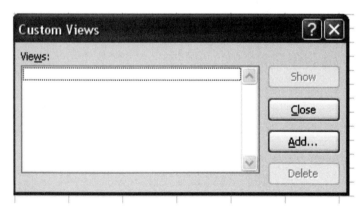

Figure 9–35. The Custom Views dialog box

Click **Add**. Type "newview" in the **Name** field. Note that the current print settings and hidden rows, columns, and filter settings will all be saved by the View. Click OK. Then unhide column C, and click **Select All** in the Country filter, restoring the UK records to view. Then Click View ➤ Custom Views, click on "newview," and click **Show**. All your saved settings return to the screen. Note that even if you had removed the filter completely from the range, the Custom View restores it and reveals only the USA records—just as you had saved it.

In Conclusion…

As we've seen, Excel is happy to supply you with a whole range (pun intended) of print options, designed to let you nail down exactly what you want to print. Still, print basics are pretty basic—select your print range, tell Excel about it, and let 'er rip. Now we're going to reverse our field—or medium—by moving from paper to the Internet, to describe how you can share and contribute to workbooks posted out there on the Web.

CHAPTER 10

Taking it to the Cloud: Sharing and Collaborating on the Internet

---

Note: As *Beginning Excel 2010* goes to press, Excel's Web App 2010, an Internet-based means for empowering multiple users to access and edit the same workbook simultaneously, remains a work in progress. What follows is a report of how the Web App works—as I've experienced it. But results, as they say, may vary—and the nature of Web apps is that they are much more frequently updated and modified than traditional desktop applications, so the Excel Web App may undergo changes between the time I'm writing this information, and the time you read it.

In the old days—I think it was around 2000—I was assigned to a help desk post at an actuarial firm in New York. One afternoon a fellow from the San Francisco office called me with a spreadsheet question and proceeded to attach the workbook to an e-mail, in order to afford me a closer look at the data. After giving the question due consideration, I e-mailed the workbook back with my recommendations.

Not a terribly compelling tale by today's expectations, is it? But the idea that one can toss a spreadsheet back and forth across a 2,500-mile long backyard is remarkable enough, even if we're no longer impressed by the techo-magic that makes that transcontinental game of catch possible. But wouldn't it be even better if the help desk guy could actually *see* the workbook onscreen at the *same time* as the guy posing the question, and if the two could make changes to the workbook then and there, and immediately see the results on the screen? That is, wouldn't the exchange of information be better served by hoisting it into the cloud—that is, that vast Internet-based, data-hoarding place in the sky—and making it available to anyone down here on the ground?

I think the answer to that question is yes; and something like that scenario is coming to a screen near you—*now*—in the form of Microsoft Excel's Web App 2010, a new Office 2010 free Internet-based way to access a version of Excel on your browser, which lets you grant access to your workbooks to others and enable them to collaborate with you in real time (more or less). All you need is a Windows Live ID (if you're a Hotmail subscriber, for example, you already have one, and you can get an ID with an e-mail address from any provider), Excel 2003 or later, and access to the Web. Get past that minor bureaucratic chore and you can upload your workbooks to the cloud, and make them available to anyone else at your discretion.

Of course, many workplaces *already* share their workbooks through Excel's **Share Workbook** feature. That option lets employees work collectively and simultaneously on workbooks—but that access is naturally confined to that organization. With Web App 2010, on the other hand, the whole world can be signed into your network (it *is* called the Internet, when you think about it) and grab a seat on your cloud.

Once you get your workbooks into (or onto) the cloud, you can view and edit them (within some important limits, which we're going to describe), and give them worldwide exposure—if you want to. Excel Web App 2010 works with Internet Explorer 7 and above, Safari 4 and above for the Mac, and Mozilla Firefox 3.5 and above; and you can start Excel workbooks from scratch in the Excel Web App 2010, even if you don't have the application on your PC.

That last assertion may raise an eyebrow—or two, for that matter. After all, you may ask, with that blinding glint in your eye, if the Web App lets me open and use Excel—for free, on the Internet—why then should I, or my firm, bother to go out and actually *buy* the application? Well, I'm a smart aleck, too, and I asked that very question. The answer is that the version of Excel that offers itself to you gratis on the Web App isn't fully functional, as they say in the trade. It can't do everything that your duly paid-for, desktop-housed copy can; and if you do need to do something that's beyond the Web App variety, you'll need to open the workbook on your PC (also called the desktop client), and save the activity back to the cloud. That's how it works, as we'll see.

Getting There

In order to get started with Web App and to upload your workbooks to that destination you need to access *Windows Live*, which can be navigated to via a variety of routes. You can maneuver here directly by traveling to the home.live.com address, or, for example, through Hotmail (if you need a Windows Live ID you can acquire one from skydrive.live.com). Then sign into Windows Live. You will have been assigned a *SkyDrive*, a holding area on the Net—really a cloud-based set of folders to which you can also store documents, quite apart from any Web App Excel activity. Click the *More* drop-down arrow on the menu bar on the top of the screen and click SkyDrive. You'll see (Figure 10-1):

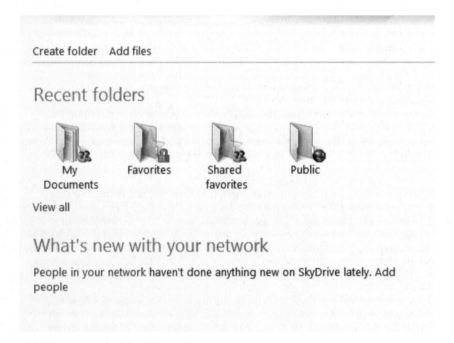

Figure 10–1. After you've accessed your SkyDrive

As with the computer-based Office programs, you'll find a My Documents folder, and in the interests of convention I'll upload the SampleSalespersonReport there, just as I would attach a file to an e-mail. To do so, click *Add files* ➤ *My Documents* in the folder list that appears, to identify the recipient folder. Then click *Browse*, and click on the name(s) of the file(s) you want to upload from your PC (Figure 10-2):

***Figure 10–2.** Where to add files to Web App folders*

Once you've uploaded the workbook, you'll see (Figure 10 -3):

***Figure 10–3.** About to view the workbook in the Web App…*

Then click on *View.* You'll see (Figure 10-4):

	A	B	D	E
1	Country 🔽	Salesperson 🔽	OrderID 🔽	Order Amount 🔽
3	USA	Peacock	10252	$3,597.90
4	USA	Peacock	10250	$1,552.60
5	USA	Leverling	10251	$654.06
8	USA	Leverling	10253	$1,444.80
9	USA	Leverling	10256	$517.80
10	USA	Peacock	10257	$1,119.90
12	USA	Davolio	10258	$1,614.88
13	USA	Peacock	10259	$100.80
14	USA	Callahan	10262	$584.00
15	USA	Peacock	10260	$1,504.65
16	USA	Peacock	10261	$448.00
18	USA	Leverling	10266	$346.56
19	USA	Callahan	10268	$1,101.20
20	USA	Davolio	10270	$1,376.00
21	USA	Peacock	10267	$3,536.60
24	USA	Davolio	10275	$291.84
25	USA	Fuller	10265	$1,176.00
26	USA	Leverling	10273	$2,037.28
27	USA	Fuller	10277	$1,200.80
28	USA	Callahan	10276	$420.00
30	USA	Callahan	10278	$1,488.80
31	USA	Callahan	10279	$351.00
32	USA	Peacock	10281	$86.50
33	USA	Peacock	10282	$155.40
35	USA	Leverling	10283	$1,414.80
36	USA	Davolio	10285	$1,743.36
37	USA	Peacock	10284	$1,170.37
38	USA	Callahan	10287	$819.00
41	USA	Callahan	10286	$3,016.00
42	USA	Davolio	10292	$1,296.00
43	USA	Peacock	10288	$80.10

◄ ►   Source Data   Sheet2

Figure 10–4. …and here it is. The Salesperson Sample Report, as it looks in the Excel Web App

You've seen these data before, but is the (inter)face familiar? Take a scrupulous look at the worksheet, and more particularly the buttons resting atop it; not what you'll see in the standard, PC-based scenario. Note as well that the default white cross symbol accompanying your mouse meanderings is also among the missing screen elements, as is, more subtly, the fill handle at the lower right of any selected range. What you're left with instead is a white arrow pointer with which you'll have to click on cells. Veteran Excel users won't be used to seeing and clicking it, but it is what it is (Figure 10-5):

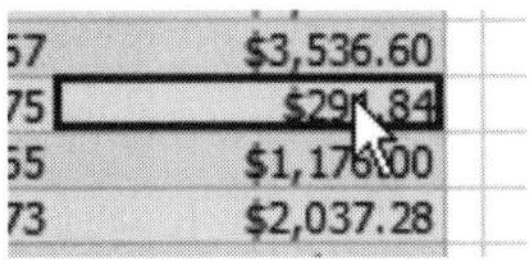

Figure 10–5. The arrow points to cells in the Web App version

But perhaps more importantly, the View of the worksheet you're seeing here is *read-only*. Neither you, nor anyone to whom you've granted access to the workbook, can enter data in this mode. To go ahead and make changes to the workbook you need to click the ***Edit in Browser*** button (you can also click the ***Edit*** link instead of View, when you open the workbook—see Figure 10-3)—and that click takes you here (Figure 10-6):

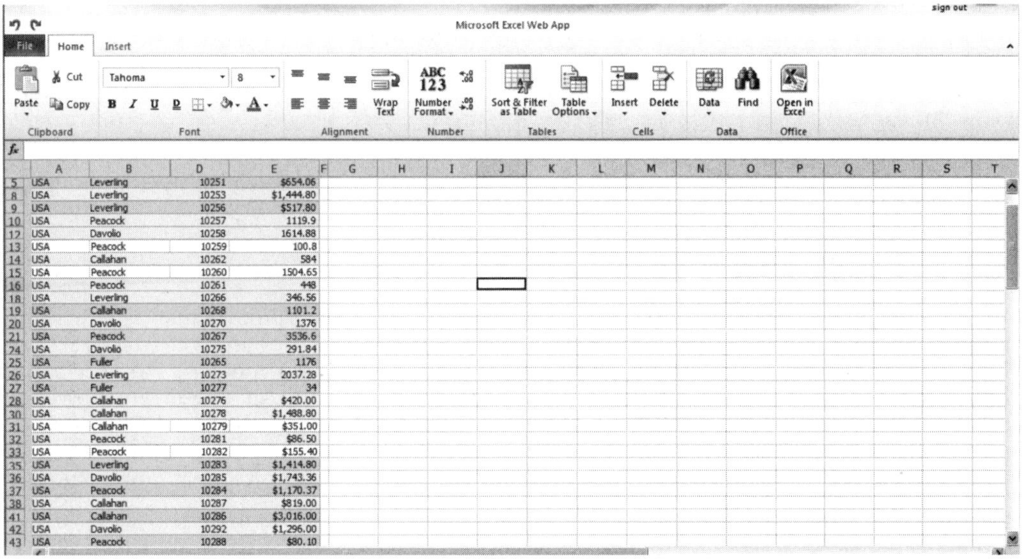

Figure 10–6. The worksheet in Edit in Browser view

Now that's more like it—sort of. The interface greeting you in Edit in Browser resembles the Excel 2010 tab and button configuration far more faithfully—but discrepancies still abound, and you'll notice them right away. For one thing, only three tabs populate the tab area, and their button contents are considerably sparer than those on your desktop equivalents. I don't know about you, but I can't even find AutoSum in there. Thus you'll need to scan these buttons closely so that you'll learn which Excel Web App command options are—and are not—available to you. Don't expect to find chart-creation, Conditional Formatting, or PivotTable construction tools here, though you can draw from Excel's formidable reservoir of functions here, and write them with the prompting of the ***AutoComplete*** feature—though that FX you see by the formula bar doesn't do anything when you click on it. And the Name Box is missing, too. You *can* sort and filter, though. Note also that you can't actively save the workbook—because Excel saves all your changes *automatically* back to the cloud. (Note: Documents saved to the Public folder are available to everyone, but in read-only mode.)

Also, don't expect lightning-quick responsiveness from the sheet. The records on the Salesperson sheet seem to unroll in stages as you scroll down the page. As a result it may take a while for all the data to kick in.

In any case, all these limitations raise the obvious question: What if I need to do more with the workbook? What if I need to add a chart or PivotTable to the mix, so that I can display these objects to my virtual colleagues viewing the workbook in their browser?

The answer lies in the ***Open in Excel*** option, which appears in two—really two-and-a-half—places, either after you've opened the workbook in the Web App (Figure 10-7):

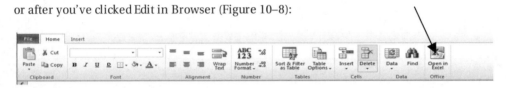

Figure 10–7. The Open in Excel option

or after you've clicked Edit in Browser (Figure 10–8):

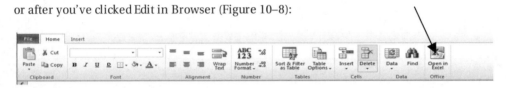

Figure 10–8. An alternative route to the Open in Excel option

The half place? If you click the File tab in either of the above views, a drop-down menu likewise reveals Open in Excel, too. Whatever you click, Excel flashes a few prompts at you, one of which asks you if you trust the download source—because what you're really doing is downloading the workbook temporarily back to your PC. Once the smoke clears, you're brought back to Excel—the original Excel, the one commanding your hard drive. Once here, you can sound all of Excel's bells and whistles—do whatever you want on the sheet, and then save the workbook. When you do, another prompt lets you know that the workbook is being routed back to the cloud. At this point your browser window turns blank (Figure 10-9):

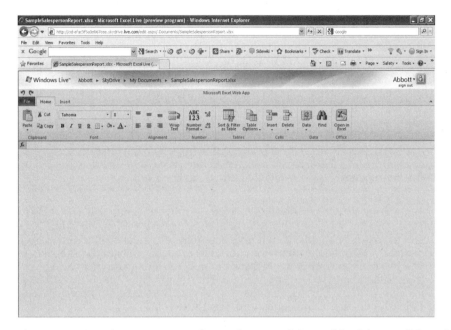

Figure 10–9. *Your browser screen, after you've opened the workbook in your PC version of Excel*

It's as if you've temporarily *moved,* and not copied, the sheet back to your PC. Now click the Workbook name prompt at the top of the screen (above the ribbon), and open the workbook again. Your changes should be available.

And by "available" that means, among other things, that once you've constructed (or reconstructed) a PivotTable back at the ranch on your home PC and saved it back to the cloud, any data entry changes you *then* make while accessing the workbook via your SkyDrive *will* be reflected in the PivotTable—at least they will once you click the ***File*** tab➤ ***Data*** ➤ ***Refresh Selected Connection*** option. (Figure 10-10):

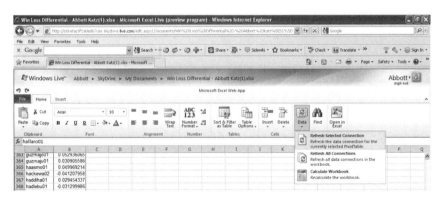

Figure 10–10. *Where to refresh a PivotTable in the Web App*

(Note the sub-legend beneath this command states "Refresh the data connection for the currently selected PivotTable.")It also means that any chart you've added to the Web App version (after it's been constructed on your PC and then returned to the cloud) will be automatically updated when you change any of the contributing data—as you're changing them back on the cloud.

To sum up here—Working with Excel on the Excel Web App 2010 grants you three different levels of workbook access:

- *View*—lets you view the worksheet in a read-only state; you can however refresh a PivotTable or chart in View if another user has changed the data.

- *Edit in Browser*—lets you enter and sort and filter data, and change formatting.

- *Open in Excel*—opens the workbook in Excel proper, allowing you to implement any and all of the application's features. Saving any changes here saves them back to the cloud, whereupon it's made available back in the Excel Web App version.

You can also initiate a brand new, Web App-based workbook by getting into your SkyDrive, clicking the folder in which you want the workbook to appear, and clicking *New ➤ Microsoft Excel Workbook ➤ Create*, and enter the workbook name (you'll note here that you can also mint new documents in the Web App for other Office applications, too). You'll be brought to a blank workbook, and you're ready to go. To delete a workbook, click on the book name in its folder, and click Delete.

A few words may also be in order about the File tab, presented in slightly different guises both in the initial Web App workbook view (before you click an edit option) as well as the Edit in Browser view. In that first View, clicking a file triggers this drop-down menu (Figure 10-11):

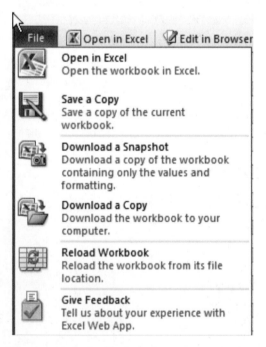

Figure 10–11. The file drop-down mnenu in the initial Web App view of a workbook

We've already discussed the Open in Excel option. *Save a Copy* produces a copy of the workbook *on the cloud, not on your hard drive. Download a Snapshot* does what its legend promises—by casting the entire workbook into a kind of Paste Special-Values version—but it sends the download to your PC, not the Web App, as does *Download a Copy*, and that copy is likewise dispatched to your hard drive, and completely detached from the Web. *Reload Workbook* is a rather odd option. It discards "any changes since you last opened the workbook…" according to its accompanying caption, but since Reload Workbook is only available in the Web App's read-only view—in which you can't make changes anyway—what can this mean? It seems to mean this: if you changed or added data to a table—a table that supplies the data to a PivotTable in that workbook—in the Edit in Browser view, and then close the workbook and reopen it in that initial View, you *can*, even here, refresh the PivotTable, whereupon the data change will appear, and will impact the PivotTable. But if you then click Reload Workbook the workbook will revert to its pre-refresh appearance, before the data changed the PivotTable. No—you're not likely to click this one too often.

Clicking the File tab once you've begun to edit the workbook in the browser serves up a couple of other options, while deleting Reload Workbook from its drop-down (because changes made here are automatically saved—and so there's no way to reload the workbook *without* the changes). When you click *Where's the Save Button?* Excel simply musters an onscreen prompt declaring "In Excel Web App, there is no save button because your workbook is being saved automatically."

Permission Granted: Sharing Your Workbooks

Of course the Web App is really about the ability to work on documents collectively, anytime and anywhere. And as the author of your workbooks, you can decide who's going to be able to view and even change your data. And the means for implementing those decisions are pretty easy.

Before you proceed, keep in mind that granting access to an individual to view and/or modify a workbook is really a collective decision, too; that's because affording workbook access to a colleague means giving him or her that degree of access to *all* the files in the folder. Save ten workbooks to a folder, and that person gets to see and/or change any of them.

To award colleagues access rights to your data, return to SkyDrive, and for illustration's sake click on My Documents. Because I've already uploaded that Salesperson workbook here, I see (Figure 10-12):

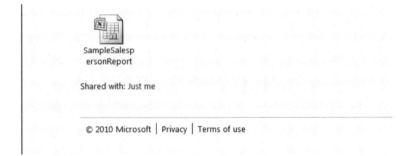

Figure 10–12. All by my lonesome: My Documents, before its contents are shared

Click on *Just Me*, and you'll be brought to the *Edit permissions* screen (Figure 10-13):

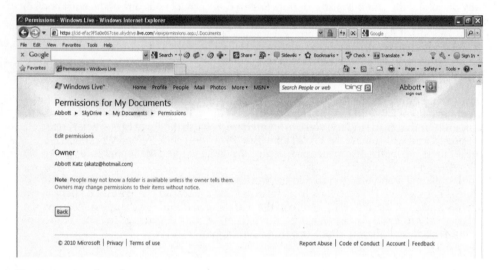

Figure 10–13. The Edit permissions screen

Click Edit permissions and you'll be brought to your list of existing e-mail contacts stored under your Windows Live ID (you can import these from your AOL, Facebook, Linkedin, etc. accounts. In my case my existing Hotmail contacts were automatically posted here.), beneath an *Edit Permissions for My Documents* title. Exactly what you see will vary in part by how you've organized your contact categories, if you have any, but everyone should see a *Public and Networks* heading, beneath which you'll see the designations *Everyone* (public) and *My Network*, that latter category consisting of, to quote the SkyDrive's text, "Anyone you add to your profile or to [Internet] Messenger." (Your profile is an area—see the top of figure 10-13 for its link—containing basic biographical information about you, to which you can selectively grant access to others.)

You can also click the check box alongside *Everyone*, and the whole world can *view*, but not edit, your data in that folder. Tick the box by My Network, and a drop-down menu appears, presenting you with two options: *Can view files*, and *Can add, edit details, and delete files*. Just click your choice and the appropriate access level is selected. If you've compiled additional names in categories, ticking the box adjoining a category calls up the same drop-down menu, and that pair of access selections.

But you can also add individuals to your access list who aren't already listed anywhere in your categories or your network. Type that person's e-mail address (her Windows Live ID) in the *Individuals* field at the bottom of the screen. In the interests of science, I'm entering another e-mail address of mine, yankinlondon, as the person who'll be able to view and edit my workbooks (Figure 10-14):

Figure 10–14. *Self-nomination: Adding an individual to my permissions list*

I'll graciously ignore the wisecracks about my shortage of friends, and continue. Having made the selection(s), you'll see (Figure 10-15):

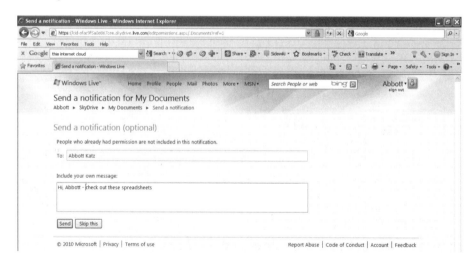

Figure 10–15. *Where to grant degree of access to an individual*

Then again, assign level of access. Don't forget to click Save, too. When you do, you'll be brought here (Figure 10-16):

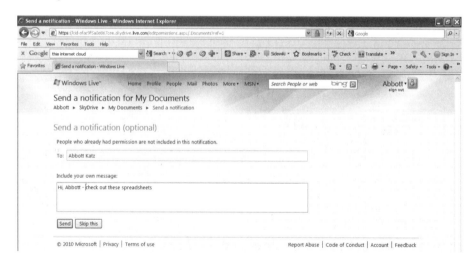

Figure 10–16. *Giving notice: Informing your contact of permission to access your workbooks*

Write a note in the message space if you wish (I'm on a first-name basis with myself) and click Send. An e-mail appears in the designee's inbox (Figure 10-17):

Figure 10–17. Start spreading the news: The notification about workbook access

Click *View Folder* and you're brought directly to the *owner's* My Documents folder, where the colleague—that is, the person who's been given access rights—can view and/or edit the workbook, depending on the level of access the colleague has received. The message should be retained in the Inbox, because it's here where that access originates on subsequent occasions—by clicking View Folder.

Hey—You! Get *Onto* My Cloud*!*

I don't know if Mick Jagger is on your contacts list, but once the owner's folder appears on the colleague's screen, he can open any one of its workbooks and edit it in the browser, just as the owner can, and they can edit the book simultaneously, with all edits making their way into the book, for all to see. If by some unlikely chance two users find themselves working in the same cell at more or less the same time, the last edit "wins"—that is, its data takes over the cell—at least until the next edit. What you *can't* do is open the workbook back in Excel (on your PC) and work on it there while others are editing the workbook.

And as users access the workbook, this little tally pops into the lower right of the worksheet (Figure 10-18):

Figure 10–18. You're on notice: who's editing your workbook

Click the small arrow to the right of that count and a "People editing this workbook" window pops up, recording the e-mail addresses of the people currently at work on the sheet—so you know who's out there at any time.

In Conclusion…

If you've got your head in the clouds nowadays—and I'm no stranger to that territory—you've finally got it in the right place. The next big thing—once it gets off the ground (so to speak)—is the migration of data from your—and everyone else's—PC to that massive Internet cloud hovering high above us, raining down its riches anywhere on planet Earth. Perhaps hard drives and CDs will go the way of floppy disks and other quaint data repositories, once *all* your data is saved to the virtual stratosphere. Excel's Web App is one more step in that lofty direction. See you up there.

APPENDIX A

■ ■ ■

Working With Range Names

What's in a Name? Plenty, if it's a Range

It's easy enough to understand how to identify a range – e.g., A34:R78 refers to all the cells camped out between A34 and R78, *including* those two cells which hold down the upper left and lower right corners of the range. But that reference isn't as informative as it could be. You might want or need to know what kind of data populates a range, be they test scores, income figures, or population statistics. As a result, Excel lets you *name* a range and use it in a formula, so that an expression such as

=SUM(A6:A20)

could be rewritten to read

=SUM(Income)

where the word "Income" represents or acts as a proxy for A6:A20, which could be listing a collection of income data. Naming a range helps you, and anyone else who may be viewing the workbook, to quickly understand what the range is about, and can also ease the formula writing process. After all, it may be simpler to type

=AVERAGE(tests)

than

=AVERAGE(B15:B112)

which requires you to remember those range coordinates, and/or drag down all those cells.

And there's another reason you might want to name a range, one I alluded to about 300 pages ago. I wrote there about naming a range which consists of exactly one cell. If that cell – say C1 - is applied repeatedly to different formulas – say a constant grade bonus of five points entered in that cell, added to a series of test scores listed down a column – I'd have to write something like

=A3+C$1

and then copy that formula down the column in order to add the five points to all the other exams listed down the A column. The dollar sign establishes an absolute reference, whereby the 1 in C1 is held constant. But if you name C1 Bonus, for example, you can write

=A3+Bonus

without having to worry about those dollar signs. Naming a range automatically holds its cell references constant, no matter where you copy it.

Naming a range is easy, although as usual Excel offers you more than one way to achieve this end.

In order to get the hang of this, first download the Range Names workbook from the book's page at www.apress.com. The simplest approach to range naming is to select the range you wish to name, click in the name box, type the name, and press Enter. Thus if you want to give a name to the range A6:A20, select those cells, click in the name box, type Income or any other name you wish, and tap Enter (**Note:** multi-word range names such as test scores must be joined by an underscore: test_scores. If you omit the underscore you'll trigger this error message: "You must enter a valid reference you want to go to, or type a valid name for the selection."

The latter half of that caution refers to range names, the first half, to the *navigational* role played by the name box we referred to in chapter 2. It's perfectly legal to name a range with just one letter – a, or p, something equally spare – and while a one-lettered range name won't tell you too much about the range, it's obviously easy to apply to a formula. Note that your named ranges will be listed when you click the drop-down arrow alongside the name box; click any such name and Excel will immediately highlight that range on your workbook. (Figure A-1):

Figure A–1. The Income range name as listed in the name box

An alternative way to compose a range name is particularly apt when your range is topped by a named header row. Let's say cells A6:A20 feature a header named Income in cell A5. Select that A6:A20 (note that you need not select A5) and click the Formula tab ➤ Define Names in the Defined Name button group. You'll see (Figure A–2):

New Name	? X
Name:	Income
Scope:	Workbook
Comment:	
Refers to:	=Sheet1!$A$6:$A$20
	OK Cancel

Figure A–2. Defining a range name from a header row

Click OK, and the range is named. Note the range does *not* include row A5, the row which contributed that name (as you can see, you could have entered a diferent name in the Name field, though doing so would have defeated the purpose of calling upon the header row. Excel decides on the range namehere by grabbing onto the *label* - Income – in the immediately preceding cell. Had a *value* been stored in A5 – well, Excel won't drum up a range name from there; you'll have to make one up yourself.

While we're at it, here are some other range naming rules:

- Range names can contain up to 225 characters
- They must *begin* with a letter
- You can't define a name that resembles a cell reference, e.g., X345. X345Score is legal, though.

That last criterion needs to be refined a bit, and points up a subtle downside which besets named ranges. Because the pre-2007 releases of Excel were confined to 256 columns, it was permissible there to name a range XAA321, for example, because that name refers to a cell which doesn't exist in those versions. That same reference won't be accepted as a range name by Excel 2010, however – because cell XAA321 *is* a perfectly valid address in 2010.

Note also that you can use the Define Names dialog box to assign a name to a *value*. That is, you can enter a value in the Refers to field instead of cell coordinates, and the name you assign to that value can be used in formulas as well (Figure A–3):

Figure A–3. Here, an actual value is assigned a name

The Scope field is a bit more obscure. Note that Workbook is set as the default scope- and that means that this range name can be deployed in any cell in the workbook without additional qualification. Thus if I name the range A6:A20 in Sheet 1 Income and leave the Workbook scope default in place, I can write a formula such as

=AVERAGE(Income)

in *Sheet 2* as you see it above. If, however, I define the scope of A6:A20 as Sheet1, I'd have to write the above formula in Sheet 2 this way:

=AVERAGE(Sheet1!Income)

Obvious question, then: why bother to restrict the scope here to Sheet1? It requires more work to write formulas this way. The answer is that you may want to name a second range, this one in Sheet2, as Income too, and so you'd need to identify the particular sheet in any formula reference to distinguish between the two Income ranges However, if you do confine the scope of this formula to Sheet1, you can still write

=AVERAGE(Income)

in Sheet 1 itself. Write exactly the same expression in Sheet2 and it'll refer to that range in Sheet2.

The Comment field lets you enter a description of the range you're naming, thus explaining to other viewers of the workbook exactly what you had in mind using the name.

You'll also note that the Define Name command features a drop-down arrow. Click it and you'll see a rather quirky option, Apply Names. Apply Names lets you replace a standard range reference in a formula with its name, if you've devised that name *after* writing the formula. For example, if you've written

=AVERAGE(A6:A20)

in a cell and *then* named A6:A20 Income, you can click in any blank cell, click Define Name ➤ Apply Names, and click Income, which will be listed (Figure A–4):

Figure A–4. The Apply Names dialog box

The above formula will now read

=AVERAGE(Income)

And so if you've named five different ranges *after* you've already written formulas containing their actual cell references, you can click any blank cell, select Apply Names, click on all five range names in the Apply Names dialog box, and those names will replace the cell references in all the formulas. Yeah – that blank cell thing is quirky indeed.

As indicated, once you've named a range you can apply it to a formula. You can simply type, for example

=AVERAGE(Income)

Or you can start to write the formula, and when you get this far

=AVERAGE(

click the Use in Formula button in the Define Names button group. If you do, you'll see (Figure A–5):

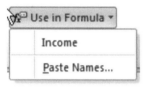

Figure A–5. Using a range name in a formula

(Needless to say if you name several ranges, all of their names will appear in the drop-down menu.) Click Income and that name will be inserted into the formula. On the other hand, you could also starting typing

=SUM(Inc

at which point you'll see the name Income appear in the auto complete function menu (Figure A–6):

Figure A–6. Pick and choose: the range name, via autocomplete

And once you click the Use in Formula button you'll likewise notice the Paste Names option, a slightly ambiguous one – because it suggests you can paste a range name into a formula. But we just did that, and without the assistance of this command. But Paste Names does two very different things. Clicking Paste Names activates a dialog box bearing two options – Paste List and OK. Clicking Paste List won't insert a range name into a formula – rather, it'll simply *list* the ranges you've named somewhere on the workbook, beginning in a cell of your choosing.

Let's say, for example, I've supplemented the Income range name with a second named range, called Staff, occupying cells K6:K12 and headed by the name Staff in K5. Click in cell E14 and click Paste Names (Figure A–7):

Figure A–7. The Paste Name dialog box

Click Paste List and you'll see (Figure A–8):

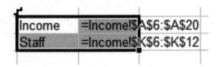

Figure A–8. The ranges in your workbook, listed

We see that indeed, the ranges are simply listed on the selected worksheet, in this case starting in E14 (and thus the screen shot above spans cells E14:F15) with both names and range coordinates reported. Paste List can be a handy means for keeping track of the whos whats and wheres of all your named ranges right there on a worksheet, without having to return to any dialog boxes to learn that infomation.

But click the OK button in the Paste Nanenes dialog box and you get something else entirely. If I click in cell B6, the cell to the right of the first income figure, and click Use in Formula ➤ Paste Names ➤ Income ➤ OK, I'll see Figure A–9):

Income	
$ 34,567.00	=Income
$ 56,012.00	
$ 21,345.67	
$ 43,879.00	
$ 27,802.00	
$ 39,457.92	
$ 60,456.00	
$ 81,345.00	
$ 17,678.00	
$ 23,789.00	
$ 61,789.00	
$ 70,348.00	
$ 53,789.00	
$ 31,568.00	
$ 28,581.00	

Figure A–9. Pasting a named range – sort of

Press Enter and you'll see 34567 – the contents of cell A6. But the formula bar view for that cell will display =Income. What that means – at least what that means *here* – is that pasting the *name* of the range Income in B6 posts the data in the corresponding Income cell only - which is A6 in this case. If I copy the result in B6 down the B column, I'll return each corresponding value down the A column- even though each one of those cells will actually state =Income. You're reporting each individual value for each cell comprising the Income range – even though each of these cells is referenced by =Income – which of course stands for cells A6:A20 – the whole range. I know what you're thinking – this one is pretty quirky, too.

Thus clicking OK in Paste Names requires - before you click OK - that you click in cells which must *line up with,* or correspond to, the cells in the range name being pasted. If you carry out the Paste Name command sequence in cell B4, for example – a cell which does not correspond to any Income range cell in the A column – you'll see the #VALUE! error message in that cell after you press Enter.

Naming Many Ranges – at the Same Time

The next option in the Defined Names button group – Create From Selection – dates back to Excel's antiquity. Click on the Bowling Scores sheet tab on the Range Names workbook and select cells F10:I15 – a range which contains a collection of bowling scores as well as name and game-number labels (and make sure you've selected the labels). Click Create From Selection, and you'll see (Figure A–10):

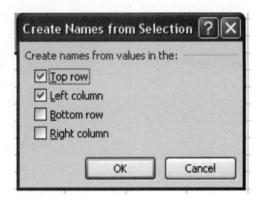

Figure A–10. The Create Names from Selection dialog box: Generating range names from the data

Click OK and nothing really seems to happen on screen. But click the down arrow by the name box (Figure A–11):

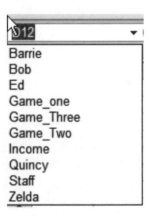

Figure A–11. Voila: Range names from the selection

Something *did* happen. Excel has fashioned a range name for *each* row and column in the range you selected, by appointing the data in the top row and left column as respective range names. Click on Bob, for example, and Excel will highlight cells G11:I11 – those cells which appear to the immediate right of Bob's name. Thus Create from Selection is a fast way to assign range names to individual rows and columns of data, by grabbing onto labels that top each row and sidle each column. (Note, by the way, that the Game One, etc. labels were rewritten as Game_One, and so on, because range names cannot contain spaces.)

The Name Manager – Tracking Your Ranges

The final and largest button inlaid into the Defined Names button group is the Name Manager. Click it and you'll see (Figure A–12):

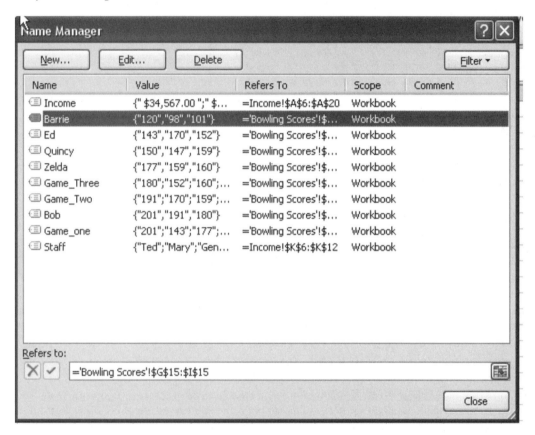

Figure A–12. Range finder: the Name Manager dialog box

Most obviously, the Name Manager lists all the workbook's named ranges, identifying their location, some of the values populating the cells in the ranges, and their scope and any comments about the range. By clicking Edit after clicking on a range name you'll be brought to an Edit Name dialog box, which enables you to both change the range's name as well as the range's coordinates. Click on a range name and then clicking Delete will naturally delete the range's name – but *not* the data in its cells (you can also do the same by clicking on a name and tapping the delete key). Clicking the Name header sorts the ranges names in A-Z order.

The Filter button displays a list of options by which you can selectively view certain of your named ranges (Figure A–13):

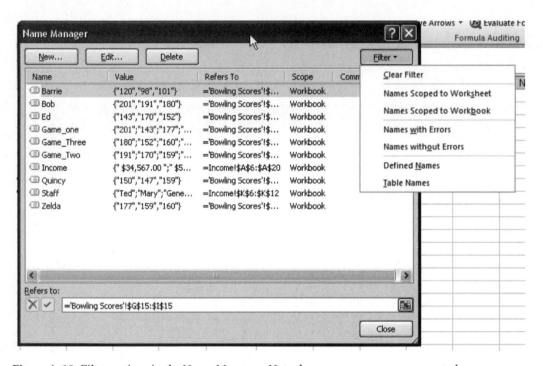

Figure A–13. Filter options in the Name Manager. Note the range names are now sorted.

The Names with Errors filter option lists only those ranges containing any values which exhibit an error message, e.g., #REF or #VALUE!.

In Conclusion...

Range names can add a measure of ease-of-use to the formula writing process, and can inform the user—and her colleagues—about the contents of a range. On the other hand, there is a view that range names should be used with caution, as there's some evidence that they may hobble the spreadsheet error debugging process. Your decision to name ranges will depend, as usual, on the purposes you bring to your workbooks, and their complexity. But for straightforward formula writing tasks they're good to know about.

APPENDIX B

■ ■ ■

Keyboard Shortcuts

What follows is a list of selected Excel 2010 keyboard shortcuts, culled from Microsoft's more comprehensive listing(you can view all the shortcuts by tapping F1–itself a shortcut–calling up Excel's 2010 help component, and clicking the Keyboard Shortcut link). I've added explanatory comments where I thought they'd help.

Remember that you can activate ribbon and button group commands by pressing the ALT key, which instates what Excel calls Key Tips atop the ribbon:

These too could qualify as keyboard shortcuts (see Chapter 1).

By definition, a shortcut offers swifter way to execute a command that would otherwise be carried out a bit more slowly with the mouse – and that's often true, considering a) where your hands are currently positioned and b) that you can actually *remember* the shortcut. If you can't, the time you spend looking it up defeats the purpose, and you'll wind up with a longcut instead. And because shortcuts are so numerous, you're not likely to commit too many to memory. There's nothing wrong with that, but learning the ones that do work for you can indeed save you time and streamline your work routine. So here goes.

Control Key Combinations

CTRL+SHIFT+)   Unhides any hidden columns within the selection.

CTRL+SHIFT+(Unhides any hidden rows within the selection.

CTRL+SHIFT+~   Applies the General number format.

CTRL+SHIFT+$ Applies the Currency format with two decimal places (negative numbers in parentheses).

CTRL+SHIFT+%   Applies the Percentage format with no decimal places.

CTRL+SHIFT+!   Applies the Number format with two decimal places, thousands separator, and minus sign (-) for negative values.

CTRL+SHIFT+:   Enters the current time; that is, the actual time as data – not a formula result.

CTRL+SHIFT+"	Copies the value from the cell above the active cell into the cell or the Formula Bar. That is, if you click in a blank cell, this shortcut will copy any value in the cell immediately above i If that value is the result of a formula, this shortcut will paste only that value, not the formula.
CTRL+;	Enters the current date as data – not a formula result
CTRL+`	Alternates between displaying cell values and displaying formulas in the worksheet. That is, this shortcut will display a cell formula onscreen instead of its value. Tap the shortcut a second time and the value returns. This option is available for the workbook via File ➤ Advanced ➤ Show formulas in cells instead of their calculated results.
CTRL+'	Copies a formula from the cell above the active cell into selected cells, or the Formula Bar. The copied formula cell references change as per relative cell references. You need to select the source cell along with the destination cells at the same time.
CTRL+1	Displays the Format Cells dialog box.
CTRL+9	Hides the selected rows.
CTRL+0	Hides the selected columns.
CTRL+A	Selects the entire worksheet. If the worksheet contains data, CTRL+A selects the current region, that is, an area of cells populated by data (e.g., a table) – if you click in that region. Pressing CTRL+A a second time selects the entire worksheet. If you click in a blank area o the worksheet, CTRL+A will initially select the entire worksheet.
CTRL+B	Applies or removes bold formatting with alternating taps.
CTRL+C	Copies the selected cells.
CTRL+D	Uses the Fill Down command to copy the contents and format of the topmost cell of a selected range into the cells immediately below.
CTRL+F	Displays the Find and Replace dialog box, with the Find tab selected. This works similarly to the Find and Replace option in Word. Also available on the Home ribbon ➤ Editing button group ➤ Find & Select.
CTRL+SHIFT+F	Opens the Format Cells dialog box with the Font tab selected
CTRL+G	Displays the Go To dialog box, as does F5.
CTRL+H	Displays the Find and Replace dialog box, selecting the Replace tab.
CTRL+I	Applies or removes italic formatting with alternating taps.
CTRL+L	Displays the Create Table dialog box. Equivalent to CTRL+T.
CTRL+N	Creates a new, blank workbook.
CTRL+O	Displays the Open dialog box to open or find a file.
CTRL+P	Displays the Print tab in Microsoft Office Backstage view.
CTRL+R	Uses the Fill Right command to copy the contents and format of the leftmost cell of a selected range into the cells to the right.
CTRL+S	Saves the active file with its current file name, location, and file format.

CTRL+T	Displays the Create Table dialog box.
CTRL+U	Applies or removes underlining with alternating taps.
CTRL+V	The classic Paste command. Inserts the contents of the Clipboard at the insertion point and replaces any selection. Available only after you have cut or copied an object, text, or cell contents.
CTRL+ALT+V	Displays the Paste Special dialog box, enabling you to paste only the *results* of a copied formula, by clicking the Values option in the dialog box. If, for example, a formula in cell A17 states =SUM(A2:A13) and yields 3224, Paste Special will return only the value 3224 in the destination cell. It will not copy the formula. This option is also available via the Paste button in the Home ribbon and on the Paste shortcut menu.
CTRL+W	Closes the selected workbook window.
CTRL+X	Cuts the selected cells.
CTRL+Y	Redo; that is, it undoes the last command you've undone via Undo. But it also repeats any last command or action, if possible.
CTRL+Z	Uses the Undo command to reverse the last command or to delete the last entry you typed. Successive CTRL+Zs continue to undo the immediately previous command.

Function keys

F1	Displays the Excel Help task pane.
	CTRL+F1 displays or hides the ribbon.
	ALT+F1 creates a chart of the data in a current range in which you've clicked, on the worksheet contaning the data.
	ALT+SHIFT+F1 inserts a new worksheet.
F2	Edits the active cell and positions the insertion point at the end of the cell contents. It also moves the insertion point into the Formula Bar when editing in a cell is turned off. This keystroke draws a temporary border around the cells that contribute to any formula in the cell you're editing. Thus tapping F2 on a cell containing =AVERAGE(A6:A10) will trace a border around cells A6:A10. An easy way to identity cell relationships.
	SHIFT+F2 adds or edits a cell comment.
	CTRL+F2 displays the print preview area on the Print tab in the Backstage view, as does CTRL-P.
F3	Displays the Paste Name dialog box. Available only if there are existing names in the workbook.
	SHIFT+F3 displays the Insert Function dialog box.
F4	Repeats the last command or action, if possible.
	CTRL+F4 closes the selected workbook window, as does CTRL-W.
	ALT+F4 closes Excel. As usual you'll will be prompted to save your changes should you not have already done so.

F5	Displays the Go To dialog box.
	CTRL+F5 restores the window size of the selected workbook window.
F6	Switches between the worksheet, ribbon, task pane, and Zoom controls. In a worksheet that has been split (View menu, Manage This Window, Freeze Panes, Split Window command), F6 includes the split panes when switching between panes and the ribbon area.
	SHIFT+F6 switches between the worksheet, Zoom controls, task pane, and ribbon.
	CTRL+F6 switches to the next workbook window when more than one workbook window is open.
F7	Displays the Spelling dialog box to check spelling in the active worksheet or selected range.
	.
F8	Turns extend mode on or off. In extend mode, Extended Selection appears in the status line and the arrow keys extend the selection. Extend mode allows you to select consecutive cell with the keyboard arrow keys without requiring you to hold down the Shift key. Tapping F8 a second time toggles this command off.
	SHIFT+F8 enables you to add a nonadjacent cell or range to a selection of cells by using the arrow keys. That is, after having selected one range, tapping this shortcut lets you click elsewhere and drag or key-select another range, even as the original range remains selected.
	ALT+F8 displays the Macro dialog box to create, run, edit, or delete a macro.
F9	Calculates all worksheets in all open workbooks. You'll rarely use this one nowadays. You might, however, if your workbook features thousands of formulas which are going to be recurrently impacted by new data entry. On a slow computer, that process can be rather time-consuming. If this is the case, you can click Formulas ➤ Calculation ➤ Calculation Options ➤ Manual, which prevents Excel from recalculating formulas when you enter new data. F9 will then calculate the worksheet when pressed. The Calculate Now button on the Calculation button group calculates the workbook in which you've clicked. Note that when you enter new data in manual calculation mode, a "Calculate" prompt will appear in the lower left of the status bar, reminding you that you've entered new data which needs to be recalculated. That's a good thing to know, because if you overlook the need to recalculate, you'll be working with "old" data – that is, you'll be proceeding with values which have yet to be updated.
	SHIFT+F9 calculates the active worksheet only. If, however, other worksheets in the workbook refer to values in that active sheet, they won't be updated by this command.
	CTRL+ALT+F9 calculates all worksheets in all open workbooks, regardless of whether they have changed since the last calculation.
	CTRL+F9 minimizes a workbook window to an icon.

F10	Turns key tips on the ribbon on or off. Pressing ALT does the same thing.
	SHIFT+F10 displays the shortcut menu for a selected item.
	CTRL+F10 maximizes or restores the selected workbook window, equivalent to clicking the lower tier of maximnize-minimize buttons in the upper right of your screen.
F11	Creates a chart of the data in the current range in a *separate* Chart sheet.
	SHIFT+F11 inserts a new worksheet.
F12	Displays the Save As dialog box.

Other shortcut keys

ARROW KEYS	Moves one cell up, down, left, or right in a worksheet.
	CTRL+ARROW KEY moves to the edge of the current data region (data region: A range of cells that contains data and that is bounded by empty cells or datasheet borders) in a worksheet.
	SHIFT+ARROW KEY extends the selection of cells by one cell.
	CTRL+SHIFT+ARROW KEY extends the selection of cells to the last nonblank cell in the same column or row as the active cell, or if the next cell is blank, extends the selection to the next nonblank cell.
	LEFT ARROW or RIGHT ARROW selects the tab to the left or right when the ribbon is selected. When a submenu is open or selected, these arrow keys switch between the main menu and the submenu. When a ribbon tab is selected, these keys navigate the tab buttons.
	DOWN ARROW or UP ARROW selects the next or previous command when a menu or submenu is open. When a ribbon tab is selected, these keys navigate up or down the tab group.
	In a dialog box, arrow keys move between options in an open drop-down list, or between options in a group of options.
	DOWN ARROW or ALT+DOWN ARROW opens a selected drop-down list.
BACKSPACE	Deletes one character to the left in the Formula Bar. If you *select* the cell's contents in the Formula Bar, Backspace deletes all those contents, just as selecting a word in Word and pressing Backspace deletes the entire word.
	In cell editing mode, it deletes the character to the left of the insertion point – as in Word.
DELETE	Removes the cell contents (data and formulas) from selected cells without affecting cell formats or comments.
	In cell editing mode, it deletes the character to the right of the insertion point – as in Word..

END	END turns on what's called End Mode. In End mode, you can then press an arrow key to move to the next nonblank cell in the same column or row as the active cell. If the cells are blank, pressing END followed by an arrow key moves to the very last cell in the row or column – that is row 1048576 or column XFD.
	END also selects the last command on the menu when a menu or submenu is visible.
	CTRL+END moves to the last cell on a worksheet, to the lowest used row of the rightmost used column. But see the additional discussion about this in Chapter 2. If the cursor is in the formula bar, CTRL+END moves the cursor to the end of the text as does END.
	CTRL+SHIFT+END extends the selection of cells to the last used cell on the worksheet (lower-right corner). If the cursor is in the formula bar, CTRL+SHIFT+END selects all text in the formula bar from the cursor position to the end—this does not affect the height of the formula bar.
ENTER	Completes a cell entry from the cell or the Formula Bar, and selects the cell below (by default).
	Opens a selected ribbon (press F10 to activate the menu bar) or performs the action for a selected command.
	In a dialog box, it performs the action for the default command button in the dialog box (the button with the bold outline, often the OK button).
	ALT+ENTER starts a new line in the same cell – a kind of a manual Wrap Text, when entering data in that cell.
	CTRL+ENTER fills the selected cell range with the value you're currently entering. That is, if you select A1:A10 and type 45 in A1, CTRL+ENTER – *instead* of ENTER - will copy 45 to cells A2:A10.
	SHIFT+ENTER completes a cell entry and selects the cell above.
ESC	Cancels an entry in the cell or Formula Bar.
	Closes an open menu or submenu, dialog box, or message window.
	It also closes full screen mode (achieved via View tab ➤ Worksheet Views ➤ Full Screen) when this mode has been applied, and returns to normal screen mode to display the ribbon and status bar again.
HOME	Moves to the beginning of a row in a worksheet.
	Moves to the cell in the upper-left corner of the window when SCROLL LOCK is turned on.
	Selects the first command on the menu when a menu or submenu is visible.
	CTRL+HOME moves to the beginning of a worksheet.
	CTRL+SHIFT+HOME extends the selection of cells to the beginning of the worksheet.
PAGE DOWN	Moves one screen down in a worksheet.
	ALT+PAGE DOWN moves one screen to the right in a worksheet.
	CTRL+PAGE DOWN moves to the next sheet in a workbook.
	CTRL+SHIFT+PAGE DOWN selects the current and next sheet in a workbook.

PAGE UP	Moves one screen up in a worksheet.
	ALT+PAGE UP moves one screen to the left in a worksheet.
	CTRL+PAGE UP moves to the immediately previous sheet in a workbook.
SPACEBAR	In a dialog box, performs the action for the selected button, or selects or clears a check box.
	CTRL+SPACEBAR selects an entire column in a worksheet.
	SHIFT+SPACEBAR selects an entire row in a worksheet.
	CTRL+SHIFT+SPACEBAR selects the entire worksheet, behaving as CTRL-A.

■ ■ ■

Error Messages

Nobody's Perfect

To err is human, but most duly certified members of our species have a vested interest in setting their errors right, particular because other humans (bosses, for example) are likely to be rather displeased if they don't. And make no mistake - it's nearly a law of nature that in the course of your Excel activity you *will* make mistakes. Take it from the party of the first part.

Needless to say, Excel is well aware of the near inevitable, and equips its users with a range of tools and informational alerts that try and pinpoint errors and help turn them into usable data.

Now, there are errors and then there are *errors*, and the ways in which Excel responds to these will vary. In that regard, there are at least three kinds of errors we need to consider:

1. *Simple data entry errors*: If, for example, Johnny scores a 92 on his history exam but his careless instructor enters 29 in her Excel-based gradebook, there's nothing Excel can do about it, at least not directly. It will be left to the instructor to devise a data validation rule or an IF statement that might be able to anticipate and repair this kind of misstep. By the same token, if you want to cite cell A16 in a formula but type A17, Excel won't stop you either. As capable as it is, Excel can't read your mind.

2. *Formula-blocking errors:* By this I'm referring to a class of mistakes which violate the rules of formula writing. Commit one of these and Excel prevents you from going ahead until you rectify the mistake. For example, if I enter

=COUNTA23:A49)

you'll provoke this caution (Figure C–1):

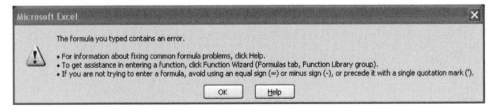

Figure C–1. You can't get there from here

And you won't be able to proceed without remedying the problem. Or if you want to divide the averages of cells C11:C13 by the value in D23 and write

=AVERAGE(C11:C13)D23

You'll spark this advisory (Figure C–2):

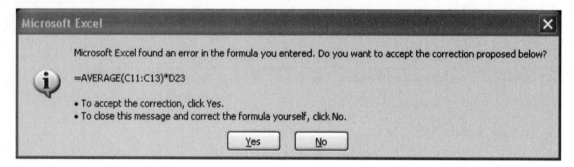

Figure C–2. *Just trying to help*

Note that Excel's recommendation isn't what you had in mind, but you'll need to rewrite the expression in any case.

3. *Formula-acceptable errors*: What I'm referring to here is a collection of formula-writing errors which Excel will *allow* you to enter in the cell, but will then record as an error in that cell. There are several classic such errors:

a. *#DIV/0!*-Try to enter say, =A12/0 in a cell and you'll be allowed to do just that, but this error will be posted in the cell. You can't divide a number or a cell-referenced value by zero.

b. *#N/A*-Appears, for example, if you're working with a lookup table and write something like this:

=VLOOKUP(R34,W12:X20,2,FALSE)

And the value in R34 simply doesn't appear in the first lookup column – and by adding FALSE you'd specified an exact match.. That value is Not Available.

c. *#NAME?*-Appears when you mistype a function name, e.g.,

=SUMX(A4:V45)

or don't surround textual formula entries with quotes, e.g.

=IF(C24>65,pass,"fail")

d. *#REF!*-This flashes in a cell when you cite a non-existent cell reference, which requires a bit of explaining. If you enter

=A17+D32

and then delete row 17, you trigger the #REF! message, and the cell itself will record

=REF!+D32

What's curious about this message is that even though you've deleted row 17, another row 17 moves in its place, of course – the row which had heretofore occupied row 18. But that "new" row 17 won't stave off the error message.

e. *#VALUE!*-Appears when your formula tries to work with textual data inscribed between the parentheses, but you wanted to work with numeric values, e.g.,

$$=MAX(SCORE,3,4,6)$$

But keep in mind that if you write

$$=MAX(A6:A10)$$

And some of the entries in that range are textual, the formula *won't* report an error-it will simply ignore the textual data here and consider the numeric values only. (Note that if you had named a range of values SCORE in the first formula, Excel *would* have computed the result).

In addition, Excel supplies you with a collection of Formula Auditing tools gathered into a button group on the Formulas ribbon which help you identify the cells contributing to the formulas you compose, and as such can help you isolate sources of error (Figure C–3):

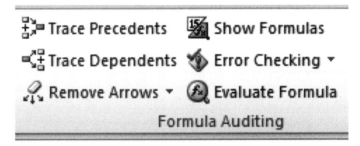

Figure C–3. The Formula Audting button group

The Trace Precedents and Dependents buttons enable you to visually flag those cells which impact a formula result (precedents) and the ones which are impacted (dependents). Thus if we write

$$=A34+B22$$

in cell D18, A34 and B22 serve as *precedent* cells to the result in D18. Say A34 contains 42 and B22 23. Click in D18 and click Trace Precedents. You'll see (Figure C–4):

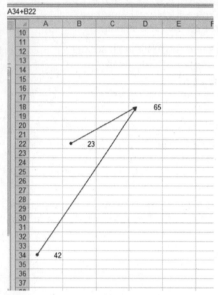

Figure C–4. Setting a precedent: Identifying precedent cells

Then click Remove Arrows. Now click A34 and click Trace Dependents. You'll see (Figure C–5):

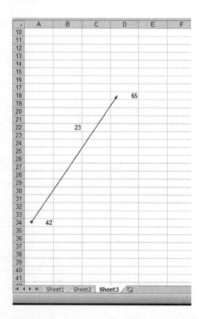

Figure C–5. Dependin' on you : D18 depends in part on A34 for its result.

We see that D18 requires, or depends, on A34 (in addition to B22) for its result.

The Error Checking option is a particularly apt one if you're having trouble determining exactly where and why an error, or errors, have been perpetrated. Clicking the Error Checking button sets in motion a dialog box which flits from error to error on your worksheet (not the entire workbook), and describes each one. Say you're entered =8/0 in cell A12 and AVERAGEX(D67:D10) in B21 (it doesn't matter if the cells in that range are blank). Click Error Checking and you'll see (Figure C–6):

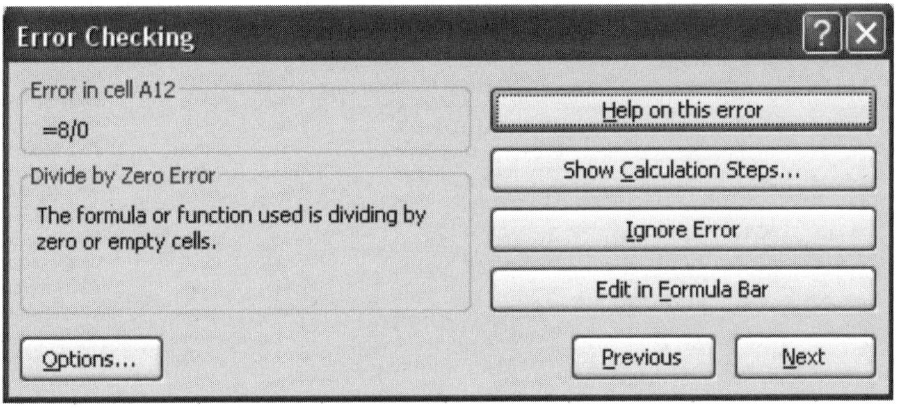

Figure C–6. The Error Checking dialog box

Note the report of the type of mistake that's been committed in A12. Click Next and the error checker will streak to the site of the next error–B21 (Figure C–7):

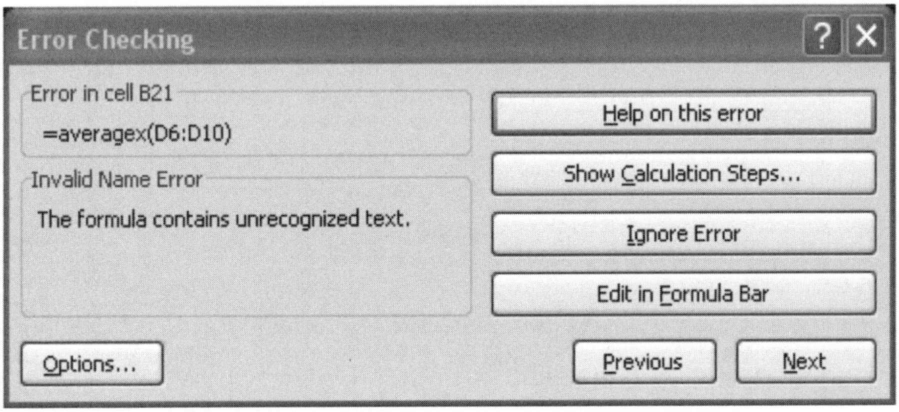

Figure C–7. Error prone, aren't I?

And so on. Clicking Show Calculation Steps opens an Evaluate Formula dialog box in turn, which in our latter case will disclose (Figure C–8):

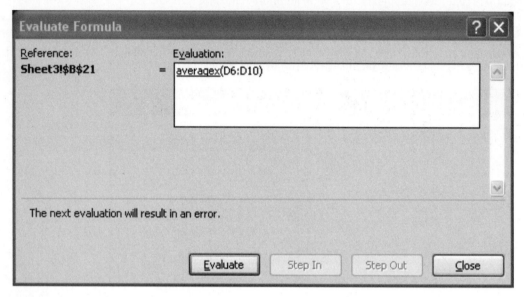

Figure C–8. Note the legend, foretelling the error evaluation which will result when you click Evaluate….

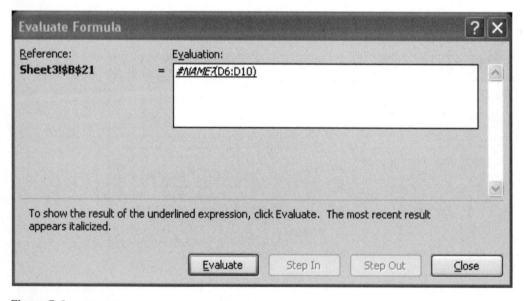

Figure C–9. …as we now see

While the command sequence is a bit convoluted, you get the idea. Excel diagnoses the error in a couple of clicks. Note as well that the Evaluate Formula button in the Formulas button group takes you directly to the Evaluate Formula dialog box you see above.

Index

■ ■ ■

■ Q

■ R